Praise for *A Portable Iden...*

CW00550828

"Like most women who have read *A Portable Identity* my first the book when I made my first move! The authors have provided an caught up in that inevitable challenge we all have faced upon relocati book is an excellent resource to help women find their own answer to that question (again and again, as it's helpful for people making multiple moves), with the help of exercises, solid advice and personal experience from two authors who are professionals as well as accompanying spouses."

Robin Pascoe, The Expat Expert, Author of Four Best-Selling Books on
Expatriate Life, and Inspirational Speaker

"This book explores territory that no other book does. It deals with the reality of moving overseas, when life is radically shifting. I have lived overseas for most of my adult life, and I believe this book is a huge contribution to the expatriate experience. It addresses every aspect of the impact of the move: mind, body, and spirit."

Kacie Liput, Corporate Expatriate Wife and
Community Organizer

"Anyone ever to encounter and navigate the endless and exhaustive details involved with moving and living overseas will appreciate the meticulous care and thought that went into this primer. The exercises for planning for, and understanding the different stages, emotions, and thought processes that accompany such a move are terrific, not just for the move itself, but for a very effective and smooth assimilation of this kind of life-changing experience. I will be giving this one to many of my friends who are also contemplating living and working overseas."

J.K., International Business Consultant,
Washington, D.C.

"Like many other women who accompany their husbands overseas, I started to think I was going crazy! But, after attending a workshop facilitated by the authors, I realized what I was feeling was completely normal. By using the skills and exercises that Debra and Charise illustrate in their book, you can get back on your feet and transition into your new lifestyle overseas."

Tracy Garringer, Former U.S. Embassy Expatriate Wife,
Bangkok, Thailand

"...I have long felt a lack of information about how crucial it is to know yourself and what is important to you. This knowledge can help you find or develop what you need in order to thrive in a foreign environment...*A Portable Identity* does a thorough job of addressing the issue...Even for someone not interested in answering questions, the book's sometimes painfully honest personal accounts provide riveting examples of the challenges of adapting to life overseas. Men who are "trailing spouses" will have to mentally change the pronouns, but should find it equally useful. *A Portable Identity* belongs in the personal library of every expat: it is a definite "must-buy"!"

Jan Fischer Bachman, Managing Editor, Foreign Service Lifelines,
Associates of the American Foreign Service Worldwide

"The authors do not hide behind professional expertise but lay themselves bare, and reveal themselves with all their faults as well as their personal strengths. To read the book is to share in their personal sagas. At the end of the book, you feel like you have an intimate personal relationship with each of these very special women. *A Portable Identity* encourages a woman to take the time needed to get in touch with herself. The book achieves its objective of providing the means to "cope, grow, and handle moves with grace and joy"."

Carol Usher, Canadian Social Worker living and working in the UK, and
Book Reviewer for Tales from a Small Planet, a website for expatriates

"By presenting their own stories of identity confusion and changes, Bryson and Hoge have given us an excellent plan of action to deal with our own personal and cultural adjustments in the overseas settings. This is a book that should not just be read. Rather one should take the time to complete the exercises and reflect on the wisdom enclosed in this work."

Thomas A. Rodgers, M.D., Former Regional Psychiatrist,
U.S. Department of State

"I've counseled hundreds of expatriates having adjustment problems during the fifteen years that I ran the CIWEC Clinic Travel Medicine Center in Katmandu, Nepal. It would have been nice to be able to refer them to this carefully crafted book that gently guides the reader toward a knowledge of herself that can allow her to be comfortable in any environment."

David R. Shlim, M.D., Medical Director, Jackson Hole Travel and
Tropical Medicine, Jackson Hole, Wyoming

"There is an abundance of self-help books on the market, but this unique workbook gets you to sit down and take on the task of putting your sense of "self" back where it needs to be when coping with a new and different environment. This book is not just about coping with change, but how to get back that person (yourself) you feel you may have lost in the move."

Donna Ayerst, Family Liaison Office Publications Coordinator,
U.S. Department of State

"…We forget the power of the individual to take the opportunity expatriation brings both to take stock of, and even refashion her life…Fortunately for partners everywhere, Bryson and Hoge have rectified that situation by creating *A Portable Identity*…Their experience combined with their counseling backgrounds gave them the skills to develop this honest, informative, and user-friendly workbook for partners…*A Portable Identity* goes to the heart of the dilemma women face once abroad. By working through Bryson and Hoge's book, the partner will emerge with an energized new identity."

Valerie Scane, Editor of Families In Global Transition's Website, Writer
and Speaker of Expatriate Issues, and Corporate Expatriate Wife,
Jakarta, Indonesia

A Portable Identity:
A Woman's Guide to Maintaining
a Sense of Self While Moving Overseas

by

Debra R. Bryson, MSW and Charise M. Hoge, MSW

A Portable Identity:
A Woman's Guide to Maintaining a Sense of Self While Moving Overseas

Copyright © 2003 and 2005 by Debra R. Bryson and Charise M. Hoge

Cover design by Sandra Guiloff
Cover photo of Debra Bryson by Ryan Wagner, Prestige Portraits
Cover photo of Charise Hoge by Razi Studio of Potomac
Diagrams, including The Wheel, by Shelley Kurgan

ISBN 0-9765682-0-9

Revised Edition

Transition Press International

P.O. Box 564
Glen Echo, Maryland 20812
http://www.aportableidentity.com

Printed in the United States of America

Table of Contents

Acknowledgements

Many people supported us along the way to help bring this book to fruition. We'd like to thank Joan and Steve Neubauer of Word Wright International for editing and publishing the first edition of this book. We are grateful to them for sharing their knowledge and expertise about the world of publishing. We'd like to thank Robin Pascoe for her time, encouragement, and wisdom. Her support gave us the confidence and courage to create Transition Press International and to publish this revised edition of *A Portable Identity.* We'd like to thank Shelley Kurgan for sharing her creative abilities by giving our primitive pencil drawings of our diagrams, including The Wheel, a professional look. We'd like to thank Sandra Guiloff for her insightful artistry as the illustrator of our book cover. We'd like to thank Dr. Tom Rodgers for his discerning advice and suggestions, and Audrey Forga, Tracy Garringer, Mara McFadden, and our husbands for helping us edit various components of the book. Their input was invaluable.

We'd also like to thank the staff at the Community Services of Bangkok for their support when we began this endeavor in 1992 by conducting workshops on this topic. We'd also like to thank the expatriate women we met in Thailand as well as the women and men who have lived abroad who we met during the writing of this book, for their words of encouragement and validation of the need for this book.

We'd like to thank our parents, Joe and Darlene Buehler, and Charles and Dorothy McFadden, for providing us with the foundation for who we are today. We'd also like to thank our families and friends for their unending support and encouragement while we worked on both editions of *A Portable Identity* and our other endeavors to reach out to expatriate spouses worldwide. We'd especially like to thank our daughters, Seneca and Siana Bryson, and Alex and Amelia Hoge, for their patience and understanding while we spent time away from them to complete this book.

Most importantly, we'd like to thank our husbands and partners in life.

To Brad from Debra—Throughout our lives together, you've always encouraged and supported me by giving me the space to pursue the dreams and passions of my heart. Thank you for your precious gift of time and self during the writing of this book.

To Charles from Charise—Thank you for the adventure of our lives together, including bringing me overseas and opening my world to new opportunities. I'm grateful for your continual support and faith in my endeavors; especially for the freedom I've enjoyed in writing this book.

We dedicate this book to expatriate women around the world.

You are the inspiration for this book.

Preface

Who We Are

The idea for this book began in Bangkok, Thailand. We both have Masters' degrees in Social Work, and were employed as counselors at a community organization in Bangkok that provided mental health counseling to the expatriate community. However, our paths crossed and our lives touched primarily because each of us moved overseas in support of our husband's career.

As expatriate wives, Charise lived in Bangkok for four years and Debra, for three. We both overcame great obstacles to work overseas. Charise became the first graduate student in the history of the social work program at the University of Georgia to fulfill an overseas internship.

Soon after arriving in Thailand, Debra discovered that she was prohibited from working in her profession because of her husband's employment at the U.S. Embassy as a diplomat. This propelled Debra to become the primary advocate for spousal employment issues at the U.S. Embassy in Bangkok. In part, because of her efforts, the embassy and the Royal Thai government agreed to allow spouses of embassy employees to work legally in Thailand.

Why We Wrote this Book

The decision to write this book resulted from four key factors:
   · our personal experiences with moving to a foreign land;
   · our conversations with other women in our role as expatriate spouses;
   · our professional work counseling and conducting workshops with women overseas;
   · our discovery of the need for more in-depth information about how moving
   overseas affects a woman's identity and a plan to deal with the changes that occur.

Our Personal Experience

We decided to write this book because of our experiences as women moving to a foreign land. We each experienced a range of feelings, thoughts, and behaviors after moving abroad that we had not anticipated. Only later did we understand how much moving overseas affected our identities. Throughout the book, we'll elaborate more on how moving to a foreign country affected each of our identities, and how we dealt with these changes.

Conversations with Expatriate Spouses

The second reason we wrote this book developed from our interactions with other expatriate spouses. As expatriate spouses ourselves, we often met other expatriate wives of husbands with careers overseas. These women had been overseas for variable lengths of time, ranging from less than a year to over twenty-five years. As newcomers to the expatriate lifestyle, we expected life as an expatriate spouse to be enviable and luxurious. Most expatriate spouses in Bangkok had a higher standard of living than they did in their home country: they had maids, drivers, and many opportunities to attend social engagements. Spouses also had more free time on their hands because they were "relieved" from working (although for many women, it didn't feel like a relief). In most cases, spouses were prohibited from working in Thailand.

Some women seemed content, satisfied, and fulfilled with their role, while others seemed dissatisfied or unhappy. During social engagements or conversations, these women often expressed their dissatisfaction with the expatriate experience. They often talked about the things wrong with Thailand, her people, and ways of life. They complained about how their maids or drivers didn't carry out their jobs properly. They longed to return to their homelands, and often discussed plans for their next home leave. When these women took the risk of speaking honestly, they often confessed to feeling dissatisfied, bored, confused, unsettled, angry, depressed, or resentful of the expatriate lifestyle.

We wondered why some of these women were so unhappy when they seemingly had so much. What was the root of their unhappiness? We found the experiences and feelings of some of these women mirrored our own early experiences in Bangkok as well. We wanted a better understanding of what was occurring with other women and with us.

Workshops and Professional Observations

A third reason we wrote this book emerged from our professional work. As counselors, we worked with women who sought counseling during a crisis, or for personal growth. Many of these women entered the counseling process for depression, anxiety, adjustment difficulties, or marital conflict. We focused on these women's symptoms as related to clinical diagnostic conditions, or as problems with adjustment to a foreign country, and provided treatment accordingly. In providing treatment to women who sought counseling for adjustment difficulties, our goal was to help them adjust and adapt to their new environment.

We assured them that adjustment to a foreign country was a normal process, lasting six months to one year or more, the current thinking and common practice among professionals in the field. However, given what we knew about ourselves and other expatriate women we interacted with, we had a sense that something else was going on but didn't know what.

On our own time, we began to meet to discuss what we thought might be happening with these women and concluded that they were suffering from a loss of identity and we decided we wanted a better understanding of this loss. We began reviewing the literature but found little information on the subject. What we did find typically portrayed these women as having everything—money, leisure, support, and therefore were not "in need."

In 1992, we began to develop workshops for Western women living in Thailand. They focused on the effect an overseas move had on a woman's identity. To develop our workshops, we drew from our personal experiences, our discussions with other expatriate women, many hours of brainstorming, and our professional experience. We also researched related topics and drew from the fields of human development, women's issues, and social work.

Our workshops evolved as we learned from each other and from each of the participants. Their willingness to share their stories touched us. At each step of the way, the women encouraged us to do more: to develop more workshops; hold longer workshops; offer more written materials; and, conduct more workshops for couples, families, and employers.

Charise also attended a mental health conference where she met other professionals living and working throughout Asia. She presented our work and the model we developed at the conference. We received encouragement from colleagues to share this information with other professionals working in the field of counseling. Our colleagues wanted written information to use with their clients or within their communities. We had begun to understand what happens to women's identities when they move overseas.

Need for More In-Depth Information and a Plan

The fourth factor that led to our decision to write this book is the need for more in-depth information on how moving overseas affects a woman's identity and the need for a plan to deal with the changes that occur. Other authors acknowledge that women experience changes and losses of identity when they move overseas. However, those books primarily focus on other aspects of the overseas move. *A Portable Identity: A Woman's Guide to Maintaining a Sense of Self While Moving Overseas* focuses entirely on the topic of identity in relation to every stage of the move. Our model of *The Wheel* offers spouses a plan for taking charge of the changes in identity that occur during an international relocation. This type of information is critical for spouses, their partners, the sending organization, human resource managers, and international relocation specialists in order to ensure the spouse's success overseas.

Introduction

The Untold Story

Image of Life as an Expatriate Spouse

To some, life as an expatriate spouse compares to a modern-day fairy tale. In exchange for a woman's willingness to enter expatriate life to support her husband's career, she accepts an adventure to move to a foreign land and gains a comfortable living arrangement. She will likely acquire more wealth, more personal time, and more help to maintain her house and family needs. It's easy to see why she would seize such an opportunity. But the fairy-tale image of expatriate life is like a veil. It hides the untold story of women's lives overseas. It does not begin to describe the reality of a woman's experience.

When a woman leaves her homeland, she experiences a loss of the familiar, of continuity, connection to her surroundings, and contact with people who have been central to her life. When she lands on foreign soil, she plunges into a new country and culture, often very different from her own. She must quickly learn how to navigate in her new surroundings. Overnight she becomes an expatriate spouse, the "wife of," or a "dependent of," her husband or partner. She must make new friends and carve out a new path for herself.

Historically, the ways in which an expatriate spouse manages the effect of so much sudden change in her life, as well as her feelings about these changes, have been her personal struggle. When an expatriate spouse experiences difficulty because of the multitude of changes and losses in her life, most believe that something is wrong with her, that she's not adjusting well. The consequences to women and their families have been distressing.

According to Nancy J. Adler, "The spouse's dissatisfaction, which often leads to early return, is the single most frequently reported reason for failure on a foreign assignment. Nearly half of 300 surveyed companies have brought families home early due to the reported unwillingness or inability of the spouse to adapt."[1]

Although adjustment to a foreign culture is necessary for a woman's successful overseas experience, it's only part of the story. If we continue to focus on the prevailing view that something is wrong with the individual if she experiences problems after moving overseas, the more accurate story of what actually occurs to her when she moves overseas remains untold.

The Key

In *A Portable Identity* we focus on revealing this untold story. **We believe the key to understanding a woman's experience when she moves overseas is simply this: an overseas move affects a woman at the deepest level of who she is, her identity.** An overseas move changes the fundamental structure of a woman's life and her sense of self and replaces organization with chaos.

The process begins the moment a woman discovers she will move overseas. Internally, she may experience this as twinges of anxiety whose origins she can't trace. During the move itself, as a woman leaves familiar roles, relationships, and surroundings behind, she may feel that she is losing her identity, or parts of it.

Once she arrives abroad and starts interacting with a different culture and takes on new roles and relationships, her identity becomes even more vulnerable. This vulnerability may come in the form of self-questioning or self-doubt about who she is. Or she may find herself experiencing one, two, or a whole gamut of emotions and behaviors that seem out of character for her. For example, she may find herself feeling tearful, irritable, angry, or frustrated. Or she may feel resentful, hopeless, or numb. She may find herself feeling depressed, impulsive, or anxious. To distract herself from her feelings, she may find that she eats too much or too little, drinks more alcohol, or shops excessively. In an attempt to avoid her feelings, she may withdraw from others, or use fantasy as a way to escape her situation. She may notice these feelings and behaviors spilling over into her relationships, and she may have difficulty relating to her husband, partner, or her children.

A woman in this situation may not realize that what she is experiencing could be a reflection of the enormous impact the overseas move has had on her identity. Until now, there has been a lack of in-depth information available to her on this topic. All too often she's had to pick up the pieces of her life and try to make sense of it by herself.

Who this Book is For

We wrote *A Portable Identity* primarily for women who move overseas in support of their husband's career, either for the first time or any move after that. Our book is devoted to helping a woman in this situation understand:
   · how her identity is affected at each stage of an overseas move;
   · why thoughts and feelings she may experience during the move are normal within the
     context of so much change;
   · why she may be having difficulty in her new life overseas;
   · how she can decide to take charge of the changes that occur in identity while living abroad;
   · how she can make choices that will help make the overseas life a happier and more
     meaningful experience.

Note: We originally wrote *A Portable Identity* for women because the majority of accompanying spouses are female, our professional work has primarily been with wives of male expatriates, and our own personal experience is that of women supporting our husbands' careers overseas. However, based on feedback from those who have read this book and from professionals in the field of international relocation, the content of the book may also be applicable to male expatriate spouses (a growing population) and to the international expatriate woman pursuing her own career. In essence, *A Portable Identity* is about taking charge of change, regardless of a person's given situation.

Professionals who work in the field of international relocation, such as human resource managers, relocation specialists, and employee assistance professionals will also benefit by reading *A Portable Identity*. They will develop greater awareness and understanding of this critical topic for spouses, and the book provides them with a valuable expatriate resource that they can provide or recommend to spouses moving and living overseas in support of their partners' careers.

How to Use this Book

You, the spouse, are the central character of *A Portable Identity: A Woman's Guide to Maintaining a Sense of Self While Moving Overseas*. The book is written from the perspective that you have already moved overseas because this is when you are most likely to become aware of the impact of the move. However, you can begin reading the book in the pre-departure stage of your move. We encourage you to start at the beginning and follow the order of the book, as each chapter and each section builds on the previous one. In Chapters 1 through 5, your story of how the overseas move has affected your identity will unfold as you record your answers to the questions and exercises in these chapters. (Note: If you are in the pre-departure stage of the move, complete Chapters 1 through 3 only. Then, after you move, resume reading the book starting with Chapter 4.) In Chapter 6, we introduce The Wheel, a model we developed that you can use to help reconstruct your identity. In Chapters 7 through 20, we guide you in applying the various components of The Wheel to your own life. By using The Wheel, you'll take charge of how your identity takes shape.

This book provides interaction between you, the reader, and us, the authors. We step out of our traditional counselor roles to share our personal experiences about moving overseas with you for several reasons. First, we want to let you know that you're not alone in what you may be experiencing. Expatriate women often live in remote corners of the world, in places where privacy may be an issue or where personal growth opportunities are limited. We hope our stories will encourage you to write your stories. Secondly, we use our stories as true-life examples of the concepts we present in the book.

Please accept our support and encouragement as you strive to better understand how your overseas move has affected your identity.

Disclaimer

Our primary purpose for writing this book is to help you understand how moving overseas affects your identity. Although this book in part evolved from our professional work, counseling and conducting workshops with women in Bangkok, Thailand, don't use this book in lieu of therapy. If you currently, or while completing this book, experience emotions or behaviors that you're unable to manage on your own, we encourage you to seek professional help and support.

Part One

Your Identity in Transition

Chapter 1

The Starting Place: Your Identity
Before the Decision to Move Overseas

How You View Moving Overseas

Your perception of moving overseas to support your husband's career probably falls somewhere between enthusiasm and resistance. You may view the move as a positive opportunity: a chance to explore exotic lands, have extra support to maintain the household, take time off from a career, or enjoy not working. You may view the decision to move overseas more negatively: as a necessary nuisance for your husband to advance in his career, as an interruption to your own career path, or as an obstacle taking you away from important roles, places, and people in your life. In this case, when you agree to the move, you do so reluctantly. We both found ourselves at opposite ends of the continuum when we first discovered we'd be moving overseas.

Debra:

I remember the day I learned that my husband, Brad, and I would move to Bangkok, Thailand. Brad came home from work like any other day. We made and ate dinner, then went for a walk, something we often do, especially when we have something important to talk about. As we walked, Brad told me that his assignment with the State Department had come through and we'd be moving to Thailand within the year.

"Finally," I thought. "I'm ready to go."

My mind immediately started to spin off into a fantasy about what my life would be like there. I saw myself confidently walking down unfamiliar streets, meeting local people along the way, and, of course, being readily accepted and liked by them. I saw myself eating exotic foods and learning to speak the language fluently. I saw us exploring and traveling the country together on the weekends. I thought it would be fascinating to be a part of the embassy community. I looked forward to the opportunity to meet and socialize with foreign dignitaries. I wanted to pinch myself. I couldn't believe moving overseas was finally going to happen.

Charise:

When my husband, Charles, told me he had a job offer in Bangkok, I could sense his excitement. The opportunity to live in Asia and develop research projects in tropical medicine thrilled him. Moving overseas would be a boon to his career as a doctor.

As he expressed his desire to go, I thought, "Where am I in this plan? Does he realize what he's asking me to give up? Does he know that I dread such a move?" I felt hurt and helpless. We had just moved two years earlier to Atlanta, which was a mutual decision. I was just beginning a new career as a social worker and was still in graduate school. I was afraid that by moving overseas, I'd lose everything that I'd already accomplished. When I expressed these concerns to Charles, he promised to help me find a way to work overseas. He knew another American doctor in Bangkok whose wife was working as a counselor. He said he'd make inquiries for me. While he thought he was helping to ease my anxiety, he didn't know the extent of my fear.

The idea of Asia terrified me. It was "too foreign." I had lived in Central America as a child, and in Europe during college, but Asia seemed like another planet to me. I felt that I didn't have the skills to master living there. I viewed the move as a detour, undermining my confidence in my abilities and derailing me from my goals.

⋨Exercise: Reflections ⋩

In this exercise, we'd like you to identify what you thought about the move overseas to support your husband's career.

How did you view the move? Did you see it as a positive opportunity or as something negative? Or, did your feelings fall somewhere between the two?

_____
_____
_____
_____
_____
_____

What were some of your thoughts and feelings about making the move overseas?

_____
_____
_____
_____
_____
_____

Reality of Moving Overseas

Although every woman has diverse views and images of the move overseas as well as different experiences after arriving abroad, women who move to support their husbands' careers have something in common: loss and change.

Debra:

During the first few months in Bangkok, as the ever-present newness began to wear off, it began to sink in that I was in Thailand. This would be home. I began to miss the familiar life I had in Washington, D.C. It seemed odd to me that just a short time before I was ever so willing to "give it all up" for this adventure. I began to question myself and the decision I had made. I felt sad and lonely; yet I was also glad we made the move. I had been so excited about it.

This wide range of feelings made no sense to me. At times I found myself feeling irritable, or crying over a minor frustration, or for no apparent reason. I told myself that I just needed time to adjust. I missed my family and friends in the U.S. Everyone seemed so far away, so untouchable. The phone calls to my parents were a vivid reminder. The voice delay and echo on the line as we talked made it difficult to maintain a natural flow of conversation. I found it difficult to be honest with them about my feelings. I shared the details of my adventures and my positive feelings, but awkwardly omitted anything painful. I didn't want to worry them, besides, they were never too thrilled about me moving overseas in the first place. They liked their children close by; with the overseas move, I was now farther away from them than ever.

Charise:

I recall the moment I came to understand that Bangkok was my home. We were already there, well into a three-month stay. We had chosen our house after a month in a hotel, and our household belongings had arrived. We had a semblance of order and our daily routines of rising, gathering at the breakfast table, going our different directions to work and school, and coming back to a clean house filled with the enticing smell of dinner in the making.

During this early settling-in period we took a four-day holiday to the beach a few hours' drive south of Bangkok. We stayed at a resort-style hotel where costumed, smiling Thai staff catered to our needs. This offered a reprieve from the scorching sun and the whims of our three-and-a-half-year-old.

After four days, we loaded our car for the drive home, and soon entered the press of Bangkok traffic. We emerged from the main streets into the smaller lanes of our neighborhood and arrived in our driveway. While this was no surprise, it seemed I was in the wrong place. I was anticipating returning home from the beach but it looked like just another shelter from the sun. I wanted my other home in the States, not the prospect of settling in for a long stay. A very long vacation. A very long time away.

Exercise: Reflections

This exercise will help you identify the thoughts and feelings that you've experienced since moving overseas.

What thoughts and feelings have you experienced since arriving at your new destination?

_____
_____
_____
_____
_____

Have you been confused or surprised by any of your thoughts or by any of the emotions you've felt? If yes, which ones and why?

_____
_____
_____
_____
_____

What reasons have you attributed to thinking or feeling the way you have?

_____
_____
_____
_____
_____

Do the thoughts and feelings you've experienced since arriving at your new destination match the thoughts and feelings you had anticipated before the move? Please explain your answer.

_____
_____
_____
_____
_____

You may have moved into a more comfortable situation by moving overseas. However, your answers to the above questions may reveal that your thoughts and feelings don't match what you expect of a person who is "more comfortable." Your thoughts and feelings may seem strange to you. You may feel a sense of urgency to find some way to overcome the difference between what you're experiencing internally and the situation you're in with all its perks. You may have been looking forward to the move, and now you may feel that something is wrong with you for feeling the way you do. Or you may not have wanted to make the move, and now you may want to blame yourself, your husband, or your situation for feeling the way you do. You may fear that what you're experiencing right now may stay with you throughout your overseas stay.

Regardless of how you initially viewed the move overseas (whether you viewed the move more positively or more negatively, or somewhere in between), don't deny the thoughts, feelings, and behaviors you've been experiencing. It is important to understand your experience in the context of the multitude of changes and losses you now face. Your thoughts and feelings very likely reflect the degree to which your identity has changed.

In the following section, we'll help you better understand the range of thoughts and feelings you've been experiencing since moving overseas. We'll do this by exploring in-depth the concept of identity, and by helping you construct a picture of your identity before the move.

What is Identity?

People define identity in both complex and simple ways. In its simplest form, identity is who you are, everything about you, all the qualities and traits that make you a unique, one-of-a-kind individual. Identity includes your personality. It separates you as an individual and explains why you seek out others. You often seek people similar to you and sometimes people very different from you.

Identity is a complex concept because of the many traits and characteristics that make you unique. Your identity begins to form in the womb before birth and evolves as you develop, learn, grow, and experience new things throughout your life. If someone asked you to define your identity, how would you do this? How would you describe every unique quality that in total makes you who you are? It would be an impossible task.

Our Definition of Identity

We define identity as a composite of four main facets:
- your internal view, or the way you view yourself;
- the effect of external factors on your identity, such as the ways others view you and how your identity is affected by those things around you;
- the roles you occupy;
- significant relationships you have with others.

Let's begin by looking more closely at each of these four facets. We're not saying that you as a woman are defined as four separate and equal parts. Instead, we use these four main facets as reference points to help you look deeper within yourself. Understanding them will help you look more in depth at the multitude of components that make you unique.

Viewing identity in this way gives you greater self-awareness. The significance of each facet largely depends on how you define yourself. For example, you may define yourself primarily by how you think and feel about yourself, or you may define yourself primarily through your relationships with other people. Another possibility is that you may define yourself primarily through the way others see you, or through the roles you occupy. We think that having this more detailed and deeper understanding of your identity is critical to comprehending the effect of the overseas move on you.

As you read the section below, think about yourself and your own identity. Within each area, we have provided questions to help stimulate your thinking as you reflect on yourself and your life. As you proceed, you may also come up with questions of your own that better apply to you. After reading through the section below, you will complete an exercise that will help you apply this information to your own identity.

The Four Facets of Identity

Internal View of Self

The first facet that in part makes up your identity is your internal view of yourself which includes:

Your perceptions of yourself: How do you view yourself? Do you like yourself? Do you think you're a nice person? Do you think you're not quite good enough? Do you think you're okay? What characteristics or adjectives would you use to describe yourself?

Your beliefs: Do you believe in a Higher Power (e.g., God, Buddha, Allah)? Do you believe in equal rights for women? Do you believe in democracy? Do you believe in a national identity (e.g., Americans = baseball, hot dogs, apple pie, and Chevrolet; British = afternoon tea)? What are some of your beliefs?

Your values: Do you value a family, a career, or some combination of the two? Do you value time with your family? Do you value your private time? Do you value money? Do you value helping others? What are some of your values?

Your attitudes: Do you generally have a positive attitude about your life, or do you feel more hopeless and out of control? What are some of your attitudes?

Your likes and your dislikes: Do you like to wake up early and have your first morning cup of coffee or tea reading the paper before anyone else gets up? Do you like the excitement of the city, or do you like the quiet solitude of the country? Do you dislike the cap being left off the toothpaste? Do you like or dislike change? Do you like new opportunities? What are some of your likes and dislikes?

Your gender: What is your perception/view of being a woman? What does it mean to be female? Do you feel comfortable in your skin? Does being a woman mean you're a nurturer? Does it mean you can be assertive and even aggressive? How do you feel about being a woman?

Your body image: How do you view your body? Are you happy with your body image or are you never happy with your body image (e.g., "If I could only lose that last five pounds!")? How would you describe your body image?

External Factors Affecting Identity

The second facet that in part makes up your identity is how external factors affect you.

The way others see you: What do your friends, family, and colleagues think of you? Do they view you as competent, lazy, nice, funny, or someone who can be counted on? Do they view you as responsible or irresponsible? Are the opinions of others about you, important to you?

Societal influences: What messages do you get about yourself from society? What kind of messages do you get about being a woman? A homemaker? A career woman? Are you homogeneous with your society or do you isolate yourself? Are you set apart in some way? What societal influences affect you?

The community you live in and are involved with: Are you accepted in your immediate community? Do you fit in, or do you experience some form of prejudice or discrimination? Is your community safe, or is it filled with violence? What is your community like? How involved are you in your community?

The impact of the culture in which you live: Your culture is like a pair of glasses through which you see the world. Your culture is interwoven into every aspect of your existence. One definition of culture we like comes from *The Survival Kit for Overseas Living: For Americans Planning to Live and Work Abroad* by L. Robert Kohls. This definition of culture encompasses a broad range of factors that when combined, describe a person's culture.

In Kohls' book, culture is defined as: "An integrated system of learned behavior patterns that are characteristic of the members of any given society. Culture refers to the total way of life of particular groups of people. It includes everything that a group of people thinks, says, does, and makes—its systems of attitudes and feelings. Culture is learned and transmitted from generation to generation."[2]

How would you describe the impact of your culture on you? As you think about this, ask yourself some of the following questions:

What are some of your home country's cultural values that affect your identity? Does your culture value working hard? Does your culture value family? Does your culture value leisure time? What are some of the attitudes and beliefs in your culture that help define you? Does your culture believe in and advocate equality for all people? Or does it have rules about certain types of people? What message does your cultural background give you about being a woman?

Roles

The third facet that in part makes up your identity is comprised of the roles you occupy.

Roles help define who and what you are and what you do: You occupy roles that you were born into, such as gender roles. You also have roles within the family such as parent, wife, daughter, and sibling. Some we choose for ourselves, and some come to us through other means, for example, occupational roles, community roles, student roles, and leadership roles. What are some of the roles you occupy?

Roles have culturally defined expectations and rules for interpreting and judging appropriate behavior: How does your culture define and interpret your role as a woman? As a wife? As a career woman? As a working mom? Are you within the norm for your culture, or are you seen as non-traditional? What are some of the expectations and/or rules for the roles you occupy?

Your self-esteem is affected by the roles you occupy: How do you view and feel about yourself and the roles you occupy? Do you like or dislike the roles you occupy? Does what you do make you feel good? How do your roles affect your self-esteem?

Significant Relationships with Others

The fourth facet that in part makes up your identity is comprised of the significant relationships you have with others.

The role of relationships in a woman's identity: The current thinking in the field of psychology and in women's psychology is that as women, our identities are strongly connected to our relationships with other people, our husbands, partners, families, friends, and/or colleagues. This doesn't mean that we depend on others for our existence in an unhealthy or negative way. Women do develop separate, autonomous identities, but in context of the important relationships in our lives.[3]

Significant relationships in your life: How important is your husband, partner, or family to your identity? How significant of a role do your friends play in your life? Do you have close relationships with colleagues or your neighbors? Who are the most significant people in your life? How important are these relationships to you? How do your relationships help define you?

Exercise: "Who Was I?"

This exercise allows you to apply our concept of identity, which we have just described, to your situation. You may already have a pretty good sense of yourself, and know how you would respond if someone asked you to define your identity. Or you may have more of a vague or general description of yourself. The purpose of this exercise is for you to put more self-awareness into your own definition. Because you're trying to gain a better understanding of how your identity is affected when you move overseas, it is essential that you have a clear understanding about how you defined yourself before the move.

We encourage you to do this exercise when you have sufficient time to explore it thoroughly, since many of the succeeding exercises will build off of this one. You may want to do it over several sittings until you feel confident about it. If you need to do it over a period of time, that's fine.

To begin, if this is your first move overseas, take yourself back to the time *before* you moved overseas. If you've moved overseas more than once, reflect on your most recent experience. (Note: You can also apply this exercise when you move from one foreign country to another, or when you return to your homeland after living in a foreign country. If you are in the pre-departure stage of your move, this exercise will reflect your identity as it is now, and the questions below will refer to your current situation.)

Whether you've been overseas a few months or a year or more, think about yourself and your life before you made the move. Think about where you lived, your surroundings, the community you lived in, and your daily activities. Reflect on the way you thought about yourself and your likes and dislikes. What kind of attitude did you have and what were some of the things you believed in? What were some of your roles in your family and in your community? Were these roles ones you chose for yourself, or were they given to you by circumstance or by others? Who were the most significant people in your life at that time? What impact did these people have on your life and on you as a woman?

Under each of the four facets of your identity (internal view, external factors affecting identity, roles, and significant relationships with others), write several descriptions that help define you at that point in time. You may want to refer back to the questions we provided under each of these areas in the previous section. This exercise is to be a reflection of your identity before moving overseas. Remember, the way you respond to each area is very personal and unique. There is no right or wrong answer.

"Who Was I?"

Under each category, write several descriptions that defined you before the move.

Before I moved overseas to _____, my identity, my sense of self, my view of me, my uniqueness =

Internal View of Self

My perceptions of myself:

_____
_____
_____
_____
_____

My beliefs:

_____
_____
_____
_____
_____

My values:

_____
_____
_____
_____
_____

My attitudes:

_____
_____
_____
_____
_____

My likes and dislikes:

_____
_____
_____
_____
_____

My gender:

_____
_____
_____
_____
_____

My body image:

_____
_____
_____
_____
_____

External Factors Affecting Identity

The way others saw me:

_____
_____
_____
_____

Societal influences:

_____
_____
_____
_____

The community I lived in and was involved with:

_____
_____
_____
_____
_____

The impact of the culture I lived in:

_____
_____
_____
_____
_____

Roles

Roles I occupied:

_____
_____
_____
_____

Culturally defined expectations and rules for interpreting and judging appropriate behavior for the roles I occupied:

_____
_____
_____
_____
_____

In what way(s) was my self-esteem affected by the roles I occupied?

_____
_____
_____
_____
_____

Significant Relationships with Others

Who were the most significant people in my life?

_____

_____

_____

_____

_____

How important were these relationships to me?

_____

_____

_____

_____

_____

How did my relationships help define me?

_____

_____

_____

_____

_____

Reflections on "Who Was I?"

Debra:

I can vividly recall the time I completed the "Who Was I?" exercise. Charise and I were in the process of developing our material for a workshop and had constructed the exercise as a tool to use with women who would attend. (The first exercise was in a somewhat different format from the one you just completed, but the content and focus were the same.)

I was sitting at my dining room table in Bangkok and decided to complete the exercise. Charise and I had talked a lot about the individual areas and our responses to each area, but I thought I'd complete the exercise in written format to see if it would capture what we anticipated it would.

The impact on me was incredible. As I went through each section, thinking about my responses to the questions and writing down my answers, I was overcome by the realization of how dramatically my life had changed since I boarded the plane and made the move to Bangkok. All the little things that had been a part of my daily life had vanished.

I recalled how I used to enjoy checking the mail after work, taking a walk with my husband *after dinner, or going on a solitary run to think. I now missed those things terribly. By contrast, I now had to rely on my husband to receive mail. Walks with him were infrequent because of the heat and his long work hours, and I put away my running shoes after stray dogs chased me on several occasions.*

I also realized how far away I was from family and friends, and how important those relationships were to me. The organizations I had been a vital and active member of now seemed very distant. As I sat there at the table, I found my heart longing for my old life and I felt pulled to return to the familiar. Sadness overcame me and I found myself unable to control the tears that rolled down my face.

Charise:

When Debra suggested that she and I complete the "Who Was I?" exercise to test it out, I was a little taken aback. I wasn't eager to delve into the quagmire of my own moving process. I wanted some professional immunity, the ability to distance my personal self from my work. However, I agreed to look more deeply at my former life. Finding a quiet moment at home, I sat, with paper in hand, on the wooden elephant chair belonging to my landlord. The huge chair dwarfed me as I prepared to open some small window to what had been my life just a year ago.

At best, I made brief and sketchy notes, not even full sentences. I couldn't relate the person on the paper with the person sitting in the elephant chair. The dancer that I had been was not dancing anymore. The student I had been was now a full-fledged counselor of expatriates. The wife I had been was no longer responsible for taking care of the house and its chores. The mother I had been now had a full-time nanny. None of these changes happened gradually. Their impact was sudden, dramatic, and unreal. I didn't feel sad or elated. I felt scared. I sat with myself wondering what I would become as a person with such privilege. I felt old. I was no longer playing at life or struggling to get somewhere. I had arrived.

✧ Exercise: Reflections ✧

In this next section, we'd like you to take some time to reflect on what it was like for you to complete the exercise "Who Was I?"

What was it like for you to complete this exercise?

_____

_____

_____

_____

_____

_____

_____

_____

_____

What were some of the thoughts and feelings you experienced as you went through this exercise?

_____
_____
_____
_____
_____

Does anything stand out for you about yourself as you reflect on *"you"* before the move overseas?

_____
_____
_____
_____
_____

What discoveries did you make about the significance of each area to your definition of your identity?

Internal View of Self:

_____
_____
_____
_____
_____

External Factors Affecting Identity:

_____
_____
_____
_____
_____

Roles:

_____
_____
_____
_____
_____

Significant Relationships with Others:

_____
_____
_____
_____
_____

If certain areas were more significant to your identity than other areas, what is your understanding about why this was so?

_____
_____
_____
_____
_____

How did you feel about yourself as a person before your move overseas?

_____
_____
_____
_____
_____

How would you rate your satisfaction with your identity before moving overseas on a Scale of 1-10? (1 = low, a more negative self-view, unhappy, not satisfied with your identity. 10 = very high, a more positive self-view, very happy, very satisfied with your identity.)

Numerical rating: _____

Write a few words that describe the numerical rating you gave yourself:

_____
_____
_____
_____

What thoughts or feelings do you have about this numerical rating?

_____
_____
_____
_____

Chapter 2

Stories and Diagrams: Clarifying Your Identity

In the "Who Was I?" exercise in Chapter 1, you looked at the separate pieces that make up your identity. In the Reflections exercise, you highlighted your thoughts and feelings about your identity before your overseas move. In this chapter you'll continue to build on these two exercises by putting these pieces into a context, a whole. You'll do this by writing a story and making a diagram about your identity before your decision to move overseas. This will provide an even deeper understanding of yourself before the move.

Identity Before the Decision to Move Overseas: Sharing Our Stories

Before we guide you to write your own story and diagram your identity, we'll share our stories and diagrams with you. This will help you write your story and construct your diagram later in this chapter. Within our stories, we highlight our roles and relationships by underlining them. After writing our stories, we use that information to construct our diagrams. As we highlight roles and relationships, we include our internal view and the external factors affecting our identity. Remember that internal view and external factors affecting identity are inextricably linked to roles and relationships. By diagramming roles and relationships, we can create a pictorial representation of our identities before the decision to move overseas.

Debra's Story: Identity Before the Decision to Move Overseas

Before I moved to Bangkok, Thailand, in the fall of 1991, I lived in Washington, D.C. with my <u>husband</u> Brad. Brad and I met in 1982 in Springfield, Missouri, where we both went to college. I remember the nights we spent talking about his plans to one day live and work abroad. As I listened to his thoughts and dreams about living overseas, I had no idea that one day it would be a dream we would share as a couple.

After we graduated from college, Brad moved to Washington, D.C., to work at the U.S. Department of State. Over the next several years, Brad traveled around the world for his work and I worked as a social worker for the Platte County Department of Family Services in Kansas City, Missouri. The geographical separation strained our relationship, and we stopped seeing

24

one another for about ten months. Although the time apart was difficult, it helped both of us realize that we wanted to be together.

As our relationship became more serious, we decided to marry. Brad told me that he needed to move overseas very soon for his job. He knew that his career plans would affect my plans and he feared that one day I might resent him for that. We had both worked hard through college to earn good grades, and we both had strong career goals. He didn't want his plans to interfere with mine. I naively thought that as long as we were together, everything else would work out. Even though I knew my career plans would change, I accepted the idea of moving overseas, but it seemed like a far-off future concern not worth worrying about. I focused on my upcoming marriage and my more immediate move to Washington to be with him.

After Brad and I <u>married</u>, I moved to Washington from the Midwest. I had difficulties the first year as I attempted to adjust to all the changes associated with moving and a new marriage, as well as leaving my job, family, and several close friends. After I eventually settled in, I embraced the hustle-bustle lifestyle associated with living in the nation's capital. I felt like a <u>Washingtonian</u>. I rode the subway to work and walked around downtown on my lunch hour. Brad and I often went out to dinner at one of the many ethnic restaurants around town. On the weekends we explored the city and surrounding areas, rode our bikes on the bike trails, and spent time preparing for the next work week ahead.

At this point in our lives, Brad and I both focused on our careers. Brad often went out of the country on business. I spent <u>long hours at work</u> trying to prove myself and <u>joined organizations that reflected my career interests</u>. It seemed there were never enough hours in the day, and as time went on it seemed like most of my time, and our time as a couple, revolved around <u>work-related activities</u> and <u>friendships</u>. We had made a <u>few friends in D.C.</u>, but it was difficult to get together with them frequently.

I found myself missing my <u>family</u>. I'm one of five children and my parents and three of my brothers and their families all live in Kansas City, Missouri. My other brother and his family live nearby in Lansing, Kansas. I now felt like I was more of an outsider to the family than ever. I also found myself missing the <u>long-term friendships I had in the Midwest</u>. I've known one friend since childhood and another since high school. Though I tried to maintain contact with my family and friends, the relationships changed because of the geographic distance. I was lonely for closer contact with my family and friends, but since that wasn't possible I devoted my time and energy to my work.

After working in several social work positions I realized that to advance further in my career, I'd need to return to graduate school to earn my Master's degree in Social Work. I quit my job and returned to graduate school full-time. Graduate school consumed all my time and energy and I pursued it with the same passion and enthusiasm I had previously devoted to my work.

While in graduate school, the opportunity to move overseas came up for Brad. The possibility excited me. I was thrilled at the opportunity to move overseas, live and work abroad, learn about another country, and meet new people. I had always adapted well to stress and change, and I had no reason to think that moving overseas would be any different. Brad bid on countries where he would be challenged career-wise and I could also work. We were a dual-career couple and I was in the prime of my career. I never considered the possibility of not working.

Before we made the move to Bangkok, I completed my Master's degree in Social Work with a specialization in mental health counseling. I was working as an <u>outpatient counselor</u> and was in the process of <u>completing the professional licensure requirements</u> necessary to practice as a private practitioner. This was the goal I had set for myself. Most of the <u>organizations I belonged to reflected my career choice</u>. I was also a <u>member of Beta Sigma Phi</u>, a woman's organization, and a <u>member of The Missouri Society of Washington, D.C.</u> Most of my <u>friends were professionals in the mental health field</u>. My reading reflected topics germane to my profession. I <u>exercised</u> on a regular basis. My <u>role as a social worker/counselor</u> heavily influenced the way I saw myself.

Debra's Diagram

My diagram highlights key roles and relationships that defined my life just before the decision to move to Bangkok. This diagram shows my identity at that time.

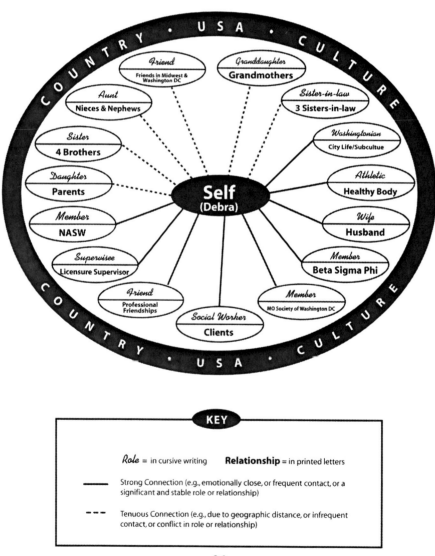

Debra's Comments on Her Diagram

Several things stand out in the diagram of my pre-move identity. First, I already had strained relationships with people I felt the closest to in the Midwest because of the geographic distance. Second, my husband was my primary support system; my other support systems were mainly through work-related activities, organizations, and professional affiliations. Third, I made the startling discovery that although my picture seemed full, my work defined my life. A major portion of my time and energy focused on professional pursuits, professional affiliations and organizations, and friendships developed through work. I wondered how this had occurred.

Looking back, I began to question the impact of the move I made from the Midwest to the East Coast to get married. I can vividly recall missing my family and friends in the Midwest, and all that had been familiar to me there. At times I questioned whether I had made a mistake in marrying Brad. I sometimes wondered whether I truly loved my husband, since I felt so unsettled. I was lonely, but I also felt guilty for those feelings since I had been so excited to marry Brad and move to Washington. Instead of considering the impact of the move on me, I attributed the feelings to "adjusting to marriage." Others reassured me that the first year of married life was the most difficult, that what I was feeling was normal for a newlywed, and that I shouldn't worry. So I chalked my feelings up to being a newlywed and pursued my career with a vengeance.

In retrospect, I think I attempted to use work to replace my missing relationships and everything familiar to me before the move. Before the move to Bangkok, the move from the Midwest to D.C. had already affected me, but I didn't understand it. I especially didn't understand how significantly it would continue to affect me when we moved overseas.

Charise's Story: Identity Before the Decision to Move Overseas

Two years before I moved to Thailand, I had been <u>married</u> for seven years, built a career in <u>dance therapy</u>, and given birth to a <u>daughter</u>, Alexandra. Just before Alexandra's first birthday, we moved from our home in Baltimore to Atlanta for my husband's new work assignment. Within the first few months in our new home, I discovered that dance therapy jobs in the Atlanta area were scarce and dwindling because of recent budget cuts. I felt panic about my newly dependent state. Suddenly my husband provided all the income and I mothered a one-year-old full-time. This situation reminded me of my own stay-at-home <u>mother</u> and the fact that she and my father eventually divorced.

My mother, in the course of rebuilding her life, was living near her brother and sister in Memphis, Tennessee. By moving to Atlanta, I had come geographically closer to her as well as to my only surviving grandparent. By moving to the south of the U.S., I returned to my ancestral roots, as personified by my <u>grandmother</u> who still lived in a small town in Mississippi. She was a petite woman with a feisty and playful spirit who could entertain Alexandra for a couple of hours without any signs of fatigue. My <u>sister</u>, my only sibling, also lived in the Atlanta area with her husband. She and I had had a history of lengthy phone conversations, primarily about how our mother was doing.

By living in the same city, my sister and I could visit and forge a more direct relationship *with one another. We had more opportunity to connect in ways outside of our mutual concern for our mother. My <u>father</u>, who was living overseas, was delighted to be able to visit my sister and I together. He made several brief stopover visits. He was here and gone and here again, breezing through our lives with his joy of reuniting, and then returning to his world of high finance and expatriate living.*

While my extended family became more united by this move to Atlanta, I hadn't made any friends. My husband's job required him to take periodic trips out of state. We were unable to plan for these trips, because they were in response to sudden medical concerns of epidemic proportions. This meant that we typically had only a day or two's notice of an impending trip. My life revolved around other people's needs and I felt I had very little control. I wanted something of my own design in this life picture. I spent a year trying to piece together a career in dance therapy, and instead ended up making it into the dance community. I joined <u>two dance-performance groups</u>. The rehearsals and performances were part-time, and not very lucrative. But I did feel a connection to myself while dancing that I didn't feel very often in my daily life.

The demands of mothering a toddler often overwhelmed me. My husband traveled for weeks at a time and I felt left behind. I resented that I maintained the home front while he advanced his career. We developed separate lives, and I found this frustrating. Many days I felt frazzled and anxious and wanted to run away. I angered easily. At the same time, whenever I held Alexandra, I felt a great tenderness. I felt her vulnerability, and mine as well.

Alexandra anchored my emotional life because she required constant attention. I felt a huge sense of responsibility for her. Eventually, I found support for her care from two sources: <u>a neighbor who provided daycare in her home</u> and my sister, an English professor with no children of her own who enjoyed helping out as an aunt.

In the second year, I chose daycare because of the demands of my schedule. Alexandra made friends with a girl next door and several other neighborhood children. I saw <u>their families</u> often; we took walks together, went to the school playground, or gathered at each other's houses. After awhile, I felt less like a newcomer and more like part of the community. While I didn't develop close friendships with my neighbors, I did share a rapport with them as parents of young children, and enjoyed observing the children develop friendships.

With support for my mothering role from my neighbor, sister, and community, I enrolled in <u>graduate school</u> for a Master's degree in <u>Social Work</u>. The camaraderie of <u>my fellow students</u>, many of whom were at a similar stage of life, boosted my morale. The future looked bright and exciting. I felt content and full of direction and purpose.

At this time, I began working with a <u>counselor</u> because my program encouraged students to learn about the counseling process first-hand. When my counselor asked me how I wanted to use the sessions, I had no idea. I had never put myself at the center of an interaction like this. Over time, I appreciated the ease with which my counselor shared her own experience as a mother, encouraging me to break my silence on the difficulties of my life. At home I fumed and complained, but then persevered and exhausted myself when I felt stressed. Discussing other ways to manage was a great relief and I learned other strategies for taking charge of my life. I continued to dance and somehow managed to juggle studies, periodic rehearsing, and mothering for the next ten months. I focused on doing well in school because it was my ticket out of my feelings of dependency. I became a high achiever.

Charise's Diagram

My diagram highlights key roles and relationships that defined my life just before the decision to move overseas and provides a picture of my identity at that time.

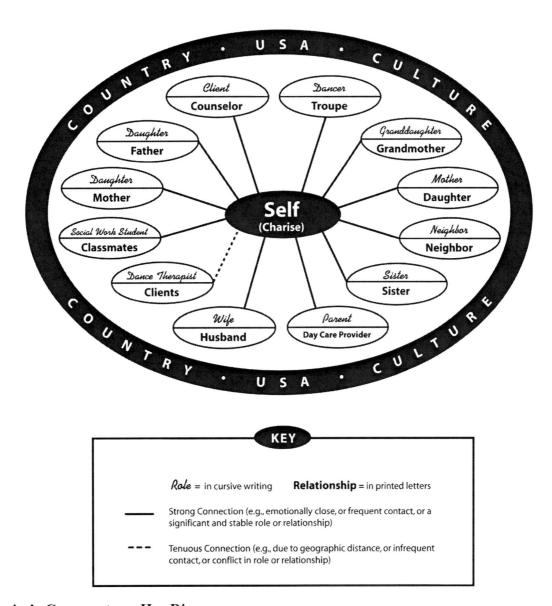

Charise's Comments on Her Diagram

My diagram shows a prevalence of family relationships. The move to Atlanta brought me closer to my parents, sister, and grandmother. I grew closer to family members while my role as a mother intensified because of my husband's absences. My dance therapy ambitions languished and lingered as a distant memory.

The completed picture shows a snapshot of my identity during the second year of life in Atlanta, just before the overseas move. As a dancer and social work student, I had acquired several sources of support for my non-familial roles. Also, I had begun to feel a part of a community within my neighborhood. I can still remember how my outlook and my mood shifted in that second year. The feelings of frustration and anxiety that characterized the first year began to subside. I focused on expanding my career goals and felt energized. I could tolerate my daily life better, even though I had less time for rest. Before entering graduate school, the feeling of fear, of not knowing what my future would hold, drained me. It undermined my ability to maintain the tasks of daily life. Caring for the house, the meals, and our child brought little joy. I felt lost as a housewife. The decision to pursue social work took the burden off of my housewife role, since it offered a way back into the job market. I felt more balanced in my activities and more secure in myself. This feeling gave me a more stable sense of my identity.

Exercise: Your Identity Before the Decision to Move Overseas

This exercise will help you look back and write about your identity before your move overseas. You'll need to decide at what point in time to begin. The beginning of your story may be a few months before the decision to move overseas, or a few years. Certain earlier events that link you to the move may be important to remember. You'll build upon the sketch that you began in the "Who Was I?" exercise. Focus on roles and relationships you identified in this previous exercise. Your story should include significant events, the rhythm of your daily life, your goals, and your feelings about how your life was going. After you write your story, go back and underline all roles and relationships as a reference for you to use when you construct your diagram.

You may feel a strong resistance to looking back and re-experiencing the emotions that surrounded that time in your life. Pace yourself, distance when you need to, and know that you're highlighting a piece of a longer story.

Part One

My Story: My Identity Before the Decision to Move Overseas

Part Two

Constructing Your Diagram

The steps below explain how to make your diagram based on your story. Your diagram will reflect your identity before your decision to move overseas.

Step 1: In the space provided, begin to construct your diagram by drawing a small circle in the center which represents your core self. Write the word SELF in the middle of the circle.

Step 2: Go back and look at the roles and relationships you've underlined in your story.

Step 3: For each role and relationship you underlined, draw an oval in the space surrounding your core self. Divide each oval in half by drawing a horizontal line through it. In the upper half of the oval, write the name of the role in cursive writing. In the lower half of the oval, write the name of the relationship in printed letters.

Step 4: Connect each of these outer ovals to the center circle with a line. The type of line you choose should reflect the degree of stability, or closeness, of each role and relationship in your life *at that time*. Use a solid line (————) to indicate a strong connection to a particular person or a role (e.g., emotionally close, or frequent contact, or a significant and stable role or relationship). Use a broken line (- - - - - -) to indicate a more tenuous connection to a particular person or role (e.g., due to geographic distance, or infrequent contact, or conflict in role or relationship).

Step 5: Look at your picture and make sure it's complete.

Step 6: Enclose the whole picture by drawing a large circle around all of the radiating ovals. Draw a second circle outside of the first circle, leaving about a quarter inch between the two. These two outer circles and the space between them are like a boundary. This boundary represents the country and culture you live in. At the top and the bottom of your picture, in the quarter-inch space between the two outer circles you just drew, write the word *country*, then fill in your home country or the country from which you moved, then write the word *culture*.

My Diagram

This diagram highlights key roles and relationships in my life just before my decision to move overseas and shows a picture of my identity at that time.

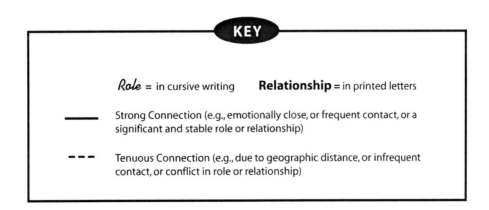

My Comments on My Diagram

In the space below, write about any discoveries you made while making your diagram. This could include thoughts and feelings that emerged, the significance of particular roles or relationships, and any other impressions about this picture of your identity at that time.

_____
_____
_____
_____
_____
_____
_____
_____
_____
_____
_____
_____
_____
_____
_____
_____
_____
_____

In this chapter, you've gained a clearer understanding about yourself before the overseas move. In Chapter 3, we'll look at the effect of your decision to move overseas on your identity.

Chapter 3

Aftermath and Departure:
Your Identity After the Decision to Move Overseas

The process of leaving home begins long before your departure. It begins with your decision to move. How you feel about your decision (e.g., resigned, excited, ambivalent), touches your life in many ways. As the awareness of your decision unfolds, you make choices about what to do and how to relate to other people. To highlight what happens to your identity when the overseas move begins, please complete the following exercise.

Exercise: "Who Was I?" (Part 2)

The Effect of the Decision to Move Overseas on Your Identity

Locate your completed "Who Was I?" exercise from Chapter 1. Next, take a highlighting marker, pen, or pencil and mark each description of yourself that the overseas move affected. This should cover the period from the time you first decided to move until you leave your home country.

For example, if you wrote down under Internal View of Self that you valued being close to your extended family and you began to wonder how you'd maintain contact with them, highlight this description. If you wrote down that you liked to exercise in a gym and began to wonder if this would be possible in your new country, highlight this description. If you began to wonder how women are viewed in the new country, perhaps questions about gender and body image began to arise. Highlight these descriptions.

Place a mark on each or any of your descriptions of yourself that was somehow affected, left behind, or changed in some way because of the decision to move. Even if it was only slightly affected, go ahead and mark it. Even if you just started thinking about that description of yourself, go ahead and mark it.

Under External Factors Affecting Identity, for example, when you told friends and family about the move, how did they view you? Did their view change? Were you envied or did others try to make you feel guilty for moving? Did they have any affect on you? If so, highlight these descriptions of yourself. If your community and culture would change, highlight these descriptions.

Under Roles, would you leave anything familiar? For example, if you worked outside the home, would you leave a work role? If you were active in your children's school, would you leave any volunteer roles? Would your role as mother change in the new country if you have household help there or if you leave older children behind to attend college on their own? If any of these roles would change, highlight these descriptions.

Under Significant Relationships with Others, when others learned of your move, did any relationships change? If so, highlight these descriptions. For example, did others pull away from you? Did you pull away from others close to you? What happened as you said good-bye? Did you make promises to write? Did you notice any changes in your support systems? Were your connections and contact with others, your affiliations with organizations, or your activities affected? If so, highlight these descriptions.

After you've completed each of the four facets of identity–internal view of self, external factors affecting identity, roles, and significant relationships with others–and you've highlighted the descriptions of yourself that were somehow affected when the overseas move was introduced into your life, proceed to the next section.

Reflections on the "Who Was I?" Exercise, Part 2

Charise:

The step of highlighting what the move would change was automatic and took no thought whatsoever. I highlighted everything. Even my views of myself changed because they were linked to particular roles and relationships. I questioned certain personal qualities because there would be little opportunity to express them. For example, I didn't feel graceful anymore because I associated this quality with dancing. The shape of my body was so closely linked to dancing that I wasn't sure what I looked like without it. Maybe, over time, I'd turn into some solid, heavy, clumsy piece of flesh. Maybe I'd become unattractive to myself and to my husband. Maybe my marriage would crumble. Fear grew as I discovered how strongly my self-perceptions were tied to my activities. I lost a sense of consistency with the past and felt my foundations crumbling. The past had blown up under my feet and I had to establish all over again where the ground was.

Debra:

On the same afternoon that I completed the "Who Was I?" exercise, I continued with the next step and proceeded to highlight all the descriptions of myself that would be altered or changed because of the overseas move. As I highlighted description after description of myself, I remember feeling stunned and sat in disbelief. I had highlighted almost every description of myself! I knew that my life had been greatly affected by the move overseas, but didn't realize to what extent until I saw it written in front of me.

I had an even more painful realization that afternoon. As I reviewed my answers to each facet I had highlighted, I didn't like that work defined so much of my life. I realized that almost everything I identified with in my previous life had changed or vanished. With the overseas move to Bangkok, my life had changed so much I no longer recognized it.

❧ Exercise: Reflections ❧

Read the following paragraph, then close your eyes and spend some time with your thoughts and feelings about what you just experienced.

As you completed the "Who Was I?" exercise, Part 2, what happened as you highlighted each of the descriptions of yourself that was affected by the decision to move? What were some of the feelings and thoughts you experienced? Did you feel confused? Angry? Sad? Numb? Happy? Did you feel a loss? Did you feel it was positive or negative? Was there relief to let something go? Did you feel in control or out of control? Did you feel like you were still you, or did you feel like you were being torn apart or fragmented in some way? Who are you? Are you the same person? What is happening to your identity? Do you feel whole? Do you feel like something is missing? Who are you now?

After you've spent some time reflecting, record some of your thoughts and feelings below.

_____

_____

_____

_____

_____

_____

_____

_____

_____

_____

_____

_____

_____

_____

_____

_____

_____

_____

_____

_____

_____

_____

_____

_____

How would you rate your satisfaction with your identity after you became aware of the move on a Scale of 1 - 10? (1 = low, a more negative self-view, unhappy, not satisfied with your identity. 10 = very high, a more positive self-view, very happy, very satisfied with your identity.)

Numerical rating: _____

Write a few words that describe the numerical rating you gave yourself:

_____
_____
_____
_____
_____

What thoughts or feelings do you have about this numerical rating?

_____
_____
_____
_____
_____

The Effect of the Decision to Move and the Departure on Identity

When you decide to move overseas, your identity begins to shift. In this section, we'll continue telling our stories that we began in Chapter 1. We'll describe the events in our lives just preceding our moves, then we'll illustrate the changes that occurred to our identities before we entered the foreign country. As our stories unfold, we'll redo our diagrams based on the repercussions of these events. You'll see our diagrams take on a very different look. Our stories will serve as examples to follow as you write and diagram your story later in this chapter.

Charise's Story: The Effect of the Decision to Move and the Departure on Her Identity

My husband, Charles, dreamed of moving to Asia for years. He longed to return to the part of the world where he'd lived as a teenager. While in medical training, he went briefly to Thailand to work on a research study and made contacts in the overseas medical world. Near the end of his two-year assignment in Atlanta, he received a call about a research position in Bangkok. He'd have to join the Army to take this job, but it was the opportunity he'd been waiting for so he agreed.

"I'm selling my soul for a few years," he told me.

Although the move to Thailand interrupted my social work training, I didn't ask Charles to refuse the offer. I had accepted his dream of Asia for years already, knowing that one day I'd go there with him. The timing was abrupt, though, and it meant giving up many things just as I had

38

them securely in place. My social work training was not completed. I had my network of neighbors and classmates. My daughter had her first budding friendship. I had become more skilled as a modern dancer. I liked the diversity of my life. I wanted to stay in Atlanta longer than two years and I had ideas about renovating the upstairs of our house.

Because of the impending move, I started losing my enthusiasm for my social work program. I felt helpless and knew I'd have to throw away everything I had worked so hard to get. When I finally got the nerve to call my advisor at school to tell him what was happening, he was surprisingly optimistic. His parents had worked in Asia, and he felt that there might be an opportunity for me in this move. He suggested that I overload my courses the next semester so that by the time of the move I'd only have one requirement left: a six-month internship. I'd have to locate an organization in Thailand that could provide such an internship placement. Then I'd have to prepare a proposal for the Dean of Students.

With my advisor's encouragement, I became my own advocate to complete my training overseas. This had never been done in the history of the school, but I had a promising case. I was a good student. Charles knew of a community services organization in Bangkok run by an American social worker. This organization was willing to take me as an intern. The alternative route, breaking up my family for six months so I could complete my program in the U.S., was unacceptable to me. I presented my case to the Dean who agreed to make an exception for me. Contracts were signed and I felt relieved and excited about the plan to complete my Master's degree. I'd move overseas not only to support my husband's work, but to build my own career path.

My awareness of the move crept in slowly over the months of preparation. I learned a new dance performance piece, even though I'd only perform it one time. I didn't want to stop the momentum of performing since I didn't know where dance would fit into my life once I moved. I held on. The performance was in June. I spent the next few weeks teaching my part to the woman who would replace me.

Next I began the household sorting and packing process. Charles and I decided which household items could be left behind and stored for several years. Then we decided what to carry with us and what would be shipped. Whatever we shipped would take two to three months to arrive. Alexandra created her own portable suitcase with a fanny pack that she strapped around her waist and filled with an assortment of toys. The weight of this bag defied logic. How could a three-year-old carry so much? It was her entire world of play. When the day came to say good-bye to her day care provider, she didn't know this was a final hug and smiled brightly while we cried.

My social work class and neighbors organized two farewell parties. These parties seemed like wakes. Everyone got a final view of me before I left them. I already felt like somewhat of a ghost and had started to detach, yet wanted to stay. I felt bombarded emotionally as my current and future life came crashing together and pulled me in different directions. I surprised myself by bursting into tears at my last social work practicum class. We were each given a chance to speak, and as I talked about not having the support of my class for my internship overseas, my voice trembled and my body started to shake. Then I cried, and everyone grew silent. I caught a glimpse across the circle of another woman crying. She and I had shared mothering woes together. She had managed to stay in the program while having a baby. We were defeating the

39

odds. When I looked at her, I felt our connection and our strength even through our tears. Maybe this, I thought, would carry me more easily to Thailand.

I suffered one more loss before our move: my grandmother died. My father, sister, and I were with her the last few days in the hospital. She looked like a teenager on her bed; she had scarcely any lines in her face. Her labored breathing was her last effort to stay alive. She waited for us to be with her and then she peacefully departed. She had staged her exit without any great drama and chose a wise time to leave us to our scattered lives. After all, I was taking her only great-grandchild halfway across the world for several years. My sister was divorcing her husband of twelve years and was moving to New York. My father's second wife was dealing with the effects of a recent diagnosis of multiple sclerosis. My grandmother would no longer be a central organizing force in our lives, rallying us together for splendid feasts at her table. We would miss her very much.

My sister, with her new single status and her new job, packed her belongings and asked my father to help her drive a U-Haul® truck up the East Coast. She promised to visit us in Thailand next summer. Neither of us cried when we said good-bye. We had a habit of looking at each other with the recognition that life was changing dramatically but we would survive. We did this when our parents told us they were divorcing. That look between us was like holding hands to steady our balance.

My counselor organized a ritual for my last session, including the lighting of candles and a farewell hug. I felt some relief at leaving this counseling relationship. I knew that the move had allowed for a closure that I wouldn't have known otherwise. How do you leave someone who has provided you with a sense of importance and direction? I walked out of her clinic detached from my emotions. I thought that I could check this one off my list of good-byes and move on with my life.

I found it most difficult to leave our house. I felt that I had let it down somehow. We sold it after only two years. We wouldn't return. Not only that, but strangers would move in. On the day they arrived, the house was empty except for our suitcases. We would spend our last night in a hotel. I walked through each room, stroking the walls, apologizing for leaving. In the midst of my ritual the new family burst through the front door. Their children ran around shouting, voices echoing off the high ceilings. Suddenly I was an intruder and it was time to leave.

I felt a choking sensation in my throat as I got in the car. Alexandra's best friend and dad smiled and waved. I sank into the passenger seat, unable to muster a smile. I looked down the hill that led to the playground and remembered some good times there. As my husband backed out of the driveway, I looked back at our house. I felt homeless. Too much had been taken away and I wanted to burrow into a hole and sleep. By the time we arrived at our hotel, my head was aching. The next day, we boarded the plane.

Charise's Diagram

The leaving process begins in the months before the move. Therefore, I already need to change my diagram based on my story, even before the move. Losses are already at hand and roles and relationships already shift. The diagram is a reflection of my identity just before I boarded the plane for Bangkok.

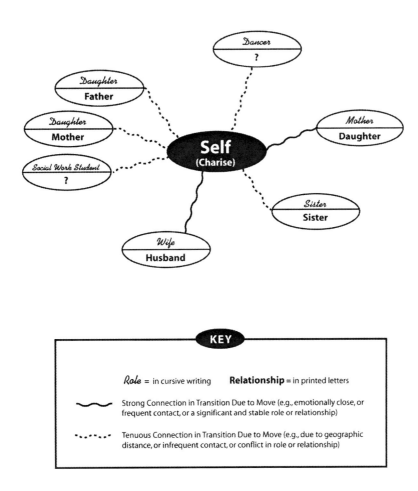

Charise's Comments on Her Diagram

The diagram looks incomplete because the outer circle–the one representing my country and culture–is gone. Certain roles and relationships that I had to leave behind are gone. Roles and relationships with my family of origin have become distant. Ongoing roles and relationships that were going with me are shifting. The remaining picture of my identity looks unstable in comparison with my previously fleshed out and balanced picture.

The instability of my diagram reflects my internal experience just before the move. While I had agreed to the move, and planned for it, I felt like a dead weight dragged and bobbing along behind the furious momentum of change. My world had collapsed around me. I felt stunned.

Debra's Story: The Effect of the Decision to Move and the Departure on Her Identity

When Brad explored the job at the U.S. Embassy in Bangkok, we were both excited. We had always dreamed and talked about doing this. It was truly a dream come true. I resigned from my job and organizations. As we made our plans to move, sold our car, put our house on the market, took Thai language lessons, and said good-bye to family and friends, I was full of anticipation and excitement.

I felt lucky to have this chance of a lifetime. Daydreams about exploring my new neighborhood, city, and country filled my thoughts. I pictured all the people I'd meet, not only Thais, but other Americans and people from other countries living abroad, too. I thought about what our home would look like. As an expatriate spouse, I knew I'd have to entertain. Was I ready for this? I went to classes while still in the States to help prepare. I wasn't worried about work. I had already found an organization in Bangkok that provided a variety of services to the expatriate community, including mental health counseling. After I sent them a copy of my resume, they invited me to contact them upon arrival to discuss employment as a counselor. Former residents of Bangkok told me that many women worked there and I looked forward to practicing my profession abroad. Before leaving the U.S., I felt that I was walking on clouds. I was so excited about the move and all it had to offer that the irritating details of the move seemed minimal, or at least tolerable.

I think the impact of our decision to move overseas finally hit me when we took off from Dulles International Airport in October 1991, bound for Bangkok. As I sat on the plane, I felt strange and numb. I didn't feel happy or sad. I felt emotionless. I wrote in my journal about my activities earlier that morning before we had left our hotel. It was dark, rainy, and very early. Our packed bags awaited the taxi driver, but nonetheless I kept roaming around the rooms, searching. I went through each room and looked under the beds, checked behind the doors, and looked in drawers. At first, I thought I was checking for forgotten items. Yet, I knew at some level this was too easy an explanation. I sat on the plane with my journal in my lap listening to my inner self. As I wrote, I discovered that instead of searching for forgotten items, I was really searching for safety, security, and my sense of belonging. I wanted to collect and find everything that had already departed from my life.

As I sat writing, I realized that all the parts of my known world were spread out or being left behind. We had scattered our physical belongings, which represented the life we had created up to that point. Some were in storage, others were in Thailand, and some were in transit and not due to arrive for months. We had left our families and friends behind. I knew that some of our relationships would not stand the test of time and distance. I had left my job and professional support system behind. In short, I was leaving almost everything that reflected me. The only things left were myself, my husband, a few personal documents, and some clothes. I realized I was not sure when I would return. The 14,000-mile journey to Bangkok suddenly became a very vivid reminder of how far away we were going from everything and everyone we knew.

I'll never forget how I felt that day. As the tears rolled down my face, I felt suspended in time. Although I knew where I was moving to, I didn't know what it would be like, what I'd be like, or what my life would be like. I was acutely aware of everything I was leaving behind and I felt all the changes and losses deep in my soul. I felt that everyone I knew was gone, or out of my life in a way that was unfamiliar to me. It felt like I was floating. I had no home in the U.S., and I didn't have a home abroad yet, either.

I was leaving everything and everyone I loved in my country and despite my high hopes of meeting new people and making new friends, I felt friendless and odd. I felt sad, but didn't understand why–I had been looking forward to this move. As the plane continued to climb and carry me towards my new destination, I held many contradictory feelings. I felt an incredible longing to return to my old life and simultaneously felt incredible anticipation and excitement for what might lie ahead.

Debra's Diagram

As I sat on the plane bound for Bangkok, I slowly became aware of how much my life had already changed, but was only marginally aware of the significance these changes would have later. My job, organizations, friendships, relationships, and many of my support systems were far away. The diagram reflects my picture of my identity the day I left for Bangkok.

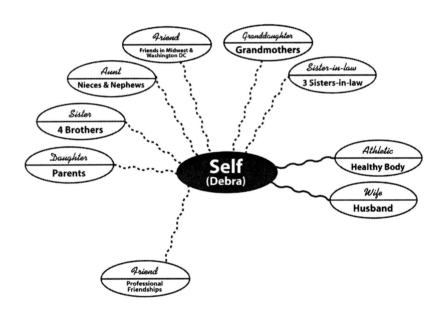

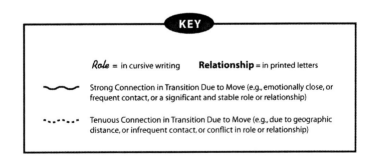

Debra's Comments on Her Diagram

My immediate reaction to my diagram was that everything had changed and I wanted to distance myself from it. I preferred looking at the diagram as a detached observer because this was less disturbing. My identity seemed distorted, unattractive, and disconnected. I did not like this picture, and preferred the previous fuller and complete picture of my identity. I forced myself to sit with the more barren picture of my altered identity. As I did, I felt alone and detached from the things left in my life because nothing looked or felt the same.

I realized how much of who I was had been defined by what I did. It was unsettling that work, work-related activities and organizations, and relationships that had been such a vital part of me were now completely gone. I felt off-balance and insignificant.

My diagram showed that my identity consisted primarily of my relationships. However, every relationship had changed or was changing. My relationships with friends and family from the Midwest were strained because of my previous move, and I knew the increased distance to Bangkok would only make things worse. The more recent friendships in Washington were also affected by my leaving, and I questioned how I could maintain them from so far away. The task seemed overwhelming. As I continued to look at my diagram, I felt only marginally connected to the people I cared the most about. I feared that this would grow worse with time as I remained so far away. As I sat with the barren picture of my identity, I became overwhelmed by loneliness and sadness.

Exercise: The Effect of the Decision to Move and the Departure on Your Identity

In this exercise, you'll explore and write about your decision to move overseas. By doing this, you'll build on your story from Chapter 2. You'll also expand your "Who Was I?" exercise, Part 2, that we did at the beginning of this chapter.

In your story, include your thoughts and feelings about the events surrounding your decision to move overseas. Describe how your roles and relationships changed, what it was like to say good-bye (to friends, family, work, etc.), and what it was like to leave.

Part One

My Story: The Effect of the Decision to Move and the Departure on My Identity

Part Two

Constructing Your Diagram

To draw your diagram, you'll refer to the story you've just written, as well as the diagram you created in Chapter 2. You may also want to refer to our diagrams as a guide. The diagram you draw now should reflect the status of your roles and relationships after you made the decision to move overseas, just before your arrival on foreign soil. This diagram shows your identity at that time.

Step 1: In the space provided, draw a small circle in the center to represent your core self. Write the word SELF in the middle of that circle.

Step 2: Based on what you've discovered in writing your story and by reviewing your diagram in Chapter 2, decide which roles and relationships to include here. You may leave out any roles and relationships that will no longer be active in your life due to your move.

Step 3: For each role and relationship you've identified, draw an oval in the space surrounding your core self. Divide each oval in half by drawing a horizontal line through it. In the upper half of the oval, write the name of the role in cursive writing. In the lower half of the oval, write the name of the relationship in printed letters.

Step 4: Connect each of these outer ovals to the center circle with a wavy line. There are two types of wavy lines; a solid one (〰〜) and a broken one (·····). The wavy line shows that the connection is in transition because of your move. Use a solid wavy line (〰〜) to indicate a strong connection to a person or role which is in transition due to the move (e.g., emotionally close, or frequent contact, or a significant and stable role or relationship). Use a broken wavy line (·····) to indicate a tenuous connection to a particular person or role which is in transition due to the move (e.g., due to geographic distance, infrequent contact, or conflict in role or relationship).

Step 5: Leave out the outer circles or boundary, because you're leaving your country and culture.

My Diagram

This diagram highlights my identity via key roles and relationships after I made the decision to move overseas, but just before my arrival overseas.

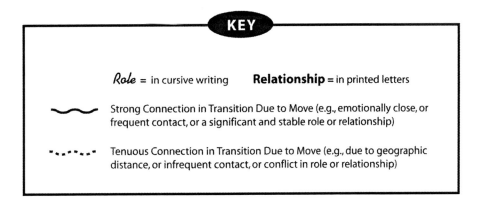

My Comments on My Diagram

In the space below, write about discoveries you made while constructing your diagram. This could include thoughts and feelings that emerged, changes in significant roles and relationships, and any other impressions about this picture of your identity at that time.

_____
_____
_____
_____
_____
_____
_____
_____
_____
_____
_____
_____
_____
_____
_____
_____
_____
_____
_____
_____

The Emotional Response

The diagram you constructed reflects how your roles and relationships changed with your decision to move overseas. As you compare this diagram to the diagram you completed in Chapter 2, the emotional impact of these changes may be very significant. The Reflections exercise below, and the Focusing exercise that follows, will help you capture the emotional impact of these changes. We'll also share our responses with you to help you through the process.

❖ Exercise: Reflections ❖

What does your second diagram look like to you?

_____
_____
_____
_____

Charise:

My diagram looked like a doodle, like a few funny scribbles on paper, not like a finished representation of my identity structure. It floated with no boundary. I had no solid people connections.

Debra:

My diagram looked incomplete and out of balance. Nothing looked solid or stable. Instead, those things that remained, primarily relationships, looked tenuous and distant. I didn't like the look of my diagram. I had the urge to fill in the empty spaces with something.

What was it like for you, on an emotional level, to build and create the first (Chapter 2) diagram, which reflected your roles and relationships before your decision to move overseas? What was it like emotionally to see the changes when you drew your second diagram which reflected your roles and relationships after you made the decision to move overseas?

_____
_____
_____
_____
_____
_____
_____
_____
_____
_____
_____
_____
_____
_____

Charise:

What an exhausting experience! I became aware of the effort I had put into setting up a structure for my life. I loved what I did and the direction and routine of my life. The first diagram contained a lot of potential for further development. My second diagram looked like I had killed something that had barely lived.

Debra:

What an emotional roller-coaster ride! My first diagram showed me at the top of the tracks ready to plunge into new and exciting adventures. I felt I had reached the top after a long climb to get there, and I felt content and secure. My second diagram seemed incomplete, and made me feel numb and empty. I realized how much energy I had spent building my life, and how quickly an overseas move changed or eliminated those efforts. I felt anxious and uneasy, like when you're at the top of the roller-coaster tracks right before you go barreling down towards the bottom. Although you want to stop it, you can't.

Did you have a physical reaction to this exercise? If so, where in your body did you feel it?

_____

_____

_____

Charise: *Yes. I felt an unsettling sensation in my belly, and a tightness in my chest.*

Debra: *Yes. I felt it in my stomach and abdomen mostly. It felt like a pit in this area.*

Exercise: Focusing

If you answered "yes" to the previous question, this Focusing exercise will help you gain a better understanding of the physical reaction you experienced in the process of constructing and comparing your diagrams. Focusing is a technique for developing awareness, originally developed by Eugene Gendlin.[4] Since this type of exercise may be new to you, we'll also share our responses to help you through the process.

Read the following paragraph once before trying the exercise. Then record your responses in the space provided.

Recall the physical reaction you identified in the previous question. Close your eyes and go back and locate the sensation in your body. Follow this sensation, and notice whether it moves, shifts, or stays the same. Breathe with it and give it space. Keep an observer's eye so that you maintain some separation between the sensation and your awareness of it. In other words, stay next to the sensation rather than inside of it. Allow any images or words to surface. Stay with this exercise as long as you need to, then spend a few minutes sitting quietly and acknowledging your body's ability to inform you of your experience.

In the space below, write about your experience and what you became aware of as you did the Focusing exercise.

_____

_____

_____

_____

_____

_____

_____

_____

Charise:

As I did the Focusing exercise, I was aware of two distinct sensations. The nauseous feeling in my belly was pulling me down into my body, commanding my attention. It was unpleasant. At the same time, the tightness in my chest pulled me out from that unpleasant sensation in my belly, like the tightness was trying to hold me up, out of the sick feeling. The two sensations tended to cut me in half and I felt split–disconnected. As I paid attention to the sensation in my chest, images emerged of people I knew in Atlanta. I felt a softening, a warmth, a desire to see these people again. It was easier to breathe. My stomach responded by settling itself. I felt sad. I felt the loss. I felt it completely, no longer split in myself.

Debra:

As I did the Focusing exercise, I felt a pit in my stomach and abdominal area. The sensation seemed somewhat hollow, yet it also felt like there was a slight burning sensation to it. It seemed black and barren. The feeling, not a new one, reminded me (as I sat next to it), of other times where situations got beyond my control, e.g., parental fighting and family discord. It also reminded me of times when I had wanted a change, e.g., breaking up with a boyfriend, going to college, moving out of my parents' home, and moving from the Midwest to the East Coast. Yet when the change happened, I was left with the same feeling. I know that my tendency has been to hold losses in my stomach and abdominal area. Over the years, I have worked on not doing this.

As I continued to focus on the sensation in my abdomen, I gradually felt it lessening a bit, and it didn't seem as binding or constricting. The sensation seemed to move up toward my throat, waiting to be vocalized. As I was able to vocalize the losses I felt, the sensation in my stomach and abdomen slowly disappeared.

The Impact of the Move

The Focusing exercise provided you an opportunity to notice feelings and sensations still active in you, even though the changes occurred in the past. When you pay attention to it, the impact of the move lives within you. If you've previously attempted to ignore or deny the impact, it may hit you rather hard right now as you examine it closely. You may be feeling particularly emotional. Remember that you've gone from a position of balance and stability in a familiar environment to an unanchored position facing the unknown. It is normal and natural to want to suppress these emotions. It may seem easier to deny the impact of the move than to face it with the awareness you've just gained. However, maintaining the denial requires more energy than proceeding with your new awareness.

Before you go on to Chapter 4, we encourage you to take some time (a few hours, a few days, or a few weeks) to pause and assimilate your thoughts and feelings that you've discovered so far.

(Note: If you are in the pre-departure stage of your move, this is a stopping point for you in the book until you arrive overseas. Once you arrive overseas, you can resume reading by beginning Chapter 4.)

Chapter 4

The Impact of the Foreign Culture on Your Identity

Your first encounter with the new culture occurs after you've just flown many hours. You're short on sleep, and still feel raw from the leave-taking process in your home country. You're not in the best condition to step into a new environment. In fact, you're probably in one of the worst conditions possible in terms of your threshold for tolerance.

Debra:

I remember that we arrived in Bangkok in the middle of the night. Our plane was late and rain poured down as we landed. It was hot and humid, and my clothes stuck to me. I was tired. Our sponsor from the embassy met us. She spoke fluent Thai and quickly got us through the airport and customs. I remember listening to all the people speaking Thai. This amazed and amused me. At some level I felt like I was in a dream and perhaps when I woke up, I'd be back in my world where everyone looked familiar and would be speaking English. At another level, I guess the reality of being in Thailand finally hit me.

As we drove into Bangkok in the embassy van, our sponsor told us that instead of taking us to a hotel, she'd take us to our temporary housing, a two-bedroom apartment. This was the first we learned about the change in plans. We arrived at about 3:30 a.m. She gave us an embassy welcome kit that included bed, kitchen and bath linens, some kitchen and cooking utensils, and a few things we could use until our air shipment arrived. She had put a few basic food items in the refrigerator so we could have something to eat in the morning and to hold us over until we could get to the market. She had even made the bed for us. Then she left with instructions for us to be at the embassy by 9:00 a.m. the next morning to begin our check-in procedures.

I remember being very tired but I roamed the apartment exploring our temporary home. It felt odd. The floors were cold and the walls were bare. I eventually went to bed, but I lay there wide awake. When I got up to go to the bathroom I saw something squirming across the floor. It looked like a snake! I screamed, ran, and jumped back into bed. My husband cornered it and said it resembled a small lizard. I pleaded with him to kill it. Brad said he thought it was harmless, but I knew I couldn't sleep with it on the loose. Again I pleaded with Brad to kill it. He reluctantly agreed, found a shoe, and hit it until it was dead. I examined the dead carcass and felt relieved and ashamed. It was so little. My fear had made my husband end its life.

The next morning at the embassy I inquired about the creature we encountered the night before. They told us it was a harmless gecko, actually beneficial because it eats mosquitoes. Although I had read a lot about Thailand before we arrived, nowhere had I learned about geckos. I was not prepared for meeting my first gecko in the middle of the night. After I learned that geckos were harmless, I felt even more ashamed that I had pleaded with Brad to kill it out of my own ignorance and fear.

We were at the embassy that first day much longer than we had planned. Although we were exhausted from our travel, the lack of sleep the night before, and our long day at the embassy, we decided to get more groceries at the commissary since it was a four day Thai holiday weekend. After completing our shopping, we were each loaded down with bags full of groceries. We walked out the front gate of the embassy to hail a taxi. It was hot, humid, and the fumes from the cars made it difficult to breathe. The taxis either whizzed by us, or after stopping to inquire where we lived, the drivers refused to take us home because it was too far for them to go to get back in time for shift change (even though it was only about three miles away). For over an hour, our attempts to hail a taxi were unsuccessful. As we stood on the sidewalk in front of the embassy with our frozen food melting and sweat dripping down each of us, my husband and I got in an argument about what to do. Brad decided to ask an embassy guard about the situation. The guard explained that Thai taxi drivers rent their vehicles for the day, and if they don't return the taxis on time, they are charged an additional days rent. The guard suggested that we might have better luck getting a taxi outside the back gate of the embassy. We lugged our groceries and our sweat drenched selves to the street behind the embassy, but our attempts to get a taxi were still unsuccessful. Eventually we went back to the commissary and requested that our bags of groceries be kept in the cooler while we tried to find someone in Brad's office who could give us a ride home. Several hours later, we finally made it back to our apartment.

Charise:

I remember walking out from the baggage claim area of the Bangkok airport and meeting my husband's new supervisor. He had come, at midnight, to greet us and help us to our hotel. He and my husband began chatting casually as if it were a normal hour to meet for conversation. I tried to be polite with my daughter clinging onto me. The Thai people tended to stare at her, smile, laugh, and make cooing sounds as if she were an adorable teddy bear. I just wanted to get out of the airport as fast as possible into the dark night; to sink into the darkness and disappear into sleep. I kept my desire in check, waiting patiently as if I were standing on a mountain of willpower. I sensed I was supposed to follow the rhythm of my husband and his boss. I felt obliged. I also felt distant, outside of their interaction.

I realize now that I started to become an outsider the night we arrived. I knew I was on my own, and naive about the ways of this new country. I'd have to figure out my own way to break into some sense of belonging here. Otherwise, I might as well sit on my suitcases and wait a few years for the flight back home.

⊰Exercise: Reflections ⊱

In this section, we'd like you to recall your thoughts and feelings about your first encounter with the foreign country.

What do you remember about your arrival overseas?

_____
_____
_____
_____
_____
_____
_____
_____
_____
_____

Does anything stand out as you recall your arrival?

_____
_____
_____
_____
_____
_____
_____
_____
_____
_____

What do you feel is significant about this memory?

_____
_____
_____
_____
_____
_____
_____
_____
_____
_____

Entering the Cultural Maze

After you arrive in a foreign country, you face many questions about your living arrangements. You must decide (or it may be decided for you) where to live, where to purchase things, where to go for various services, and so on. Even with guidance, you're bound to wander, stumble, take a wrong turn, or underestimate the amount of time it takes to accomplish things. You've now entered a cultural maze. As you attempt to find your way, larger questions loom. How will you live here? How will you handle feelings of frustration, helplessness, incompetence, wonder, curiosity, disgust, or any other of a wide range of feelings? Will you retreat, hide, engage, play, or fight your way through each day? What do your emotions and your actions say about you? How are you behaving in this new and foreign land? How does your behavior define *you*?

The purpose of this chapter is to look at how your identity is further affected by living within a foreign culture. The reason for focusing on the culture is to increase your understanding of what happens to you, and your sense of self when you take up residence in an unfamiliar culture. We'll focus on the interaction between the culture that you've internalized from your homeland and the external culture you encounter overseas. We'll discuss what an internalized sense of culture is, and help to clarify what this means to you. We'll then return to the fundamental question of who you are separate from your sense of place; separate from your home, your community, your country, and your culture.

Cultural Confrontation

You've probably heard of the term "culture shock." This term describes the experience people have when suddenly placed in a culture foreign to them. In our opinion, the term is a misnomer. It implies a reactive, passive process going on in which a person is shocked. We think it's more accurate to say that you're confronted, rather than shocked, when immersed in a foreign culture. What you hold to be true from your own cultural background gets challenged by other ways of acting and behaving. Suddenly you're confronted not only with the ways of another culture, but with what you believe based on your own cultural bias. You become aware of things you didn't necessarily need to know about yourself when you were living in your own country.

When in your own country, you're in a familiar context. To a greater or lesser degree, you've absorbed the culture you live in. This becomes your internalized sense of culture, which includes the values, beliefs, and assumptions you've assimilated from your family, community, and country.

Let's imagine that this internalized culture is a design blended into a background. Ordinarily, it's difficult to distinguish the design from the background. When you leave your home country, however, the background falls away and the design becomes prominent. Your internalized culture, which you may not have been aware of, surfaces. Two things result: one, you're more likely to feel rubbed the wrong way by the culture you meet; and two, you have a great opportunity to see how much of your self-definition actually belongs to the mandates of your culture. You'll find yourself engaged in a lively, interactive process of having your internalized cultural values and beliefs confronted by the cultural values and beliefs of your new surroundings. This is the essential definition of our term "cultural confrontation."

Debra's Story: Cultural Confrontation

The first few weeks in Thailand overflowed with numerous tasks to officially mark our arrival. Since my husband Brad would be working at the U.S. Embassy, we were required to complete all the check-in procedures at the embassy–getting our identification cards, Thai driver's licenses, and filling out paperwork to register us with the embassy and our new community. People at the embassy introduced us to other expatriates and Thais, and they showered us with invitations to get together for dinner and introduce us to our new surroundings and community. We also met our apartment building neighbors, some of whom later became good friends. Many people within the embassy community went out of their way to welcome us to Thailand and to make our initial transition easier.

While Brad worked, I kept busy establishing our new home, a difficult task at times because of language and cultural barriers. I set up the utilities, water, and paper delivery. I went out to find food markets and other necessary shops. The shelves in the two grocery stores that catered to foreigners contained many unfamiliar food items from all over the world. Some of the foods looked familiar, but were still different in the packaging, consistency, color, smell or some other aspect. The store itself smelled different than what I was accustomed to. As a result, in the beginning, I made few selections.

I attempted to tackle the obstacle and art of preparing and cooking food in a foreign land. I had found instructions on how to do this in an information packet from one of the classes I took in the U.S. These instructions included a process of soaking the food in a solution of bleach and water several times, followed by rinsing the food in purified or bottled water several times. I obsessed about making sure I got all the bleach off the food. I had visions of poisoning us by accident. It took me most of an afternoon to prepare a simple dinner. By the time it was ready to eat, I was tired from the heat and had lost my appetite. It was difficult for me to eat what I had prepared because of the process I went through making sure the food was free of parasites or harmful contaminants.

On other days, I ventured out on my own, or sometimes with new friends, to explore my neighborhood and to become familiar with my surroundings. Along the street, vendors sold food. The spices used to prepare the food smelled exotic. The food also looked more appetizing than what I was preparing at home. I was eager to try the local cuisine, but other expatriates warned me not to eat food prepared on the street in order to avoid "Bangkok Belly." The symptoms ranged from upset stomach, diarrhea and vomiting to full-blown food poisoning depending on the cause, which could be unfamiliar spices, bacteria, or unsafe food handling.

I looked forward to my daily excursions, which were both exciting and anxiety producing. Everything was so new and interesting. I felt like a small child discovering the world and I was on sensory overload. I can also vividly recall feeling somewhat detached from my activities. It was a different feeling than I had experienced previously while on vacations. While vacationing, I could explore a new place with wonderment and take it all in without feeling substantially changed or affected by what I learned or discovered because I knew it was only temporary. Now, my stay was more permanent and my new surroundings were my home.

As I explored my new environment, I searched for familiarity and some way to belong. I asked myself, "How can I fit in, when everything–the streets, the homes, the people, the climate, the food, the smells, the language, the customs–are all so different from what I know?" I, too, was viewed differently. Here, I was the foreigner. I was looked at by some of my new Thai neighbors with curiosity and with gentle, smiling suspicion.

One day when I was out walking, a small child, a little Thai boy about three years old, saw me and began crying and running from me toward his mother. He pointed at me and repeatedly screamed, "Khun me, khun me, farang, farang. Khun me, khun me, farang, farang!" What the little boy was screaming translated to "Mother, mother, white-skinned foreigner, white skinned-foreigner!"

I stopped in my tracks. I felt stunned, surprised, and sad. I now was the outsider, the unfamiliar person, someone small children would be leery of because I looked so different. This felt so odd, so out of place. For a moment, I felt ashamed of who and what I was. This was a new experience for me. I had never before felt so different, that I could look like someone others would be afraid of.

Clumsily, I attempted to speak the language. Sometimes I got frustrated with myself because I couldn't communicate in the new language. The Thais were patient with me, but I wanted to talk with them more freely than my limited vocabulary would allow. I started studying the language again because, as I struggled to speak it, I realized how much of the language I didn't know. I also developed a new appreciation for all the foreigners living in my home country. I now knew how it felt to be so different and so far away from everyone and everything familiar. It was hauntingly lonely.

Charise's Story: Cultural Confrontation

I remember that first morning as I ventured out of my hotel. There were motorcycles revving up at a traffic light, jammed between cars...fumes...the sun glaring...sidewalk food stands...cooking smells and stale air...people milling about...women in short skirts with long-sleeved shirts...children in school uniforms...a bald, barefoot monk swathed in orange cloth...people cramming into buses already filled to the doors. I felt quite conspicuous as a tall, fair, blonde, blue-eyed woman. I didn't know how to blend into the teeming life. The strong fumes from all manner of vehicles burning leaded gasoline was inescapable. I tried to breathe with short, shallow breaths as I made my way down the street.

During our first week I had no interest in exploring the city. I stayed in the hotel room as much as I could, created a play space for my daughter, and organized our clothes and belongings. Every afternoon, while my husband began his work orientation, my daughter and I slept for several hours. I had to force myself and daughter to wake up so we could sleep again at night.

On the evening of our tenth day my husband, daughter, and I went to a well-known shopping mall. At the center of the mall the space overhead revealed a group of suspended escalators, going up many floors. This was the largest mall in Bangkok, and the largest I had ever seen. The crowds moved in all directions. My husband, who had been here before, suggested that we go up to the top level to eat at a Thai food court. While I heard what he said, I couldn't comprehend his suggestion. As I looked up, I couldn't motivate myself to move toward the escalators. I felt dizzy. Just a few feet away stood a pizza shop. This became my anchor. I told my husband I'd only eat at this pizza shop. I felt foolish, yet relieved, to sit and eat familiar food in an enclosed space. When we finished eating, I wanted to return to the hotel.

Over time, my initial state of overload dissipated and the physical and sensory stress lessened. My body needed time to adapt to the tropical heat, new smells and tastes, different foods, different water, different air, and different language sounds to decipher. I struggled to feel competent, but I felt unequipped to navigate my new world. I was an alien here, and that affected how I interacted with the Thais and other expatriates.

I sought competency and control so decided to immerse myself in Thai culture in as many ways as possible. I did not initially seek out expatriate groups or clubs. My husband and I chose to live in a Thai, rather than an expatriate, community. I attended intensive language classes. I learned to drive British style, with right-hand drive, rather than hire a driver. I sought out tennis lessons from a tennis coach who spoke no English. I allowed my maid to choose our food, which meant that we ate Thai food every day. I enrolled my daughter in a Thai preschool where she was the only foreign child. I worked as a student intern at a local, non-profit organization, the Community Services of Bangkok.

This approach dramatically increased my threshold for tolerance. I learned to accept my new environment and culture. While my senses had once been assaulted, they were now stimulated. I had developed a new filter, one I could carry around with me. I had a different mindset. I now valued Thai culture. I developed new tastes, new preferences, and new ways of doing things. Though I still disliked many things, I could more easily accept this new world.

One day while walking on the street near my house, I noticed some dog excrement on the pavement. Atop that pile lay a yellow flower that had fallen from a nearby tree. This represented the perfect symbol of Bangkok: the juxtaposition of something foul with something delicately beautiful.

Your Story: Cultural Confrontation

In the space provided, write about your early experiences living overseas and your confrontation with the foreign culture. This may include the first days, weeks, or months of your stay. Focus on your initial impressions, how you managed new situations, and how you felt in your new surroundings. Revisit the events, thoughts, and feelings central to your experience as a newcomer to a foreign culture.

_____

_____

_____

_____

_____

_____

_____

_____
_____
_____
_____
_____
_____
_____
_____
_____
_____
_____
_____
_____
_____
_____
_____
_____
_____
_____
_____
_____
_____
_____
_____

⋰ Exercise: Reflections ⋰

The two questions that follow will help you further capture your early experiences in a foreign culture. We'll also share our responses to these questions.

As a newcomer, how did you experience the presence of the foreign culture in your life? For instance, did you experience the foreign culture as a friendly or hostile presence? Did you feel welcome or not in the foreign culture?

_____
_____
_____
_____
_____
_____
_____
_____
_____
_____
_____
_____
_____

Debra:

Before moving to Bangkok, I had only traveled overseas on vacation. Although I heard that Thailand welcomed foreigners, especially Americans, I didn't know what to expect. From the moment we arrived, my husband and I felt welcomed by the Thai people. When we arrived at the airport, even though our plane was late and it was the middle of the night, Thai smiles greeted us. It was refreshing after a long trip. I felt wanted. This feeling remained with me throughout our three-year stay in Thailand. As a foreigner, I felt like a distinguished guest, invited to learn more about Thailand and its culture.

The Thai people and way of life fascinated me. Their gentle ways and warm smiles soothed me. I found the Thai people to be very kind and tolerant. They were very patient with me as I struggled to learn and speak their language. My experiences with the Thai people were very favorable, and helped me feel at home in their country. In fact, after we had lived in Thailand for about a year, I returned to the U.S. to visit my family and friends and I found myself missing Thailand's people and the culture.

Charise:

I felt excluded from Thai culture at first. I desperately wanted to get inside of it, be a part of it, and didn't like being identified as a "foreigner." I felt welcome, but distant. I wanted the Thais not only to accept and include me, but to want me. Speaking Thai impressed them and simple phrases made communicating fun and created a sense of camaraderie. I decided to improve my language skills because it enhanced our interactions. Over time I found the Thai people warm, engaging, and fun.

As a newcomer, did you feel the same way about yourself as you had before you moved overseas? Please explain your answer.

_____

_____

_____

_____

_____

_____

_____

_____

_____

_____

_____

_____

_____

_____

_____

Debra:

No, I almost immediately felt different about myself in Thailand. The Thais often stared at me, but not usually in a leering way. As a white-skinned foreigner I attracted a lot of attention. By U.S. standards, I'm of average height and weight for a woman. However, in Thailand I stood taller than most women and men. I also felt differently about my body. For example, Thai women generally don't wear sleeveless blouses (although this is changing) because, traditionally, it's not proper to expose the upper arm. I became self-conscious about this and stopped wearing sleeveless clothing. I also felt more beautiful as a woman in Thailand. Frequently when I walked down the street a Thai would refer to me as "suay," which means pretty or beautiful. I must admit, I liked the attention. It was a real boost to my ego when a Thai would pass me and say, "Madame, suay."

I felt special living in Thailand because of my roles as an American and the wife of a diplomat. The Thais gave us special privileges because my husband worked at the U.S. Embassy. The Thai people like Americans very much and readily accepted me.

Charise:

No! When I first moved to Thailand, I felt awkward, tall, ungainly, and very pale. I hadn't felt this way before. In the States, I had felt small. In Thailand, I felt huge. I didn't know how to carry myself walking down the street. I received such direct eye contact that I didn't know whether to stare back, look away, or smile. I felt a great loss of privacy. I couldn't just disappear in the crowd.

As I became more adept at living in the culture, I started to feel more at ease. The better I got at the language and with navigating the territory, the more powerful I felt. My beliefs about myself were changing. I connected to the part of me that wanted the attention I was getting. I began to enjoy being looked at. Whereas I had previously thought that the Thai people looked exotic, their looks became more ordinary when they surrounded me every day. Gradually I came to feel that I was the exotic one. I was able to feel more desirable as a woman than I had in my own country.

Introduction to Cultural Confrontation Exercise

Later in this section, you'll complete a cultural confrontation exercise to further demonstrate the clashes that exist between your culture and the foreign culture you've moved into. In the table on the next page, we provide examples from our experiences that describe key behaviors of the Thai people, the beliefs, values, and assumptions of Thai culture that support these behaviors, and how our beliefs, values, and assumptions as American women compare to those of the Thais. Cultural confrontation is illustrated by the jagged lines and shows areas that conflict between the two cultures. A more detailed discussion of each of the examples follows the table.

Examples of Cultural Confrontation in Thailand

Behavior of Thai People	Beliefs, Values, and Assumptions of Thai Culture That Support Behavior	How Our Beliefs, Values, and Assumptions Compare As American Women
1. Greeting: Hands clasped together in prayer-like fashion, head bowing.	Shows respect for person's **status** due to wealth, age, or power. Status is predetermined at birth and relates to **karma** of previous existence. When everyone knows their place, there is **harmony** and **predictability.**	We believe in **equality**. We believe in **opportunity**, and **personal responsibility** for one's life. We believe that **conflict** is inevitable.
2. Putting on a smile despite the circumstance.	**Presentation** and **conformity** are most important. It is safer to keep your feelings to yourself.	We believe in **individuality** and the right to **express** yourself.
3. Relationship of women to men. Presence of large prostitution industry.	Women are a **commodity** for men's sexual needs. Married women must be monogamous. The husband can have relations with prostitutes or even take on a mistress.	We believe women are **equal** to men in terms of freedoms allowed and sexual needs.

The beliefs, values, and assumptions described in the chart above shape the behaviors of the Thai people. When you witness human behaviors, you see the beliefs and assumptions that a particular culture dictates. You experience cultural confrontation when these beliefs and assumptions clash with your own (indicated by jagged lines in the table). As an expatriate, you live within the matrix of another people's belief system that affects your behavior and impacts your belief system. Let's look at the three examples.

Example 1: Karma and Predestination

In Thailand, and in other Asian countries, the belief in status is inextricably linked to the Buddhist belief in karma and reincarnation. Individuals obtain their status as a birthright.

Thailand has overt ways of displaying this belief, such as greeting others with clasped hands and bowed heads. Americans believe they overcame such beliefs by separating from the English monarchy and establishing democracy. American culture espouses equality for all, an ideal that Americans value whether or not it truly exists. Many Americans believe they can determine their destiny. They believe they have one life to live, and strive to improve their lot. The Thais view life more fatalistically and believe their lives are pre-determined. This makes them far less safety-conscious than Americans; we frequently saw them load two adults and two children onto a motorcycle, often without helmets.

Americans find such practices irresponsible, frightening, and something to avoid. Thais believe in protective forces outside the human domain. They often wear Buddhist amulets to help guard their lives. Charise recalls the news stories that followed the crash of a Thai Air flight in 1992 that killed everyone aboard. The comments of one bereaved Thai family struck her as odd when they said that they didn't believe their father had died because he was wearing his amulet necklace.

Example 2: Facial Expressions

Thailand is often called the land of smiles because the Thai people smile so freely. However, smiles can create misunderstandings for visitors not familiar with their true meaning. When a foreigner asks a Thai person a question, many times the Thai person will smile and say "yes," which may or may not answer the question. Thais respond to a foreigner's need to be reassured and calmed, not necessarily to giving correct information. Americans believe in freedom of speech and expression, and expect a direct response to a question, even if this creates conflict.

Example 3: Prostitution and Women's Rights

Prostitution is an entrenched tradition in Thai society. Victoria Combe reported in an article in a major Bangkok daily newspaper that more than 75 percent of Thai males have visited a prostitute at least once.[5] Poor mothers often sell their young daughters as prostitutes in exchange for money or material goods, such as a television. Thais believe these young women make a positive contribution to the welfare of their families. After all, a young woman owes her mother her life, and her mother can decide her fate. Young women are the property of their mothers and men. Sexual freedom is one-sided, to the benefit of men. Many well-educated Thai women choose not to marry to avoid the entanglement of men's rights over them. These women seek to establish status based on their own merits, for example, through their careers.

By contrast, Americans traditionally fight for women's rights, and American women often take legal action to resolve inequities between men and women. When an American woman moves to Thailand, she carries with her the assumption of her equal status (or at least her right to equal status) with men. Many American and expatriate women of other nationalities feel automatically at a disadvantage as women when they move to Thailand because Thai women have not achieved equality. Most Thai women accept the traditions and long-standing beliefs that make them subservient to men. Expatriate men may feel at an advantage when they move to Thailand because the balance of power between men and women tilts in their favor. Male behavior considered unacceptable in the U.S. may be acceptable in Thailand, such as taking a mistress or going to a prostitute. This reality poses a challenge for couples that move to Thailand or to other countries with a similar culture.

Exercise: Cultural Confrontation

We'll now ask you to look at how you're experiencing cultural confrontation in the country you're living in. Outlined below are the steps for this exercise.

Step 1: Experience the foreign culture first-hand. For the purpose of this exercise, you want to get close to the foreign culture, rather than experiencing it at a distance. You may have to move out of your comfort zone, get out and mingle (according to what is safe in your location). Here are some suggestions.
   · Take local transportation.
   · Go into the marketplace.
   · Enter the local temple (or equivalent place of worship), if allowed.
   · Stand in line at a food stand.
   · Watch two people in conversation.
   · Attempt to communicate what you need or want to know. (For example, tell someone where you need to go, ask how much something costs, or indicate what you want to buy.)

Notice how people act and what they do. Notice how you must act or behave to accomplish your goals. Consider how women are viewed. The status of women will make itself evident in a country's traditions, customs, and behaviors. Pay attention to what seems funny, odd, curious, uncomfortable, or puzzling. Recognize how you respond emotionally to these situations (e.g., feeling angry, frustrated, anxious, amused, irritated, or confused).

Step 2: Write down what you noticed from your experience in the first step. Make note of anything you discovered about how people act or interact, toward you and toward each other. Also, note your responses to what you saw and experienced. To understand why people behave as they do, and why things are done certain ways, you may need to talk to other people knowledgeable about the culture, or research the culture yourself. You probably learned a lot just from your first-hand experience.

Step 3: Create a table similar to our Thailand example. Use the information you collected from your observations in Step 1 and from what you wrote in Step 2 to create your table. There are three headings for your table:
   · Behavior (of the local people);
   · Beliefs, Values, and Assumptions of the foreign culture (that support this behavior);
   · How My Beliefs, Values, and Assumptions Compare as a/an (insert your nationality) Woman.

Your experience of cultural confrontation occurs between the second and third column. Draw a jagged line between these columns whenever your beliefs conflict with those of the foreign culture. You may want to do this with a friend, or in a group. It only takes a few items (our table had three) to expose a lot of information and generate a lot of discussion.

My Table Illustrating Examples of Cultural Confrontation in _____ (Country)

Behavior of _____ People	Beliefs, Values, and Assumptions of _____ Culture That Support Behavior	How My Beliefs, Values, and Assumptions Compare as a/an _____ Woman
1.		
2.		
3.		
4.		

Comments on Your Cultural Confrontation Table

What emotions did you experience while completing this exercise (i.e., did you feel angry, frustrated, anxious, amused, irritated, or confused)?

_____
_____
_____
_____
_____
_____

Why do you think you experienced these feelings?

_____
_____
_____
_____
_____

Emotional Response

When you experience a conflict between your internalized culture and the foreign culture, you have an emotional response. You may not have been aware of your emotional response, which began when you entered the foreign culture. The exercise you've just completed brings this response to light. Your emotional response shows how attached you are to your own beliefs and values. While it may seem that your emotional response is coming from your feelings about the foreign culture, it's more about your own beliefs and how you feel when your beliefs are not validated by the foreign culture. In a sense, your identity has been threatened.

The foreign culture affects your identity because the beliefs, values, and assumptions of the foreign culture challenge your internal view, while the external factors affecting your identity have changed greatly or have vanished entirely. You may be responding to these changes in identity in a variety of ways. For instance, you may be fighting to hold onto your internalized culture because it has helped define your identity. You may be more judgmental of the foreign culture. You may find yourself criticizing or rejecting this other culture, and glorifying your own. Or you may be denying your internalized culture, cutting off your roots and erasing your history, in an effort to lose yourself and merge with the foreign culture. The bottom line is that your emotional response says something about your identity and about what is important to you. Your overseas move gives you the opportunity to become aware of how your internalized culture has supported your identity.

In Chapter 5, you'll gain a deeper understanding about how the confrontation with the foreign culture affects your identity, resulting in a state of transition.

Chapter 5

Your Identity in Transition

So far we've explored the journey of leaving home, moving overseas, and encountering a foreign culture. We've brought you to where you are now: a resident of a foreign country, an expatriate. Now we'll help you develop a clearer understanding of the current state of your identity, as influenced by the move overseas and the experience of living in a foreign culture.

In Chapter 1, we outlined the four facets that make up your identity: your internal view of self, external factors affecting identity, roles, and significant relationships with others. You then did an exercise called "Who Was I?" In this chapter, we'll use a similar format as before. In the following section, we'll review the four facets of identity, but this time the questions provided will help you think about how the confrontation with the foreign culture affects these four areas of your identity. Then, you will have the opportunity to do an exercise, "Who Am I?", which will reflect any changes in your sense of self.

The Four Facets of Identity

Internal View of Self

Your perceptions of yourself: How do you see yourself in your current surroundings? How are you behaving? Do you like yourself?

Your beliefs: Which of your beliefs are surfacing for you? Have certain beliefs become more or less important? Do you question what you believed in the past? Are your beliefs clearer or stronger than ever?

Your values: Do you have a new understanding of your own values, or are you more confused? Are your values changing?

Your attitudes: Has your attitude about your life remained the same or is it changing? How would you describe your attitude now?

Your likes and dislikes: Are you experiencing *new* likes and dislikes? What do you like and dislike about living in the country you're in?

Your gender: What does being female mean in the culture you're living in? Do you feel differently about being female?

Your body image: Do you feel any differently towards your body? Does your body seem the same to you?

External Factors Affecting Identity

The way others see you: How do people (native and/or expatriate) relate to you? How do they describe you, or talk about you? Are you aware of having an image through which other people see you? How do your family and friends in your home country view you?

Societal influences: The society you live in may be primarily expatriate or primarily foreign, depending on where you live and with whom you associate. How are you seen by the society you live in now? What impact does this society have on your experience? Do you feel accepted by this society?

The community you live in and are involved with: Are you able to find a sense of community, or do you have to create one? To what community or communities would you say you belong? What is this community like?

The impact of the culture in which you live: You've already explored the question of cultural impact in the previous chapter. In what ways does the foreign culture become a central part of your life, i.e., how does it color what you do and what you decide to do? Are there certain rules of behavior that apply to you or affect you in some way? Are you expected to conduct yourself in a certain manner?

Roles

Roles help define who and what you are and what you do: What do previous roles look like now? How is being a wife different overseas? How is being a mother different? What is it like to be a daughter overseas? How are you coping with new roles, such as "foreigner," "minority," "dependent," "ma'am" of the house, or "diplomat"? What additional roles have you sought out? Are you utilizing skills from a previous career role in a volunteer role? Have you taken on membership roles in certain clubs or groups? If you've found employment, what is your role in the workplace?

Roles have culturally defined expectations and rules for interpreting and judging appropriate behavior: What kind of rules and expectations are attached to the roles you've taken on? How do you know what is the norm for certain overseas roles, such as diplomat, military, or corporate wife? Do you feel that you fit in with these norms?

Your self-esteem is affected by the roles you occupy: How do you feel about your new roles? How do you feel about your role as a wife, as mother, daughter, or sibling overseas? Do you like how you see yourself in these roles?

Significant Relationships with Others

Significant relationships in your life: Who are the most significant people in your life? Is there a shift in significance since you moved overseas? Is there more or less time to spend with family members, such as your husband or children? How easy is it to make friends? How is the quality of contact with others? Which relationships are most meaningful to you?

Exercise: "Who Am I?"

This exercise allows you to answer the questions you've just reviewed in our outline of the four facets that make up your identity. How you answer them is up to you. The questions in this exercise serve as a guideline to provoke your thinking about how your identity is taking shape within the context of your overseas move, after you've begun to live within the foreign culture.

"Who Am I?"

Under each category, write several descriptions that define you after the move.

After I moved overseas to _____, my identity, my sense of self, my view of me, my uniqueness =

Internal View of Self

My perceptions of myself:

_____

_____

_____

_____

_____

My beliefs:

_____
_____
_____
_____
_____

My values:

_____
_____
_____
_____
_____

My attitudes:

_____
_____
_____
_____
_____

My likes and dislikes:

_____
_____
_____
_____
_____

My gender:

_____
_____
_____
_____
_____

My body image:

_____
_____
_____
_____
_____

External Factors Affecting Identity

The way others see me:

_____
_____
_____
_____
_____

Societal influences:

_____
_____
_____
_____
_____

The community I live in and am involved with:

_____
_____
_____
_____
_____

The impact of the culture I live in:

_____
_____
_____
_____
_____

Roles

Roles I occupy:

_____
_____
_____
_____
_____

Culturally defined expectations and rules for interpreting and judging appropriate behavior for the roles I occupy:

_____
_____
_____
_____
_____

In what way(s) is my self-esteem affected by the roles I occupy?

_____
_____
_____
_____
_____

Significant Relationships with Others

Who are the most significant people in my life?

_____
_____
_____
_____
_____

How important are these relationships to me?

_____
_____
_____
_____
_____

How do my relationships help define me?

_____
_____
_____
_____
_____

❦Exercise: Reflections❧

Look back through your answers in the "Who Am I?" exercise and begin to get a sense of the identity that emerges from these answers. Like looking into a mirror that gradually reflects back a clear image, wait for this image to emerge. Think about how you feel about what you see.

How would you rate your satisfaction with your identity at this point in time on a Scale of 1 to 10? (1 = low, a more negative self-view, unhappy, not satisfied with your identity. 10 = very high, a more positive self-view, very happy, very satisfied with your identity.)

Numerical Rating: _____

Write a few words that describe the numerical rating you gave yourself:

_____
_____
_____
_____
_____

What thoughts or feelings do you have about this numerical rating?

_____
_____
_____
_____
_____

Remember that the numerical rating you give yourself has nothing to do with your value as a person. It gives you information about how you view yourself. You may like yourself better if you fit a certain image. For example, if you rated on the low or high side, you may be expressing a preference for a particular kind of identity picture. You may have in mind the way your picture used to be, before the move overseas. When your picture changes a lot because of the move, it sets a new standard. In this case, the rating you give yourself reflects the degree of change to your identity.

In Chapter 1, as you completed the "Who Was I?" exercise, you also gave yourself a numerical rating. Go back to that exercise and check the numerical rating. How does it compare with the one you just gave yourself based on who you are now? These ratings help you see your self-image. Self-image can change from positive to negative or from negative to positive depending upon the circumstances in your life. With a move overseas, you should expect to see fluctuations in self-image.

Having a lower rating for "Who Am I?" than "Who Was I?" does not mean that you're less a person than you were before. Again, a change in rating reflects the changes you've experienced because of the overseas move, and how you view these changes. After such a move, you're likely to be more vulnerable and unsure of yourself. If you don't like seeing yourself this way, you'll rate yourself lower. If you're more comfortable with the changes, and with being in transition, then your rating may be higher (perhaps even higher than before the move). You may like seeing yourself in a new and different way. If your ratings have not changed much between your "Who Am I?" and "Who Was I?" answers, maybe your losses and gains to your identity have balanced out. In the space below, put into words your thoughts about how your two ratings compare.

How my ratings compare:

_____
_____
_____
_____
_____
_____
_____
_____

We'd like to continue to compare the "Who Am I?" exercise and the "Who Was I?" exercise. These exercises give you two identity pictures, one current and one past. As you look at them together, you have the opportunity to ask yourself the following three questions, which we'll examine separately below.

What parts of my identity have I kept?
What parts of my identity have I left behind?
What have I gained or added to my identity?

What Parts of My Identity Have I Kept?

Refer back to your "Who Was I?" and "Who Am I?" exercises to see what parts of your identity you've managed to retain. In the midst of so much change, where do you see continuity in the two exercises? What have you kept, or salvaged, in the process of moving overseas? For example, a love of nature may be an important value for you. If you moved from a rural or suburban setting to an urban one, you've lost easy access to nature. But if you've found another way to connect to nature (e.g., fill your balcony with plants, locate a park nearby) you've kept the importance of that value. You may have kept a role: being a mother, for instance. While you may perform that role differently in your new setting, it is still a role that you keep.

As I have shifted from "Who Was I?" to "Who Am I?" what parts of my identity have I kept?

_____
_____
_____
_____
_____
_____
_____
_____
_____

What Parts of My Identity Have I Left Behind?

Refer back to the "Who Was I?" and "Who Am I?" exercises to see what parts of your identity you've left behind when you moved overseas. We are talking about the parts of your identity that are irretrievable, *or* can no longer exist in the way that they did, because the things that supported them are gone. For instance, if you leave a job, that particular job, and your role in it, is gone from your life. If you sell your house, it is gone from your life. Consequently, the neighborhood community you were once part of is also gone. How you viewed your role as a part of this community is no longer active. Your friendship with someone in that community is cut off. That friendship, even if maintained long distance, will not exist in its previous form. You've left the close contact with your friend and are no longer able to sustain a supportive relationship in the same way.

As I have shifted from "Who Was I?" to "Who Am I?" what parts of my identity have I left behind?

_____
_____
_____
_____
_____
_____
_____
_____

75

What Have I Gained or Added to My Identity?

Look back at the "Who Was I?" and "Who Am I?" exercises to see how much has been gained or added to your identity picture by moving overseas. In the midst of recounting your losses, it's also helpful to acknowledge your gains. New situations give you new opportunities and new challenges and whether or not you like the additions, they are unmistakably there. You may find that a lot has been added to your life by moving overseas. You may be in the new role of a diplomat. Whether you live in an enclave of people from your own culture or not, you're still exposed to a new culture. In many parts of the world you're likely to have household help. If so, you have a new role as an employer and may be referred to as "ma'am." There are new ways in which you see yourself, and new ways in which others see you. You're in new relationships.

We're not asking you to decide whether what you've gained is advantageous to you or not. It could be a hindrance. We're simply asking you to look at what you have *now*, in contrast to what you had before.

As I have shifted from "Who Was I?" to "Who Am I?," what have I gained or added to my identity?

_____
_____
_____
_____
_____
_____
_____
_____
_____

State of Transition

In this chapter, you have answered the following questions:
"Who Am I?"
What parts of my identity have I kept?
What parts of my identity have I left behind?
What have I gained or added to my identity?

Your answers to these questions help pinpoint all the ways in which the experience of moving and living overseas has profoundly affected you. In both blatant and subtle ways, change has touched every area of your life. You've seen how these changes reverberate through your identity, altering the picture of who you are. Your identity picture is not the same as it was before moving overseas. Your identity is in transition, from one state of existence to another. Gretchen Janssen, in her book *Women on the Move: A Christian Perspective on Cross-Cultural Adaptation*, offers a wonderful metaphor of a crab that goes through a natural process of shedding its outer shell. Without that shell, it's fragile and without protection and hides and waits for a new shell to form. She likens the crab's shell to the woman's identity. The old identity is shed, leaving the woman more exposed and fragile. Until her identity is intact again, she will be in this fragile condition and in a state of transition.[6]

Being in a state of transition is awkward because so much is beyond your control. At first, you don't know what is happening to you. You may have lost your sense of personal power in the process of moving overseas. As an expatriate woman, you're expected to navigate your new environment *before* your identity has time to gel. The crab would never do that. She stays safely out of sight until her outer shell has re-formed. You, by contrast, continue to tackle whatever comes your way the best way that you can. It's important that you get through each day and each new task.

The way your identity was structured before you moved overseas was familiar and comforting to you. Now that your identity is in transition, you experience a range of uncomfortable or negative feelings. You may feel sadness, grief, anxiety, anger, frustration, confusion, and/or depression. So much has happened to you that you're likely to feel overwhelmed. You may find that you're more easily irritated or annoyed because you don't have the ease with yourself that goes along with a more stable identity. You may feel incompetent and helpless. These feelings may not be wanted by you, or by anyone else. They may seem to interfere with your adjustment to living overseas. You may feel compelled to get rid of these feelings. You may want to ignore them, or somehow subdue them. You may even believe that a successful overseas assignment means that you need to conquer these uncomfortable, negative feelings.

You may find yourself diverting your attention from your feelings by doing some of the following things:

· excessively filling your time with activities or shopping;
· increasing your use of alcohol;
· going on food binges;
· becoming obsessed with your appearance;
· criticizing the country to which you have moved;
· focusing on getting away from your new home (e.g., scheduling trips and/or home leaves);
· fantasizing about someone else;
· frequently gossiping;
· blaming other people for your discomfort.

This list doesn't include everything but gives examples of avoidant behaviors, that is, behaviors you engage in to avoid the feelings that are part of your inner struggle. You may be engaged in an avoidant behavior for quite a while before you even know that you're doing so. An avoidant behavior may even seem to be the norm when other people are doing it, too. It's important to note that the things listed as avoidant behaviors are not necessarily problems in and of themselves. The problem is in your *dependence* on doing these things. You're dependent when it is *essential* to your well-being to regularly engage in an avoidant behavior. Ask yourself if you could go a period of time without performing one of these types of behaviors, and you'll get an idea of whether or not it is essential for you.

When I think about how I choose to use my time, and how I interact with other people, I find that I am doing a lot of . . .

_____

_____

_____

_____

_____

Are you engaging in avoidant behaviors? If so, which one(s)?

_____

_____

_____

_____

_____

If you're engaging in avoidant behaviors, and you had to stop, how would you feel?

_____

_____

_____

_____

_____

When you look at the feelings you might have if you disengage from an avoidant behavior, they're usually the ones that you'd rather not experience. Although uncomfortable, these feelings remind you that you're in a state of transition. As an expatriate woman, it's easy to get stuck in this phase of transition where your identity has been altered. You're keenly aware of how unpleasant this phase is, and you're not likely to find anything outside of you that can alleviate your discomfort. It seems that what is happening to you is unfair. You didn't know what you were bargaining for. You may feel that no one can fully appreciate your plight. You'll want to target something *outside* of you–the movers, your husband, the weather, the lack of familiar foods–for your own discomfort. You want to blame anything associated with the move for how you feel now.

Charise:

One morning, when we were still living in a hotel, we went in search of food on the streets nearby. My husband led the way to a small open-air restaurant. He was sure the food would be better and cheaper than what the hotel offered. Since he was more comfortable with the language of food, he ordered for us. Within minutes our meal was on the table. I looked at my plate with disdain and saw my breakfast, combination fried rice. I was hungry but I picked at my food.

I looked at my husband and said, "I can't eat rice for breakfast, lunch, and dinner." I felt dismayed. He was enjoying his food. I, on the other hand, was angry at him for bringing me here, for making me look at rice first thing in the morning, and for not empathizing with how I felt. I sat there sulking as he happily finished his meal.

Debra:

I did a lot of blaming when I initially discovered that I wasn't able to work after we moved overseas. I blamed Brad for the decision to move. I blamed the State Department for giving us inaccurate information. I blamed the Thai government for changing the rules in relation to expatriate women working in Thailand. I blamed other expatriate women for perpetuating the problem, i.e., accepting the fact that they were unable to work, while not being happy or doing anything about it. Being able to blame someone or something made me feel better. For a while, I relied on this tactic. It allowed me to keep the focus off of myself. As long as I was able to blame someone or something, I didn't have to look at why I was so uncomfortable without my job. I literally felt lost, and frightened by the emptiness and anxiousness I experienced without work in my life.

Whether or not you initially wanted to move overseas, these scenarios show that you may feel you have little or no control over your situation. You may behave as if you have little influence over decisions. You may lose sight of your options. After all, you're the one going along with the decision to move overseas. Even if the decision was mutual between you and your husband/partner, you're not the one who was offered a job, a promotion, or a stint overseas. You're not the chosen one. You're overseas because of your affiliation with the chosen one. You could go so far as to say that you're not primarily responsible for being overseas. Therefore, what happens to you is the result of being put in the situation you're in. This way of thinking puts the responsibility for your situation beyond you, and beyond your ability to effect change. If you continue to think this way, you may get stuck in the state of transition we've been describing.

In order to proceed through the state of transition without getting stuck, we encourage you to examine your feelings, even if you're reluctant to do so. To return to the metaphor of the crab, it might seem easier to slap on a shell and make it fit. But this doesn't work. Instead, you'll have to tolerate feelings of discomfort, vulnerability, and any other feelings that come your way. *It's okay to feel your feelings.* There's nothing wrong with you if you feel these things. The feelings you experience as a woman whose identity is in a state of transition are normal. No matter how intense these feelings are, they are temporary. They belong to the state of transition you're in.

✍Exercise: Reflections ✌

In the space below, describe what you're experiencing on a feeling level as you experience your identity in transition. Certain feelings may have surfaced for you in the course of completing the exercises in this chapter. Use the following space to name these feelings, describing them in any way you wish.

_____
_____
_____
_____
_____
_____
_____
_____
_____
_____

The feelings you listed illustrate the full range of the emotional impact of your overseas move. A time of grieving may be at hand. You may experience the grieving gradually as you slowly absorb the shock of so much change. You may experience the grieving all at once. Or the grieving may elude your awareness and catch up with you later, perhaps even far in the future.

ೞ   ೞ   ೞ

In Part One, you've begun to recognize all the ways in which your identity is in transition because of your overseas move. You've also become more aware of the feelings you've connected with in this transitional state. In Part Two, we'll discuss the possible results of this transitional phase, as well as strategies for a positive outcome.

Part Two

The Turning Point

Chapter 6

The Turning Point: The Wheel

Up to this point, we've focused on what happened to you and your identity as a result of your overseas move. In Chapter 5, you learned that your identity is in transition, between one state of existence and another. You may feel that you don't recognize yourself anymore. Referring back to the metaphor of the crab, you may feel vulnerable and unprotected, as if you've lost your old shell and are waiting for your new one. You've gained a great deal of useful information and insight about who you were before the move compared to who you are now. But now you're at the turning point and it's up to you to decide what you're going to do with everything you've learned thus far.

When identity is in transition, one option is choosing to do nothing. However, you run the risk of a negative outcome to your overseas experience. You may find yourself very dissatisfied with your identity as it unfolds, and continue to feel that something is missing from your life. The negative or uncomfortable feelings we've discussed in previous chapters may persist if you choose not to resolve the transitional state of your identity.

However, unlike the crab, you can determine what your new shell will be like once it forms. You can shape your new identity. You can exercise your conscious will and make choices. Instead of doing nothing when your identity is in transition, you have the power to generate a positive outcome from the chaos and change. You can determine what type of shell you want and what your new identity will look and feel like. For example, self-assessment helps you determine what really matters to you; knowing this helps you incorporate these things into your new life in some form. Doing so will bring you more self-satisfaction. By making choices that will have a positive effect on your identity, you can also resolve any negative or uncomfortable feelings associated with your transitional state. This frees you to feel more joy in your life.

The Wheel

We've developed a model, which we call *The Wheel*, that functions as a vehicle to lead you out of your transitional state. The Wheel can help you reconstruct the four facets of your identity defined in Chapter 1 (internal view, external factors, roles, and relationships) that were affected by the move. By using The Wheel, you can reconstruct your identity in a way that honors your emerging self and the choices you want to make. You will become more content and satisfied with your identity because you're in charge of reconstructing it. Also, your sense of identity will be less dependent on your external environment. Instead, you'll have an identity rooted to yourself.

In the remainder of this chapter, we'll discuss what reconstructing a sense of identity means, then outline and briefly discuss the three steps involved. We'll also illustrate these three steps in diagram form so you'll have a visual image of the reconstruction process. As you'll see, the various components of each of the three steps, when combined, form The Wheel.

After providing an overall picture of The Wheel, we'll devote separate chapters to each of the three steps of reconstructing your identity. In these chapters, we'll discuss each step of The Wheel in more detail. This will provide a better understanding of each step and illustrate how the steps overlap and work together to form The Wheel. We'll also provide you with practical information about applying each step to your life and situation.

What Does "Reconstructing a Sense of Identity" Mean?

To reconstruct your identity, you start building upon your identity as it exists right now. You formed a picture of what your identity is like right now when you completed the exercises in the last chapter. Once you decide to make changes to this picture, you start adding new factors to the identity-shaping process. The identity you reconstruct becomes a composite of all the changes brought about by the move, as well as the changes you choose to implement.

Reconstructing your identity is *not* about resurrecting the person you were before you moved overseas. It isn't possible to have the same life overseas as you had back home. Even if you returned to your home and familiar surroundings, *you* would be different because of the changes you've experienced as a result of moving. When you reconstruct your identity, you can build an identity more adaptable to change and therefore more suited to expatriate life. We are talking about an identity that *you* shape, based on what you need and want, wherever you go. What results is a shell that really fits, an identity that you design.

How Do You Reconstruct Your Identity?

There are three steps in reconstructing your identity. First, we'll outline these steps. In the following section, we'll show you how these three steps combine to form The Wheel.

Step 1: Make a commitment to yourself to take charge of the outcome of the transitional state your identity is currently in.

Step 2: Draw from your five personal resources (ability to let go, ability for self-knowledge, ability to manage stress, ability to access support, and ability to be open-minded) as you need to.

Step 3: Use the seven tools (re-establishing a sense of stability and security, communication with the self, communication with others, re-establishing a support network, acceptance, seeking out internal activities, and seeking out external activities) to put into place what you determine is missing from your life.

How the Three Steps Collectively Form The Wheel

Step 1: Commitment

As we stated earlier, the first step in reconstructing your identity is making a commitment to yourself to take charge of the outcome of your identity's current transitional state. (We'll discuss this step further in Chapter 7.) You do this by making three key decisions. First, you decide that you're willing to change. Second, you decide that you're willing to grow. And, third, you decide that you're willing to take risks. By making these three key decisions, you make the commitment to direct your own growth process.

Visually, your commitment to take charge of reconstructing your identity forms the hub of The Wheel. Diagram A below illustrates the concept we have just discussed.

Diagram A depicts the first step in reconstructing your identity. In this step, you turn to your Self (represented by the large letter **S** and the area inside the circle) as the foundation upon which you'll build a new picture of your identity.

Encircling your Self are the three decisions (willingness to change, willingness to grow, and willingness to take risks), which together represent your commitment to yourself to reconstruct your identity.

Step 2: Personal Resources

The second step in reconstructing your identity, as we stated earlier, is to access your personal resources. (This step will be discussed further in Part Three, Chapters 8 through 12.) Your five personal resources are:

· Ability to Let Go;
· Ability for Self-Knowledge;
· Ability to Manage Stress;
· Ability to Access Support;
· Ability to be Open-Minded.

Visually, your personal resources are the inner spokes within the hub of The Wheel. These resources exist within you, and are surrounded by your commitment, the hub of The Wheel. Your commitment provides the motivation that puts your personal resources to work creating positive changes in your life. To illustrate what we mean, refer to Diagram B below. In Diagram B, we'll be adding on to Diagram A.

Diagram B represents the second step in reconstructing your identity. We have placed the resources within the circle that represents your Self to show that your resources are within you. In this step, you again turn within and access abilities you already possess to further contribute to your growth.

Step 3: Tools

The third step in reconstructing your identity, as we stated earlier, is using the seven tools. (We will discuss this step further in Part Four, Chapters 13 through 19.) The seven tools are:

· Re-establishing a Sense of Stability and Security;
· Communication with the Self;
· Communication with Others;
· Re-establishing a Support Network;
· Acceptance;
· Seeking Out Internal Activities;
· Seeking Out External Activities.

Visually, the tools are the outer spokes of The Wheel. You use them to reconnect you to your Self, as well as to the world at large. These tools can help you determine what factors are missing from your life, and how to put the missing factors back into place in some form. This results in an identity that is more satisfying to you. We illustrate what we mean in Diagram C below, which builds on Diagrams A and B.

Diagram C represents the third step in reconstructing your identity. We place the tools outward, as an extension of your Self, to show that you can use them to reconnect with your Self as well as with the world at large.

86

The Wheel in Motion

Diagrams A, B, and C broke down the process of reconstructing your identity into three distinct steps. These steps combine to form The Wheel, shown below in Diagram D. Diagram D is similar to Diagram C, but it is in motion. Your initial commitment to participate in reconstructing your identity is what activates and sets The Wheel in motion. This commitment also keeps The Wheel moving.

Visually, the dotted lines between each tool are used to illustrate The Wheel in motion and how your commitment fuels every other part of The Wheel. The three individual steps are inextricably linked because you can access your resources and use the tools *only* after you've made your initial commitment. The Wheel in motion also represents movement towards the positive resolution of an identity in transition.

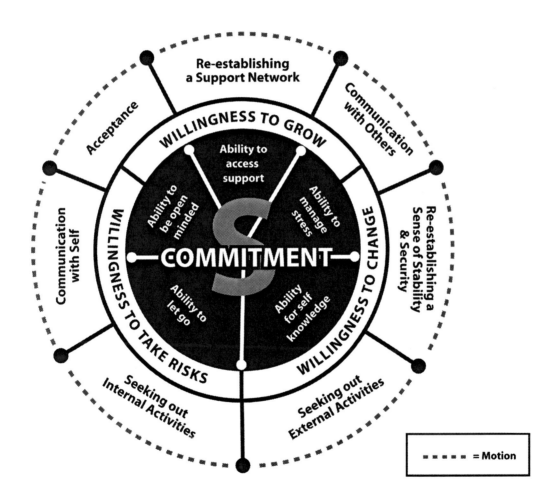

Diagram D represents The Wheel in motion. By setting The Wheel in motion, you reconstruct your identity and resolve the transitional state your identity has been in because of the move. The result is an identity you design based on what you want and need.

The Turning Point

We have guided you throughout the first half of *A Portable Identity* toward this chapter, which we consider the turning point of this book. Through exercises and sharing our own stories, we have encouraged you to pay attention to your inner responses to the move overseas. In this chapter, we have given you an overview of The Wheel, a model you can use as a vehicle to lead you out of the transitional state. We have used The Wheel ourselves, and have found it instrumental in the process of reconstructing our identities.

You're at the turning point because now it's up to you to decide where you want to go. You can either use The Wheel for yourself, or leave the outcome of your identity to chance. In the following chapter on Commitment (Step 1 in the process of reconstructing your identity), you'll have the opportunity to explore this further and make the decision about which direction is right for you.

Chapter 7

The Hub of The Wheel: Commitment

Moving overseas is like a sharp turn off the path you've been following up to now. It feels like you're suddenly in a different place altogether, sidetracked from the direction you were headed. The terrain is not the same. *You're* not the same. You've temporarily lost your bearings. Everything feels unsettled. You have an important choice to make: whether or not to walk forward into unknown territory and begin the process of reconstructing your identity.

You're at the first step of The Wheel: Commitment. Commitment forms the hub of The Wheel. In the process of reconstructing identity after an overseas move, the decision to move forward involves making a commitment to yourself to resolve your transitional state. This commitment must be in place if you are to take charge of the reconstruction process. At the end of this chapter, you'll have the opportunity to make this critical decision.

How We Define Commitment

Commitment is about making a decision within yourself. Making a commitment to someone or something means that you're deciding to pursue a certain relationship or course of action at the exclusion of other choices. By committing to one thing, you decide to leave something else behind. Commitment is about setting your eyes, soul, mind, and body toward a goal, then completing the steps necessary to achieve your goal. Commitment is about realizing that setbacks and obstacles are part of the process. It means going on even when you want to give up, or when the odds seem to be against you. Commitment is about following through with something to completion.

What does commitment mean to you?

_____

_____

_____

Is making a commitment to do something easy or difficult for you?

_____

_____

_____

Do you follow through on commitments you make?

_____

_____

_____

Commitment and the Overseas Move

In a dream, a woman moved overseas. She had recently arrived, and was with a group of people who were unknown to her. She saw people milling around, waiting for the arrival of some dignitary. She wandered over to a large swimming pool. It looked inviting, so she jumped in and began swimming. She saw another woman curled up at the bottom of the pool. She dove down to get a closer look. She knew that this woman was in trouble. She lifted her body up, thinking that this other woman must be nearly dead. As they reached the surface, the woman who had been at the bottom of the pool heaved a sigh and began crying. The woman who had rescued her held her and stroked her hair for a long time, telling her she'd be okay.

The dream is a metaphor. It depicts the possibility of a positive outcome of the transitional state your identity undergoes when you move overseas. In the dream, a woman lies passively at the bottom of a pool. Overcome, she cannot move. She has neither the strength nor the willingness to get up. Despite the fact that there are people nearby, they are not aware of her. They don't see her plight.

The woman at the bottom of the pool represents the inner struggle of the expatriate woman. She also has a counterpart: the woman who dives in and rescues her. The woman who rescues her is *the* woman herself, and represents the part of her that knows she's in need. She sees her own struggle and is willing to do something different. She makes a commitment to herself and decides to lift herself to the surface of the pool. When she does this, she is opting for a positive outcome of her struggle and she is able to emerge.

Since moving overseas, how would you describe what you're struggling with?

_____

_____

_____

_____

_____

Like the woman in the dream, what do you think it would take for you to emerge from the bottom of the pool to the surface (i.e., to take charge of your struggle)?

_____

_____

_____

_____

_____

By taking charge, how would your experience living overseas become more positive?

_____

_____

_____

_____

_____

The decision to make a commitment to yourself to take charge of your struggle and begin the process of reconstructing your identity is a very personal one. No one can decide this for you. No one can force you into it. It's up to you to decide.

However, if you're experiencing difficulties in your life because of the overseas move, we believe the only way to remedy your situation is to make a commitment to yourself to do so. As you've discovered throughout this book, growth is not always an easy process. Often painful, it sometimes requires you to confront very uncomfortable feelings. To move forward, you must be willing to be honest with yourself and to realistically assess both your strengths and weaknesses.

Personal growth can also be exhilarating. It can take you to levels of personal happiness and contentment beyond what you may have imagined. Personal growth can be freeing and liberating; it can boost your self-esteem and your self-confidence. Through personal growth you can gain the courage to take on new challenges and new risks that will enrich your life.

In the following narratives, we'll continue to share with you our stories and highlight what factored into our decisions to commit to taking active roles in shaping our identities. We do this to give you real examples of what is possible when you make a commitment to yourself to make positive changes in your life.

Debra:

When I have an important decision to make, I often "sit on the fence" a while before I make my final decision. I devote a lot of emotional energy to contemplating my various options and playing out the possible outcomes of each option in my head. While I'm sitting on the fence, I often go back and forth between my choices before I actually make a commitment to a certain course of action. It's sometimes difficult for me to make that final leap over to one side of the fence or the other because I know that making a decision to pursue one course of action means leaving something else behind. It takes me a while to reach that point.

Once I finally make a commitment to something or someone, I take it very seriously. I don't like to go back on commitments I've made. I think that's why I spend a lot of time contemplating a decision. For example, when I first discovered I was unable to work in Thailand, I hit an all-time low. At one point I considered leaving the country and returning to the United States so I could continue pursuing my career goals. My husband Brad also feared that I'd leave Thailand. I knew that if I did this, though, it would be devastating to my marriage. Instead of making an impulsive decision, I decided to tolerate uncomfortable internal feelings and sit on the fence a while and really consider my options.

The first option I considered, of course, was to leave Thailand and return to the United States. I wanted relief from my misery and to continue with my career goals. If leaving the country would provide me with the relief I was searching for, perhaps I should do it, I thought. Initially, I didn't think about the consequences of what that decision would also probably mean: the end of my marriage. My relationship with my husband had become strained anyway and part of me didn't care what happened. I just wanted relief from my misery.

But as I sat on the fence and gave myself some time and space, I allowed myself to play out the reality of leaving the country and ultimately, probably ending my marriage. I began to think about the tremendous loss I'd feel if my relationship with Brad ended. He was and is my best friend. Although my state of misery was making it difficult for me to really feel my love for him, I knew deep down that I was still in love with him.

I also considered our marriage vows and the commitment I made to Brad when we were married. I especially thought about the part of our vows that said, "for better or worse, in good times and in bad, and in sickness and in health." I thought about how easy it is to stay when things are going along smoothly, and how difficult it is when the path is bumpy or filled with obstacles. The word "commitment" kept coming to the forefront of my mind. I knew I wasn't a quitter, so why was I considering it now?

The second option I considered was to do nothing and to leave my situation to chance. However, the possibility of being miserable for the duration of our stay in Thailand was so unappealing that I only considered it briefly. I also knew that doing nothing goes against my personality and I felt too miserable not to do anything about it.

The third option I considered was to try and take charge of the situation. Up to this point, I felt that I had little control over what was going on in my life. So as I sat on the fence, I allowed myself to picture myself in Thailand the way I had envisioned it would be. I drew strength from my original desire and genuine willingness to move to Thailand. I began to let myself wonder about what my life could be like in Thailand. I pictured myself working legally in my profession counseling others and pursuing my career goals. I saw myself happy, content, and enjoying living and working in a foreign country. I saw myself exploring Thailand and getting to know her people and culture. I began to feel hopeful.

I realized that my desire to leave the country expressed the need to seek relief from the emotional impact of the overseas move, not a desire to end my marriage. If my marriage ended because I fled the country to escape my misery, I knew I'd regret it, and experience far greater difficulties related to the loss of my relationship and marriage to Brad. I knew I didn't want that. So instead of fleeing the country or doing nothing, I leaped over the fence and made a commitment to myself to stay in Thailand.

Although I was still pretty miserable when I made this decision, it gave me a sense of feeling grounded. I also decided to make another commitment to myself. I decided to face my misery head-on by pursuing a goal of working legally in Thailand, despite all the obstacles. (Since I discuss this in more detail in Part 4 in the Tool Section, I won't focus on the outcome of that process here.)

For months I continued to feel unsettled internally. But as a result of the commitment I made to stay in Thailand, I learned how to tolerate and manage these feelings better. Whenever I felt like giving up because of seemingly insurmountable obstacles thrown in my way, my original commitment was my foundation and the binding force that gave me the strength to keep going until I reached my goal.

Charise:

I remember thinking, even before I got to Bangkok, that I could not have picked a more opposite place to move to, compared with my home in Atlanta. The changes included moving from a Western culture to an Asian one; moving from a Southeastern American climate to a tropical one; switching to another time zone where daytime and nighttime are reversed; learning a language that is tonal and has its own alphabet; being surrounded by Asian people instead of primarily Caucasian people or African Americans; and, driving on the opposite side of the road. Once I arrived in Bangkok, I experienced all these changes at once, as well as others I hadn't even thought of; and these were only the external, visible changes.

My responses (which are detailed in Chapter 4) were to first barricade myself in my hotel room, and then, identify with all things Thai. In either case, I fought against change. In my early struggle, I shielded myself from the onslaught. Then I came forward with a vengeance, determined to tackle my new world and adopt Thai ways.

I surprised people with my language ability, which they didn't expect based on my looks. When I spoke Thai, I felt like a different person. It was as if I could split myself into several parts. When my tennis coach, who was married, invited me to lunch with his friends, I understood that neither my husband nor his wife were included in the plans. As a typical Thai man, he was able to maintain a social life entirely separate from his wife. As for me, I felt that I could also exclude my husband because he was not a part of this world.

The attention from my tennis coach kept me distracted from my own inner struggle. I began to depend upon his attention, whether he was correcting my serve or talking about what food he wished to introduce me to. My attraction to him was a strong force to contend with. Being at the tennis court was where I felt most intimate.

The physicality of the game demanded me to be fully in my body. As with dance, being in my body meant being in the realm of emotions and the expression of emotions. Tennis became my therapy as I unleashed my frustrations, anger, and desires while running and whacking the ball across the court. My coach could take anything I threw his way and return the ball for more, encouraging me to be faster and stronger.

Because my coach was facilitating the opening of my emotions, he became a powerful figure in my life. He was my link to myself, and I carried his image with me in my mind almost constantly. Eventually this left me wandering in a fantasy world. I found myself becoming glued to my fantasy, and withdrawing from my husband. As I went through the motions of my daily routine, it seemed that my real life was hovering somewhere else. I was in constant anticipation of those moments of contact with my coach; moments that stood out within long stretches of time.

One Sunday, when we both knew that my husband was traveling, he offered to cook lunch for me at my house. He prepared mussels with all sorts of seasoning, adjusting the amount of chili pepper to what he thought I could handle. I also introduced him to cheese, which he had difficulty chewing and swallowing because it was such a foreign substance to him. It was a very sensual experience, eating and tasting and chatting in close proximity for several hours. For me, it heightened the sexual attraction, even though we never physically touched. Afterwards, my desire for him continued to intensify. I felt scooped out, nearly empty of my self. Part of me wanted to slip away completely to find shelter in his arms. Part of me feared that if I did that, I'd no longer know who I was.

I couldn't contain my turmoil for very long, and it was already evident to my husband. I decided to take a risk. I made a decision to break the secrecy of my fantasy. With trust in the strength of our friendship, I decided to tell Charles what was going on. When I revealed to him my longing and my struggle, he listened. Then he told me that he had harbored his own fantasy of having a Thai mistress. His fantasy had begun even before we moved to Thailand.

His admission helped me understand why I had felt like I was tagging along in this move, and why I had not shared his enthusiasm. Now, I was a mirror for him. I had split myself in the same way he had. We were pushing each other away with our fantasies. He wanted this to stop. He wanted us to start over, with honesty and trust at the core of our marriage. I felt that I had already gone so far out of the circle of our marriage that I didn't know if I could come back. He offered his support and his willingness to watch me work through my uncertainty.

My decision to be honest extended itself further. I confronted my coach, who had never said anything directly about his feelings. I expressed my confusion about our relationship. He stared at me quizzically, still holding on to his social graces. I felt like a fool. Perhaps I was wrong, and had invented the tension between us. I continued to look directly into his eyes, waiting for a response, practically shaking from my boldness. Finally, his face changed and his shoulders collapsed. He said he felt just as confused as I did. I laughed. I was instantly relieved that he had admitted the truth, and validated my own feelings. Then we were silent, without smiling, without pretense. I was aware of the absurdity of our situation. Here we were, standing on the tennis court, confessing to having feelings for each other in full view of the school where his wife worked and their children studied.

At that very moment, I knew my fantasy was falling apart. The intimacy that I could so easily imagine could not be so easily accomplished. There were too many complications, too many people involved, and the attraction was too strong. After a moment or two, he picked up his racket and told me to get mine. We began to play tennis, as usual. Afterwards, I apologized to him for speaking out so suddenly. I told him I wanted to remain friends. He joked that it was better to be friends than enemies. I thought, but never said, that it was better for us to be friends than lovers.

We continued to meet for our lessons. We did not, however, get together alone again. If I saw him in a social setting, it was now in the company of my husband. I had made a decision to stop splitting myself, to stop excluding Charles. Charles and I were developing a stronger relationship through our honesty and our lengthy talks.

I still felt ungrounded in myself; pulled by my longings and didn't know where to go or what to do. I was afraid to recommit to Charles. Ultimately, I realized that I needed a better understanding of myself. I became willing to grow. I made a decision to talk to a counselor. This was the beginning of unearthing my own pain. I learned that I had involved my coach and my husband as players, but that my pain was not about them. My pain was mine alone. It was wrapped around my longing to be intimate and to feel love. It was about relating to others and relating to myself. It was about acknowledging how I saw myself and what I believed about my changing identity.

As soon as I took back my longing, which I had neatly packaged into a fantasy and displaced onto someone else, I felt my pain. It was almost unbearable. I had no idea how much I had been hurting. I felt the hurt of all the years of coolness and distance that had built up between Charles and me. I felt the old hurt of the distance between my own parents, and how much I had wanted them to be close. I felt the pain of wanting to trust someone and being afraid to do so. I wanted to anesthetize my pain. I had always toughed it out, but now I felt weak and vulnerable. I needed support, and now I had to rely on those who were offering support (Charles and my counselor).

This degree of need and willingness for outside support was something new for me. Having set out to prove I could tackle this overseas assignment all on my own, even avoiding supports already available in the expatriate community, I now had to admit I needed help. I became willing to change. I learned to be more accepting of support, and more receptive of the love, care, and concern of others. After several weeks of counseling, and numerous talks with Charles, I made the decision to recommit to my marriage. I was able to make this commitment only because I was willing to take risks, to grow, and to change.

Making this commitment meant leaving behind the possibility of pursuing a relationship with my coach. My attraction to my coach, as well as my desire to be with him, had not disappeared. I now understood that I could have these feelings for another man and still be in love with my husband, and still believe in my marriage. It was a matter of making a choice, and of basing my choice in what I valued.

The intimacy I had been fantasizing about was now happening in my marriage. Charles and I were experiencing a depth of intimacy and intensity of passion that I did not know was possible. It seemed as though our relationship was brand-new, finally, we were getting to know each other. I, truly, was just getting to know myself. We worked together to create a ceremony for renewing our vows. The vows we wrote were different than our first, Catholic, ones. We included the honoring of each other's growth as a fundamental aspect of our marriage. We were married, for the second time, in a small chapel with three other people present: a priest who was also a counselor where I worked, a Catholic nun to assist, and our five-year-old daughter.

No one knows your life or situation better than you. As you've seen from the personal experiences we have shared with you, an overseas move may initiate growth in ways you might never have thought possible. Others may also help you through this process, but it's your responsibility to attend to your own emotional needs. Only you can decide to make a commitment to help yourself.

⋄Exercise: Reflections ⋫

To get a sense of whether you might want to make a commitment to beginning the process of reconstructing your identity, answer the following questions.

What do you think is missing from your life? (Refer back to the exercises "What Parts of My Identity Have I Kept?", "What Parts of My Identity Have I Left Behind?", and "What Have I Gained or Added to My Identity?" in Chapter 5.)

_____
_____
_____
_____

What changes do you think you would like to make to your identity based on this discovery?

_____
_____
_____
_____

How do you feel about making changes to your identity based on your answers to the above questions (i.e., do you feel excited, fearful, hopeless, or hopeful)?

_____
_____
_____
_____

Do you welcome change or do you fear it?

_____
_____
_____
_____

If you fear change, how can you give yourself permission to feel your fear and tolerate it while also proceeding with making changes anyway?

_____
_____
_____
_____

Decision Point

It's now time for you to decide whether you want to make a commitment to yourself to reconstruct your identity. This involves making three key decisions. In the following space, write down your responses to each of these decisions.

Decision 1: Decide if you're willing to change. Being willing to change means that you want a change in your identity. Are you willing to change? Please explain your answer.

_____

_____

_____

_____

_____

Decision 2: You must decide whether you're willing to grow. Being willing to grow means allowing yourself to be vulnerable and letting your guard down so that you can see aspects of yourself more clearly. Are you willing to grow? Please explain your answer.

_____

_____

_____

_____

_____

Decision 3: You must decide whether you're willing to take risks. Taking risks means stepping outside your comfort zone and completing the steps necessary to support your growth. The willingness to take risks involves taking action based on your willingness to grow. Are you willing to take risks? Please explain your answer.

_____

_____

_____

_____

_____

If you responded negatively to any of the above questions, you may not be ready to commit to reconstructing your identity. You may want to pause here and explore further why you responded this way. If you decide this isn't the time for you to begin the process of reconstructing your identity, you can always choose to return to this first step when you're ready.

If you responded "yes" to the above 3 questions, you've just completed Step 1 of The Wheel by making the commitment to be in charge of reconstructing your identity and direct your own growth process. You're bridging the opportunity to *make* change. By deciding to take responsibility for how your identity will take shape, you're making a shift. You're shifting from a passive role as a recipient of change to an active role as an agent of change. Like the woman in the pool, you've decided to be your own heroine. The heroine in you remembers who you are at your core, at the deepest level of your self or soul. The diagram below shows the configuration of your commitment in The Wheel we first illustrated in Chapter 6 (**Diagram A**).

In Parts Three and Four we'll continue to guide you to return to the essence of who you are or who you can be, by helping you tap into the heroine within you. This will allow you to reconstruct a sense of identity that includes and honors who you are at your core, or soul.

Part Three

Personal Resources:

The Inner Spokes of The Wheel

Chapter 8

Overview and Resource #1: Ability to Let Go

Personal Resources

In this chapter, we assume that you've completed Step 1 of The Wheel and have made a commitment to yourself to take an active role in shaping your identity. This commitment to self, which includes your willingness to grow, willingness to change, and willingness to take risks, allows you to take the next step. You're now at the second step of The Wheel: Personal Resources. Personal resources, the inner spokes within the hub of The Wheel, surround and radiate from commitment. Your commitment fuels your personal resources. Commitment to the process motivates you to summon your personal resources for reconstructing your identity.

How We Define Personal Resources

Personal resources are abilities or skills that exist within you; you don't need to go anywhere outside of you to find them. You draw from your personal resources to help you manage whatever life delivers. We have divided your personal resources into five categories:
  1) Ability to Let Go;
  2) Ability for Self-Knowledge;
  3) Ability to Manage Stress;
  4) Ability to Access Supports;
  5) Ability to be Open-Minded.

Personal resources are acquired through your life experiences. Each time you encounter and manage a situation or event, you add to your knowledge and to your abilities as a human being. The new knowledge and abilities you gain become part of your personal resources, which, in turn, are available for you to draw from the next time you need them. The diagram on the next page shows the configuration of your five personal resources in The Wheel we first illustrated in Chapter 6 (**Diagram B**).

Personal Resources and the Overseas Move

You bring your personal resources with you when you move overseas. In Part Three you'll decide which of your personal resources you need to draw from to make the changes you want. We'll look at the five resources individually to see how each one applies to your situation. After defining each resource, we'll help you determine the current condition of each one. Then we'll discuss how the overseas move affects your resources and provide exercises to help you access them.

Moving overseas provides you with the opportunity to evaluate the condition of your resources. You may find that you're better at calling upon one particular resource than any of the others. View that resource as a strength. But

Diagram B

to reconstruct your identity, you may need to call upon one or more unfamiliar or untested personal resources. By accessing that resource, you'll probably also strengthen it.

Picking and choosing which abilities you need to access will help you fine-tune your personal resources. As you work with attributes that you've previously overlooked, you can bring all your resources into a better balance. If your habit is to draw on one particular resource and neglect something else that might be useful, remember to look at them as a whole. Perhaps your situation calls for a resource you haven't previously considered or valued. Allow your attention to shift and move around The Wheel of these other resources as needed. Once you find out which resources need attention or strengthening, you know what direction to turn within the spokes of The Wheel. By accessing your personal resources, you're continuing the journey toward reconstructing your identity. You're growing as you deepen your ability to help yourself. The first personal resource we'll explore is *Resource #1: Ability to Let Go.*

Resource #1: Ability to Let Go

How We Define Ability to Let Go

Letting go means giving up your attachment to the way your life was before some event, decision, or change altered its course. The ability to let go involves coming to terms with the fact that your life or circumstances cannot remain the same. Letting go implies that you're holding onto something that needs to be released. This is not an automatic or easy thing to do. The desire to hold on is infused with the desire to feel secure. You may not want to let go of what has provided you a sense of security, whatever that may have been: your home, your job, your lifestyle, a relationship, or your self-image.

Letting go is a conscious decision that you make. In our hurry to resolve issues we sometimes forget that letting go doesn't happen all at once, but is rather a process that takes time. Letting go is a form of grieving; it occurs in stages that correspond with your readiness to loosen your grip on whatever you've been holding onto so tightly. Letting go is not about forgetting or denying or ignoring what was. Letting go is about trusting that the past will survive in you, in your memory and in your essential core self. Letting go is also about trusting that you can survive when you release your grip on the past.

Your Ability to Let Go

The ability to let go is a skill you've practiced many times in your life already. All your life transitions have involved letting go: when you left your childhood home, when you left school, when a significant relationship ended, when you married, had children, or when someone close to you died. Each time your life changed, whether because of decisions you made, your own growth process, or circumstances beyond your control, you responded. How you've responded to major transitions in your life tells you something about your ability to let go. For example, you may have cried or rebelled or celebrated or stayed quiet. You may have felt alone or supported by the company of others. You may have rushed on into the new or clung to the past.

When you think back on the most memorable transitions in your life, how did you respond?

_____
_____
_____
_____
_____
_____
_____
_____
_____
_____

What do your responses tell you about your ability to let go?

_____
_____
_____
_____
_____
_____
_____
_____
_____
_____

Letting Go and the Move

Leaving and letting go are not the same. Leaving is a physical process. When you move overseas you leave your home, your community, and your country. Letting go is an emotional process. When you move overseas you not only leave the things that contribute to your sense of identity, you also face letting go of your identity as you've known it. You may be afraid to let go. Fear of the unknown or of what lies ahead may make it difficult. When you move overseas and are bombarded with so many changes and losses all at once, you may desperately cling to your previous identity (whether you were satisfied with it or not) to have some sense of internal, emotional stability. When you cling to or crave what you once had, you're investing a great deal of energy in the past. Your attachment to the past may also interfere with your ability to discover who you are within your new life overseas. You can only be available to the present when you purposefully detach from the past. To highlight where you are in the emotional process of letting go, place yourself in the following scenario of an imaginary journey to a foreign land.

Imagine you are on a large ship crossing the ocean, making the voyage to a foreign place. You hold in your hand an iridescent shell with a deep cavern. You cannot see inside it, but it is a reminder of your identity and all that you are leaving behind. You blow into its depths filling it with your breath as you have done time and time again. It is your trumpet, which you carry with pride. From where you stand, you can see nothing but water and waves, a vast ocean. The wind pulls at your clothes, spreading them like tatters behind you. Your hair is blowing, leaving your face open to the spray of the waves. You feel the steady momentum of the ship surging forward, on and on. As you lean against the rail, your arms receive the spray of the ocean. Slowly you open your hand, and let your shell fall. As it hits the water, you close your eyes, picturing your treasure as it drops to its home in the sea. As you stand there, how do you feel? Do you want to rescue your treasure? Or does it feel okay to let it go?

This imaginary journey may reveal that you feel comfortable letting go of your identity as you have known it. Or this imaginary journey may reveal that you feel like you, or a part of you, disappears when you let go. If this is the case, remember that *you are not your identity*. You have an identity that anchors you in the world. When you move overseas, you temporarily lose that anchor because you leave behind the life you once lived and the context within which your identity existed. If you can let go and tolerate the unknown, the energy you've invested in supporting your previous identity structure becomes available to you, and you're open to new possibilities.

Are there parts of your previous identity that you're still holding onto (e.g., roles, relationships, internal view, and external factors)?

_____

_____

_____

_____

_____

Is it possible to maintain those parts of your identity structure in your current environment?

_____
_____
_____
_____
_____
_____

If it's not possible, then why is it so hard to let those parts of your identity go?

_____
_____
_____
_____
_____
_____

What parts of your previous identity are easy to let go of?

_____
_____
_____
_____
_____
_____

Based on your answers above, would you say you still feel attached to your previous identity in any way? How so?

_____
_____
_____
_____
_____
_____

If you do still feel attached to your previous identity, does this attachment interfere with your ability to be present in your current environment? How so?

_____
_____
_____
_____
_____
_____

Is your ability to let go a resource that needs strengthening?

_____

_____

_____

_____

_____

_____

How to Access and Develop Your Ability to Let Go

As we previously stated, you must make a conscious decision to let go. Remember that letting go is a process that occurs over time, at your own pace, according to your level of readiness. Once you make the decision to let go, the process begins. No one can predict how this process will unfold because it's an individual process unique to you. You should expect stops and starts. Remember that letting go is an emotional process. At times you may feel relief to let go and at other times you may feel burdened by the enormity of the task. The important thing is to stay with your process, to persevere over time.

Anything that gets you closer to your emotions will facilitate letting go. You may need to examine any lurking feelings that hold you to the past, such as guilt for leaving someone or something behind. When you think about your overseas assignment, you may experience resentment. Or perhaps you feel betrayed or cheated because life overseas is not what you expected. What you invest in these feelings only detracts from what you could be discovering about yourself in this new experience. Letting go, in these cases, may mean forgiving someone else, forgiving yourself, or forgiving life itself.

Attending to your feelings also means giving yourself permission to grieve. Grieving can take on many forms. You can cry, scream, stomp, sing, or shake. By doing something physical, you assist the release of energy that is still bound to what was. You can also release that energy symbolically by doing visualization exercises or designing and performing a ritual. Participating in therapy and therapeutic modalities, such as counseling, bodywork, or creative arts therapies, facilitates the process of letting go.

By choosing to do any of these activities to help yourself let go, you'll strengthen this resource to help you face the many challenges of living overseas. The visualization exercise on the next page illustrates one of the ways you can access and develop your ability to let go.

Exercise: Visualization

The purpose of this exercise is to focus on letting go without the requirement of moving on. The idea is to give yourself enough space to complete whatever has not felt complete about taking leave of your former life. Read the directions below, then close your eyes to practice the exercise. You can stay with this visualization as long as you like, or you can leave it and return to it another time.

Visualize a scene from your life just before moving overseas. Choose a scene that represents something that you may need to let go of. For example, this scene may be in your former home, workplace, a friend's house, or outdoors in a familiar setting. See yourself in that scene. Then see yourself walk through a door to a place you haven't been to before. This place serves as a gateway between what you've left behind and what you're about to enter (your life overseas).

Fill in the details of this place so that you create an environment where you feel comfortable in your surroundings. In this place, you feel safe and secure and can explore what you need to do to help you let go.

Use the following space to record any thoughts, feelings, or ideas that emerged for you in the course of doing this exercise.

_____
_____
_____
_____
_____
_____
_____
_____
_____
_____
_____
_____
_____
_____
_____
_____
_____
_____
_____
_____
_____
_____
_____
_____

Chapter 9

Resource #2: Ability for Self-Knowledge

How We Define Ability for Self-Knowledge

The ability for self-knowledge is the skill of learning and discovering information about yourself over the course of your life. Think of life as a school set up to teach you what you need to know about yourself. Whatever happens can be an opportunity to gain more knowledge. By its very nature, self-knowledge is never completed. You're continually uncovering different aspects of yourself. The ability for self-knowledge is about *your innate potential* to learn more about yourself, on an ongoing basis.

Your Ability for Self-Knowledge

In earlier chapters, you took a look at your internal view, how you view yourself, a view that reflects the self-knowledge you've already gained. But your internal view is limited by the fact that it is fixed in time. It reflects what you've come to understand about yourself at a certain point in your life. Otherwise, you wouldn't be able to describe it. Your ability for self-knowledge includes your internal view; it also includes your ability to bring more clues about yourself to your awareness. The following questions will give you an idea of how your ability for self-knowledge is currently operating.

Would you say that you continue to learn about yourself over the course of your life?

_____

_____

_____

_____

How are you learning about yourself?

_____
_____
_____
_____

Do you seek out activities that foster self-knowledge (e.g., workshops, therapy, writing, meditation, pertinent discussions, reading)? If so, which ones?

_____
_____
_____
_____

What is the most recent discovery you've made about yourself?

_____
_____
_____
_____

How did this discovery come about?

_____
_____
_____
_____

Do you like finding out more about yourself, or would you rather not know certain things? Please explain.

_____
_____
_____
_____

The greatest obstacle to attaining self-knowledge is the desire *not* to know. We all have a tendency to screen certain information, to deny or reject whatever we consider unpleasant about ourselves. This is normal. When you do this, you're protecting your image. It takes great courage to look past your protected self-image and view other aspects of yourself that you may not show to the world. If you can do this *without* judging yourself, you'll be more accepting of what you discover.

Self-Knowledge and the Move

Moving overseas can provide you with a great deal of information about yourself. When you shift your focus from your environment to how you are doing in that environment, you'll learn a lot about yourself. In the next section of this chapter we'll ask you questions that will give you an idea of what is meaningful to you. Your answers may give you insight about your compatibility or incompatibility with your current overseas posting or with living overseas in general.

If your answers reveal that you're not temperamentally suited to your current posting or to living overseas, this is an important discovery. Only by actually moving overseas could you ever find this out. The move must occur for you to find out what it's really like, and how you'll respond. *It's neither a mistake nor a failure if you then discover that you're not suited to overseas life.* It's simply new knowledge. What you choose to do with this knowledge is entirely up to you. Leaving is one option. Going home will prevent further problems caused by your incompatibility. Staying is also an option. You can choose to become invested in the experience and see it through to completion. You can do this even though you know that you're not particularly suited to life overseas. Despite your incompatibility, there may be something for you to gain.

Even if your situation is unpleasant or uncomfortable, your ability for self-knowledge can flourish. In fact, the *entire* overseas experience could revolve around developing self-knowledge if you want to make that your focus. Remember that you have a choice, every waking moment, about where you place your focus. Start to observe yourself and your choices. Become curious. If you find yourself feeling powerless or defeated, remember this resource. When you tap into your ability for self-knowledge, you often find the power to turn a situation to your advantage.

How to Access and Develop Your Ability for Self-Knowledge

To help you access this resource, we've designed a list of questions to stimulate your thinking about yourself. You'll be exercising your ability for self-knowledge when you answer the questions. You may answer them in any order and in any way you like. We suggest that you trust your initial responses and avoid spending a lot of time thinking about your answers.

Self-Knowledge Inventory

What do you like to surround yourself with?

_____

_____

_____

_____

When do you experience joy?

_____
_____
_____
_____

What makes you laugh?

_____
_____
_____
_____

What makes you feel sad?

_____
_____
_____
_____

What do you catch yourself doing that surprises you?

_____
_____
_____
_____

What places do you enjoy?

_____
_____
_____
_____

Whom do you think about?

_____
_____
_____
_____

Whom would you like to spend more time with?

_____
_____
_____
_____

What do you look for in a friend?

_____
_____
_____
_____

What types of situations and/or people annoy or irritate you?

_____
_____
_____
_____

What types of situations and/or people do you find intolerable?

_____
_____
_____
_____

Is change easy or difficult for you?

_____
_____
_____
_____

What helps you adapt to new or different situations?

_____
_____
_____
_____

What are your skills and talents?

_____
_____
_____
_____

Are you able to utilize your skills and talents in the country you live in?

_____
_____
_____
_____

Do you set goals for yourself? If so, what are they?

_____
_____
_____
_____

Do you feel you can accomplish your goals in the country you live in? Please explain your answer.

_____
_____
_____
_____

Where do you see yourself in the next 5-10 years?

_____
_____
_____
_____

❧Exercise: Reflections❧

In this next section, we'd like you to reflect on what you discovered about yourself by completing the Self-Knowledge Inventory.

What was it like to answer the questions? Was it difficult or easy?

_____
_____
_____
_____
_____
_____

What did you answer that you already knew about yourself (i.e., self-knowledge you already have)?

_____
_____
_____
_____
_____
_____

What did you feel you had no answer for (i.e., areas of future discovery about yourself)?

_____
_____
_____
_____
_____
_____

What did you find out about yourself that you didn't previously know (i.e., self-knowledge you've added)?

_____
_____
_____
_____
_____
_____

Does your self-knowledge tell you anything about your ability or your desire to live overseas? Do you consider yourself compatible or incompatible with living overseas?

_____
_____
_____
_____
_____
_____

When you ask yourself questions like the ones in the Self-Knowledge Inventory and the above Reflections exercise, three things happen. You reveal what you know about yourself. You discover what you don't know, and you stimulate your ability to learn more. Any type of self-questioning will uncover these three aspects. Together, they form the parameters for the scope of your self-knowledge. Once you know what the parameters are at any given time, you have something to refer to.

For instance, if you found out that you don't really know what your goals are, you've found a missing piece of your self-knowledge. Finding out what you don't know is half the battle. Once you sense its lack, you can then decide to learn more about that missing piece. How you go about this is up to you. You may need to dialogue with yourself, or with someone else. *You access your ability for self-knowledge when it's your intention to do so.* Without your intention, it's much more difficult. Having the intention is the key to letting this resource work for you. Once you commit to this path, you'll find that just about any situation can reveal something about yourself and how you choose to operate in the world.

Does your ability for self-knowledge need to be strengthened in some way? You may want to refer back to your Self-Knowledge Inventory and the Reflections exercise. Please explain your answer.

_____
_____
_____
_____
_____
_____

If you determine that you need to strengthen your ability for self-knowledge, write a statement about your plan to do this.

_____
_____
_____
_____
_____
_____

Chapter 10

Resource #3: Ability to Manage Stress

How We Define Ability to Manage Stress

The ability to manage stress involves making choices about how you respond when stress hits. Imagine that you have an internal barometer that rises and falls according to the stress you experience. The stress could stem from anything: a conflict with someone, getting stuck in traffic, a worry that you're carrying, or a change in your health or financial situation. The cause of the stress is not our primary concern when we talk about this resource. We are primarily concerned with what you do once you're stressed, and how you respond to whatever is creating stress for you. When you learn to manage your internal response to stress, you're able to remain in charge of yourself, even if the situation seems to be out of your control.

Your Ability to Manage Stress

When your internal barometer rises, you have your own signs of stress. They can include changes in heart rate, breathing, skin tone and color, facial expression, body posture, and physical sensations (e.g., tightening in the shoulders or knots in the stomach). These are all physiological changes that occur at the time of stress. When a reaction to stress persists over time or does not fully subside, more long-term symptoms can develop. These symptoms may include headaches, body aches and pains, sleep or appetite disturbances, or general irritability.

How do you know when you're feeling stressed? What are your signs of stress?

_____

_____

_____

_____

_____

_____

What do you do when you recognize that you're feeling stressed?

_____
_____
_____
_____
_____
_____

Do you acknowledge your stress and find ways to manage it (e.g., take a few deep breaths, give yourself a pep talk, go to a safe spot and vent)? If yes, what are the ways you manage stress?

_____
_____
_____
_____
_____
_____

Stress and the Move

It is important to acknowledge that chaos accompanies any move overseas. While you may attempt to weather the move gracefully, it's not a graceful process. All overseas moves involve upheaval, mess, and a great deal of confusion about how to restore order. When in your home country, you know how to get things done. You don't need to think much about how you do this. Unless something unexpected happens, you can coast along to a certain degree. When you move overseas, you must give your full attention to the task of meeting your basic needs. You're figuring out how to inhabit your new home and community. Small things challenge you every day. You have to figure out how and where to buy groceries and other things you need. This takes patience. You have to decide how to go about unpacking and setting up your household. This takes time. You must figure out how to make yourself understood to the native people. This takes effort. You look for kinship, for someone you can be comfortable with. This takes courage. The basic requirements of daily living are not easy.

Daily life becomes stressful because everything is new or different. You are navigating in a foreign environment. You may also feel that you have little sense of control. For example, you may be dependent on your husband for information from the company or sending organization. Or, if you have others helping you (such as maids or drivers), you may feel dependent on them for the accomplishment of many tasks.

To alleviate the stress you experience you may find yourself choosing behaviors that provide temporary relief, such as binging on food, drinking more alcohol, spending more money or time on things that only briefly or superficially satisfy you. However, these behaviors are attempts to get rid of or mask the stress you feel. Instead, you can decide to learn more about how you react to stress, and then develop a more effective plan to help you manage the stress you experience.

How to Access and Develop Your Ability to Manage Stress

Step 1: Assess How You Currently React to Stress

The first step is to learn about your internal barometer to stress. Take note of how your barometer operates when you experience stress. This requires you to be your own subject of study. When you feel stressed, your goal is *to become curious about how you feel,* not to judge your reaction. Instead of getting completely caught up in your reaction to stress, some small piece of you stays detached and watches the barometer. Even while you're experiencing a great deal of stress, try to experience a little bit of wonder at the same time. That little bit of wonder allows you to ask yourself some questions and find out some answers.

What types of situations or interactions send your barometer soaring? What pushes your stress-reaction button?

_____
_____
_____
_____
_____
_____
_____

How do you behave when your barometer level is high? What happens to your voice, posture, and facial expressions?

_____
_____
_____
_____
_____
_____
_____

What allows your barometer to drop to a lower level? Do you make a decision to relax, do you relax over the course of time, or do you relax with someone else's input?

_____
_____
_____
_____
_____
_____
_____

Step 2: Ways to Manage Stress

Now that you have some information about your own reaction to stress, you can make choices about what to do when you feel stressed. You always have the choice to watch your barometer and concentrate on lowering the level, rather than continuing to react. To do this you'll need to shift your attention inward, rather than focusing on what is stressing you. You're not taking the stressor away but simply gauging your reaction and adjusting your internal barometer. This will allow you to regain a sense of control. Focus on deepening your breath, or relaxing a muscle, or unclenching your jaw. You'll be in a better place to deal with the cause of the stress if you're more relaxed physically. You'll remove some of the fear and panic associated with the stress. Then you'll have a better perspective on the situation.

Learning to consciously relax your physical response to stress is a simple and effective strategy. You'll need to remind yourself to use this strategy, over and over again. If you like, you can ask someone to be your "barometer buddy," someone who helps coach you to relax. You can call this person at the time of stress or soon after so she/he can give you specific instructions that the two of you have agreed upon beforehand. You could also tape-record yourself giving these instructions, and listen to the tape whenever you need to. Or you could memorize a pep talk you can recite to yourself at the time of stress.

Allowing your sense of humor to aid you is another way to keep perspective when you're stressed. Laughter releases tension. When you lighten up, everything seems to change and you realize that the situation is not as serious or as threatening as you thought it was. You may also remind yourself of a phrase or affirmation that diminishes some of the importance or power of the stress you experience. For example, you may ask yourself, "Will this really matter in five or ten years?" Or, you may have a faith-based prayer, saying, or mantra that you can recall during times of stress.

Having a safe place to vent or let off steam can also help you to relax. Knowing that you'll have an opportunity for a physical release of energy can make it easier for you to lower your barometer when stress hits. A physical release can take on many forms, such as running, swimming, biking, or dancing. You can also seek out restful, recuperative activities. What you find restful is unique to you. It could be restful to soak in a tub, bake cookies, or read a novel. What makes an activity restful is its ability to slip you out of a hurried sense of time. You make a decision not to rush or put yourself under pressure. You choose to do something simply because you enjoy it. When you give yourself a time-out from the chaos, mess, and confusion of the move, your barometer has a chance to neutralize and you are no longer in a reactive mode. You are then able to respond to the stress in a more positive and effective way. You can stop and consider what you may be in need of, which will improve your ability to handle stress. For instance, you may decide that you need more sleep, exercise (or a different type of exercise), or companionship. Or, you may decide that you need to make a change in your eating habits, decrease your alcohol use, or spend time paying attention to your spiritual needs (such as prayer, meditation, or worship).

Step 3: Making a Plan for Managing Stress

If you're not satisfied with how you manage stress, then you're a candidate for developing a plan. Learning new ways to manage stress will make it easier for you to meet the challenges of living overseas. Effective stress management will increase your ability to experience pleasure and have fun. Your answers to the following questions will provide you with a guideline for managing stress.

My Plan for Managing Stress

How will I pay attention to my own reaction to stress?

_____
_____
_____
_____
_____
_____
_____

How will I go about relaxing my physical responses to stress?

_____
_____
_____
_____
_____
_____
_____

When I am stressed, how will I keep the situation in perspective (i.e., have a sense of humor, recall an affirmation, phrase, prayer, or mantra)?

_____
_____
_____
_____
_____
_____
_____

How will I safely let off steam when I am stressed?

_____
_____
_____
_____
_____
_____
_____

What behaviors and/or restful, recuperative activities will help me manage my stress more effectively (e.g., get more sleep, change my eating habits, decrease my use of alcohol, get more exercise, and/or pay attention to my need for companionship or spirituality)?

_____
_____
_____
_____
_____
_____
_____

How will I incorporate the behaviors and/or restful, recuperative activities I identified above into my life on a more regular basis?

_____
_____
_____
_____
_____
_____
_____

Chapter 11

Resource #4: Ability to Access Support

How We Define Ability to Access Support

Support, in our definition, means people. When you can access support, you allow certain people to offer you help. You choose these people to play a key role in your life. Because of their presence, you feel more empowered and less alone. The type of support you may have includes individuals as well as groups.

Individual supports can include husbands/partners, family members, friends, counselors, mentors, and so on. When someone provides the emotional support you need, you enjoy their company, you feel comfortable and enjoy talking together. The contact you have is meaningful to you, and usually nourishes you in some way. You feel you're being heard and cared about. You may get a boost emotionally, or you may begin to think in a new way. An individual can also be a support by providing assistance (such as a babysitter), and may or may not also be a support emotionally.

A group support can be an organization or smaller group affiliated with your church, temple, business, child's school, neighborhood, community, or a personal interest or hobby of yours. Being a member of a group provides you a niche, a place where you feel you belong. You extend yourself out into a community that accepts and includes you. Your membership in the group enlarges your sense of self and can support you when you're in need.

Your Ability to Access Support

Individual and group supports don't materialize out of nowhere. They come about through your ability to access them. Either you seek them out, or they seek you out and you accept them. Either way, you're actively involved in a process of selecting and designating your support system. To get a sense of how you participate in this process, answer the following questions.

Are you able to take risks to talk to people new to you?

_____

_____

Do you allow people to get close to you?

_____

_____

Do you have thoughts like: "I can tough it out," "I can do it on my own," or " I don't need any help?"

_____

_____

Are you comfortable asking for support when you need it?

_____

_____

Are you satisfied with the supports you have in your life?

_____

_____

⇆Exercise: Reflections⇆

The following questions will help you reflect on what you discovered about your ability to access support.

What did you discover about yourself by answering the above questions?

_____

_____

_____

_____

_____

_____

Does accessing support come naturally to you, or is it difficult for you to do?

_____

_____

_____

_____

_____

_____

Let's go one step further in evaluating your ability to access support by looking at your beliefs about support. These beliefs, whether or not you're aware of them, factor into your ability to access support. In order to better understand your beliefs about support, complete the following sentences.

When I hear the word "support," I think of . . .

_____
_____
_____
_____
_____
_____

When I think about seeking out support, I feel . . .

_____
_____
_____
_____
_____
_____
_____

Are your thoughts and feelings about support positive or negative? Please explain your answer.

_____
_____
_____
_____
_____
_____

If your thoughts and feelings about support are positive, you probably have an easier time of reaching out for and finding help when you need it. If they are negative, your ability to access support is probably compromised. When your thoughts and feelings about support are negative, they are likely to be based in a negative belief. For instance, you may believe that having support means you're a weak person. You may be invested in proving you're *not* weak by shunning help. All you're doing, in this case, is supporting your belief, whether or not this belief does you any good. Where does such a belief come from? It may be something you acquired a long time ago from your family, when they taught you what *they* believed. Any negative beliefs about support will interfere with your ability to have a supportive relationship. If you have negative beliefs, you can question their existence, as follows:

Do my beliefs and feelings about support benefit me? Please explain your answer.

_____
_____
_____
_____
_____
_____

Do these beliefs and feelings benefit anyone else? If so, whom?

_____
_____
_____
_____
_____
_____

What will happen if I stop believing and feeling this way? What will I gain or lose?

_____
_____
_____
_____
_____
_____

Do I want to hold onto these beliefs or feelings?

_____
_____
_____
_____
_____
_____

If I let these beliefs or feelings go, what other feelings or beliefs can I replace them with?

_____
_____
_____
_____
_____
_____

Now that we have examined your ability to access support in general, let's look at this resource in terms of the move overseas.

Support and the Move

When you move overseas, the loss of the supports you had in place before the move presents a major hardship. It's as if these supports were guiding hands that have slipped away. Now you feel unsteady and off balance. You've left behind significant people; everyone you connected with on a regular basis is thousands of miles away. Because of geographical distance, friends and family back home cannot support you in the same way as before. They may feel abandoned by you or did not fully support your decision to move overseas. You may find yourself needing to reassure these people that you're okay, that you're happy–whether true or not. You may become protective of them, not wanting them to worry or feel worse about your leaving. All the relationships that have been supports for you before take on a different character because of the move overseas.

If your marriage/partnership is based in a supportive relationship, an overseas move will most likely test that basis of support to the maximum. Each member of the marriage/partnership has a unique experience of the move. While living overseas, you and your husband or partner are assigned distinctly different roles and expectations which often serve to divide you. If you're living in a culture where women are viewed as subservient to men, your gender divides you, even if it was never an issue between the two of you before. You cannot deny the power of the native culture and its belief system. The culture you came from, the one that supports *your* concept of marriage and relationship between men and women, is not with you. Your extended family, parents, and in-laws are not with you. The friends that provided support for each of you and enriched your lives are not with you.

With so much of the outside support for your marriage or partnership absent, the burden now falls on you and your husband or partner to manage without it. You may feel tempted to place your need for support on him alone, but he is also struggling to meet the same need. It is unrealistic to assume that the two of you can do for each other what a group of people and an entire culture was able to do for you before. Until you can re-establish some external supports, you'll likely feel isolated. It can be distressing to discover that you and your husband or partner are not fully available in a supportive role for each other when you move overseas. It is helpful to remember that the two of you are better able to support each other when you have support around you. For more information about the stresses and challenges international relocation places on marriage, we highly recommend *A Moveable Marriage: Relocate Your Relationship without Breaking It* by Robin Pascoe.[7] In the book, the author offers candid advice and practical solutions based on her research and personal experience.

Was your husband or partner a support for you before moving overseas?

_____

_____

_____

_____

_____

_____

Has there been a change in the support your husband or partner gives you (i.e., in the type or amount of support) since moving overseas? Please explain your answer.

_____

_____

_____

_____

_____

_____

How to Access and Develop Your Ability to Access Support

The move overseas disrupts the ability for key relationships to remain supportive. This disruption will be temporary or long-lasting, depending on the resiliency of these relationships over time. In the midst of the disruption of these relationships, you may feel that support is no longer available to you. What you need to remember is that *you still have your ability to access support.* This ability is not lost or taken away but merely challenged by the changes of the move. You can still engage in the process of selecting and designating supports.

When seeking new supports, you need to keep in mind that you're looking for the factors that make an individual or group a potential support for you. Think about what you need to feel supported. Do you need to be listened to, accepted? Do you need to feel like you belong? Think back on the characteristics of the individuals and groups who were supports for you before. Is an individual support someone available and caring? Is she/he someone you like and feel comfortable with? Is a group support one that acts to include you, that welcomes your participation? You may not have found these individuals or groups yet. You may not have remembered to look for good candidates for support. To develop your ability to access support, we offer you the following exercise.

Exercise: Accessing Support

Compose a letter that expresses what you're looking for in a support, be it an individual, or a group, or both. Introduce yourself and describe what you would like from a relationship with this person or group of people. Talk about what you can bring to the relationship as well (your ideas, your friendliness, your willingness to share your experience, etc.). You don't need to share this letter with anyone. It's an exercise to engage you in calling upon your ability to access support.

My Letter

Chapter 12

Resource #5: Ability to Be Open-Minded

How We Define Ability to Be Open-Minded

The way you think and believe, as well as your general outlook, comprises a mindset unique to you. With your mindset, you develop your own understanding of each situation. You formulate your own set of opinions. If you didn't have a mindset, if you were a blank slate, you wouldn't know how to categorize your experiences. Your mindset provides a necessary frame of reference but also has an aspect of flexibility that we call "an open mind." An open mind sees beyond its frame of reference. With an open mind, you can entertain more than one way of looking at a situation. You're also able to question whether the way you tend to think and believe is limiting you. Having an open mind allows you to have new ideas, new possibilities.

Your Ability to Be Open-Minded

Your beliefs can either be flexible, or rigid. If they are more rigid, you'll only want to see what fits into your frame of reference. You'll develop tunnel vision, a characteristic that makes it more likely you'll discard or discredit what does not immediately appeal to you. You'll be judgmental. When your mindset allows for more flexibility, you're less attached to your thoughts and beliefs. You're able to incorporate a sense of wonder about the world into your mental picture. You're more curious as well as more tolerant of new ideas that differ from your own.

We have designed the following questions to give you a general sense of your ability to be open-minded. Even if you don't know how to answer, it will benefit you to ponder these questions.

How often do you stop to examine what you're thinking?

_____

_____

Are you aware of how your thoughts can lead you to a certain course of action?

_____

_____

Do you tend to believe that there is one, right way to do something?

_____

_____

When a situation does not turn out the way you imagined it would, how do you respond?

_____

_____

Are you able to brainstorm (e.g., come up with ideas you didn't think of before)?

_____

_____

Is it easy or difficult for you to change your mind?

_____

_____

How receptive are you to other people's opinions or views when they differ from your own?

_____

_____

Open-Mindedness and the Move

When you move overseas, a sequence of events unfolds. You also experience a sequence of thoughts surrounding these events. You begin having thoughts about the move before it occurs. You develop an attitude about what is going to happen in your life. Your attitude may be positive, negative, or neutral, made up of all the things you tell yourself about the move. For instance, if you tell yourself that this move will give you the opportunity to travel and experience another culture, your attitude will be a positive one. If you tell yourself that you'll tolerate this move for a couple of years because it will boost your husband's career, your attitude is neutral, at best. If you tell yourself that you have no choice but to go along with this move, despite the fact that it is disrupting your life, your attitude is a negative one.

When you move, you bring your attitude (positive, neutral, or negative) with you. In addition to what you tell yourself about the move, you also have ideas about what it will be like to be an expatriate wife. You have ideas about the country you're moving to, about how you'll live, and about whether you'll work or not. You envision your life overseas before you get there.

What kind of thoughts did you have about moving overseas before the move itself? Please include the ideas you had about the country you were moving to, and the ideas you had about being an expatriate wife.

_____
_____
_____
_____
_____

How would you describe your attitude about moving overseas?

_____
_____
_____
_____
_____

How did your thoughts and ideas before the move compare with what you experienced after the move?

_____
_____
_____
_____
_____

When you make the move overseas, you face events with a mindset that *existed before the move*. As we stated earlier, your mindset is useful and necessary, but it is only a starting point. Your preconceived ideas about the move may prove inaccurate. What you thought about life as an expatriate wife, for instance, may have been based on misinformation. Ideas you had about the foreign country may have been culturally biased. How you pictured yourself living overseas may have been an illusion. You might have glamorized living overseas, for instance. When the situation turns out to be different than what you thought, you may feel let down, disappointed, cheated, or misled. Something has gone amiss. It seems as though *the situation* has failed you.

What has really happened? If we look at your sequence of thoughts, you've created certain expectations based on your thoughts, ideas, and attitudes: your mindset. You expect your mindset to be validated by your experience. When it's not, you see the situation defeating you rather than supporting you. You have interpreted the situation based on your own expectations.

If your expectations about living overseas haven't been met, we ask you to pause to examine your expectations. Complete the following statements:

When I moved overseas, I expected . . .

_____
_____
_____
_____
_____

I expected this because . . .

_____
_____
_____
_____
_____

My expectation has not been met because . . .

_____
_____
_____
_____
_____

What can I do about my unmet expectation?

_____
_____
_____
_____
_____

We ask you to think about what you can do about your unmet expectation because that is the point you return to in your mind whenever you feel disappointed. It's important to question whether these thoughts and ideas are still tenable. Do they hold up in light of the current situation? If they don't, can you consider another way of thinking that is more helpful to your process of moving and living overseas? The ability to be open-minded is a resource you can call upon when your expectations don't come to fruition. The following sample scenario demonstrates how this resource works.

Sample Scenario

Before Amy moves overseas, she thinks she'll enjoy a break from her career, and won't mind leaving her current job. Once she begins her life overseas, however, she starts missing her job and has difficulty finding some other way to structure her day. She believes she has made a mistake by leaving her career. She begins to panic that she's stuck with her decision. Her attitude toward living overseas becomes colored by her anxious feelings, and she cannot enjoy herself. She feels trapped. Her own expectation has trapped her. She expected that she would enjoy a break from work. Her expectation was, at best, a prediction. This prediction proved wrong. She can go on feeling anxious and unhappy about what has happened, or she can opt for an open-minded approach.

By having an open mind about her situation, Amy can take a good, hard look at her expectation and its outcome. She can see that she has learned something about herself: that she finds meaning through her career, and without it she feels at a loss. This lesson allows her to reexamine exactly what part of her career is meaningful to her.

Does she like the routine of her job, the financial compensation, or the chance to express her talents? When she takes time to think about this question of what is meaningful, Amy pinpoints the essential ingredient. She might discover that the meaningful qualities she seeks can come from somewhere outside of her career as she has previously known it.

For instance, she may find that the financial component is not the essential ingredient for her. Instead, it is the consistent interaction with people and the chance to work as a team that appeals most to her. Based on this discovery, she can look into possibilities for group projects in her community. From disappointment to discovery, she can expand her way of thinking. She can shift her attitude. Her thoughts and ideas can become more flexible and less fixated on a particular result. When this happens, she can support her growth process in the move overseas.

How to Access and Develop Your Ability to Be Open-Minded

In the sample scenario, we showed how Amy could access her resource, rather than perpetuate her anxiety about her failed expectation. The choice to access your ability to be open-minded is always available to you. It requires you to stop and re-evaluate how you think and how you perceive your situation based on your thinking. The motivation to do so comes from your willingness to take a risk. By taking a risk, you renew your commitment to take charge of your own growth process. The following questions will serve as prompts to access this resource.

If I could magically change my situation in any way that I could, I would . . .

_____

_____

_____

_____

_____

_____

With this change, I would think (and feel) like this . . .

_____
_____
_____
_____
_____
_____
_____

What would it take for me to think (and feel) this way right now, with my situation unchanged?

_____
_____
_____
_____
_____
_____
_____

Am I limiting myself by how I've been thinking about my life overseas? Please explain your answer.

_____
_____
_____
_____
_____
_____
_____

Is it possible to think differently about my situation than I currently do? Please explain your answer.

_____
_____
_____
_____
_____
_____
_____

Do I believe I can learn something about myself based on my thoughts and expectations about living overseas? Please explain your answer.

_____
_____
_____
_____
_____
_____
_____
_____

Using my ability to be open-minded, what choices can I make, and what actions can I consider to benefit my situation?

_____
_____
_____
_____
_____
_____
_____
_____

ଓ   ଓ   ଓ

By completing Part Three, accessing and developing your Personal Resources, you have completed Step 2 in reconstructing your identity. You have located your personal resources within yourself and built upon your commitment to take charge of how your identity is taking shape. In Part Four, you will continue to reconstruct your identity by engaging the third and final step of The Wheel.

Part Four

Tools for Change:

The Outer Spokes of The Wheel

Chapter 13

Overview and Tool #1:
Re-establishing a Sense of Stability and Security

Tools for Change

You've probably already started thinking about the changes you'd like to make to your identity so that your experience overseas will be more meaningful to you. In order to make the changes you are seeking, you'll need to put your thoughts and plans into action. However, you'll need some assistance.

You are now at the third step of The Wheel: Tools. Tools are the outer spokes of The Wheel and provide you with the assistance you need to make the changes you seek in your identity. Tools build on the first two steps of The Wheel (commitment and personal resources), and propel you into action. This is the final step that you'll need to work through in the process of reconstructing your identity.

How We Define Tools

We define a tool as an aide that you can pick up and use to help you reconstruct your identity. Tools help you do any one or more of the following: put into place what you've determined is missing from your life; reconnect to your self and/or the world at large; and/or, create a more meaningful life overseas. By using tools, you take charge of how your identity takes shape. Referring back to the metaphor of the crab, you use tools to create "a shell that fits," based on what *you* want and need.

We have divided the tools into seven categories:

    1) Re-establishing a Sense of Stability and Security;
    2) Communication with the Self;
    3) Communication with Others;
    4) Re-establishing a Support Network;
    5) Acceptance;
    6) Seeking Out Internal Activities;
    7) Seeking Out External Activities.

The diagram below shows the configuration of what the seven tools look like in The Wheel we first illustrated in Chapter 6 (**Diagram C**).

When you make the decision to use one or more of the tools to help you reconstruct your identity, you're doing three things.

First, you're building upon Step 1: Commitment. As you recall, at the core of your commitment is your desire and willingness to grow, change, and take risks. This is what motivates you and propels you to take action and actually pick up a tool. When you pick up a tool to use, you deepen your commitment to yourself because you're taking an active role in shaping the outcome of your identity.

The second aspect of using tools is that you're building upon Step 2: Personal Resources. As we said in Chapter 8, personal resources are abilities or skills that exist within you. Tools are an extension of those resources. They are often the method used to access and utilize your personal resources.

Diagram C

And third, using tools enables you to resolve the transitional state your identity has been in since moving overseas.

Tools and the Overseas Move

In chapters 13-19 we'll discuss the seven tools individually; what each tool is, its description, and how an overseas move affects it. We'll also discuss the importance of each tool for the expatriate woman's success overseas. Through a series of questions, we'll help you decide which tool(s) you need to make your desired changes. We'll provide you with guidelines and exercises to teach you how to use each tool within a foreign culture. We'll also include our own personal narratives throughout the chapters as examples for each area that we discuss.

Although we'll present the tools as a consecutive listing in a certain order, you don't have to use them in that particular order. Depending on personality and situation, different women will use particular tools in different ways. In our own experience, we found that though we both used each tool, the manner and the degree to which we used them varied, sometimes significantly. Choosing and using these tools is a flexible process. After you evaluate your situation or circumstances, you must determine the best time and the best way to use each tool. For example, you may choose to use one tool at a time. Or, since tools often overlap and connect to each other, you may decide to use several tools at once. Or, you may find that you don't need to use a particular tool at all.

Before moving on to the following section beginning with Tool #1, you may find it helpful to refer back to the exercises in Chapter 5 that helped illustrate the state of transition your identity is in due to the overseas move ("Who Am I?", "What Parts of My Identity Have I Kept?", "What Parts of My Identity Have I Left Behind?", and "What Have I Gained or Added to My Identity?"). This will help you remember the areas of your identity in which you may want to make changes.

Tool #1: Re-establishing a Sense of Stability and Security

What We Mean by a Sense of Stability and Security

One of our most basic human needs is the need for stability and security. Meeting this need provides you with an internal foundation that allows you to more easily absorb and handle all life's events. You're grounded and you feel safe. You have a certain level of confidence and trust about your life and its direction. With a sense of stability and security, your life is fairly regular and predictable. Overall, you feel relatively content and settled internally with your existence.

The factors that give you a sense of stability and security in your life are unique to you and are all based on your personality, preferences, values, and life experiences. What gives you a sense of stability and security can change over time. It can be one thing, or a combination of factors. For example, you may feel a sense of stability and security when you're settled into a home or community; if you have a certain amount of money in the bank; or when you maintain employment and receive a steady paycheck. Other factors that provide many people with a sense of stability and security are maintaining good health, living near family or friends, belonging to a church, or having a support network.

Debra:

My home, job, and support network have always given me a sense of stability and security in my life. When these three things are in place, I feel grounded and settled. Over the years I have made a lot of moves, including several in the same city. Every time I have moved, it has been very important for me to "set up" my house before doing anything else. I think this is because I regard my home as a safe haven. When so much of my life is disrupted because of a move, my home becomes my refuge. I never feel quite content internally until I'm settled in my new home. Only in retrospect have I come to understand that my feelings of unsettledness come from feeling uprooted, and this in turn, affects my sense of stability and security.

Having a job and my own paycheck also provides me with a sense of stability and security. I have always had some form of my own income since the age of 12 when I began babysitting. I began saving money so I could provide for myself financially once I left my parents' home. I like the feeling of having my own money. It makes me feel independent. In my mind, it was a given that I'd continue to work in my profession after the move overseas.

Having a support network has always been vital to my sense of stability and security. I think this is because I grew up in a large family and I enjoy being around other people. My support network over the years has changed, based on various situations, but it has included my husband, our families, and friends. Before moving overseas to Bangkok, Thailand, when I lived in Washington, D.C., my husband was my primary support system because we already lived far away from both of our families and many of our friends. We were each other's best friend. I was glad that we'd be making the overseas move together and that we'd be able to support one another in the process.

Before moving overseas, what represented or gave you a sense of stability and security in your life?

_____
_____
_____
_____
_____
_____
_____
_____
_____
_____
_____
_____
_____
_____
_____
_____
_____
_____
_____

How the Overseas Move Affects Your Sense of Stability and Security

Debra:

The three things that have always provided me with a sense of stability and security in my life (my home, job, and support network), were all greatly affected when we moved overseas.

When Brad and I moved we lived in temporary housing both before we left the United States as well as after we arrived in Bangkok. It felt like forever. I had a need to get settled into my new home, but was unable to fully do so for some time. I felt unsettled internally. I had difficulty sleeping. I often complained to Brad. He was my link to the embassy and I wanted him to demand that the embassy get us settled. I felt like a visitor in the dwelling where we resided. Once we were assigned to permanent housing, and unpacked our boxes, I was able to surround myself with familiar objects that represented our life together. I began to feel more settled internally.

One reason we bid on Bangkok was because we were told I could work there. We were a dual-career couple, and I was in the prime of my career. As I said earlier, I had neither planned nor thought of not working. Shortly after arriving in Bangkok, I learned a very different and very painful reality.

In the midst of settling into our home and adjusting to Thailand, I contacted the Director of Community Services of Bangkok (CSB), to talk with him about employment as a counselor. During my interview with CSB, the Director told me about the services his organization provided to the community, and he also said he'd be happy to have me work as a counselor. I was so excited. I felt that getting back to work would help me feel more settled and would help me adjust to the country. I was looking forward to continuing my work. I'd find enrichment both personally and professionally because I'd be counseling and working with people from all over the world. I looked forward to the challenge.

However, as we continued to talk, the Director informed me of a slight problem. He said that every foreigner needed a work permit in order to work legally in Thailand. In many professions, foreigners were prohibited from working if it was determined that they'd be taking a job away from a Thai national. He did acknowledge that many foreigners had worked, or were currently working, without work permits. The difference now was that the Thai government was enforcing the law with more regularity. The penalty for working illegally or without a valid work permit could include a fine, imprisonment, and/or expulsion from the country. The Director stated that as a result of the Thai government becoming stricter with foreigners working in Thailand, all new employees of CSB needed to have a work permit in order to work and receive financial compensation.

I thought, "No problem. I'll just complete the necessary requirements and get a work permit."

Then, the painful reality hit. The Director of CSB told me that, based on Thai law, I'd be prohibited from working because of my diplomatic visa and my husband's job with the U.S. government. The news stunned me. I felt devastated and confused. My heart began to sink. How could this be true?

Could the government really prohibit me from working because my husband worked for the U.S. government? Why wasn't I told this before moving halfway around the world? While I was dazed and trying to comprehend the impact of his words, he then gave me another option.

I could work for CSB as a counselor, but as a volunteer; i.e., donate my professional services. He even went on to say that because my husband was employed, it was not as necessary for me to be financially compensated for my work. He said many other professional women who were also in Bangkok primarily because of their spouses' careers were in a similar position, and many of these women chose to work as volunteers or joined organizations to "fill their time."

I was speechless. My head spun. I grew angry. As a woman, and as a professional, I was insulted. I had worked hard to get to where I was, and I was not about to work for free. Did other women really just donate their professional skills or give up their chosen professions? What would I do? I didn't understand how this could happen. I felt bitter towards my husband and his employer. I felt lied to and betrayed.

My husband, Brad, was my primary support system when we moved to Bangkok, and our relationship became strained with the move. We argued a lot and we went through a very rough time that relatively few people knew about. Our first arguments centered on my frustration with our housing situation; i.e., not being able to get settled because the embassy did not assign us to permanent housing for a long time. After I found out I couldn't work legally in Thailand, most of our arguments (often nightly), took a different course. They centered around my frustration with not being able to work in my profession legally, my thoughts and feelings about the insensitivity to spouses' career needs in the expatriate community, and how women were treated in general.

I felt that as a woman, I had stepped back in time about fifty years. I was overwhelmed, angry, and miserable. I directed my anger toward Brad. I blamed him for just about everything. I felt I had given up everything to make this move with him. I was angry because my expectations, my hopes, and my plans were not coming to pass as I had thought they would. My husband was an easy target for my anger.

Brad tried to be supportive and night after night, he listened to me and tried to understand my feelings. He held me when I cried. Without my career, what would I do? I didn't want to do anything else. I probably clung to my career even more during this time because of all the other changes that were occurring. I didn't want to lose anything else beyond what I'd already lost.

Over time, Brad's patience with me wore thin. He was going through a difficult time of his own. He felt guilty and responsible for moving us halfway around the world for his job, although we had both agreed on the move initially. He was also busy establishing himself within the embassy and learning a new job of his own. Although we missed being close to each other, we reached a point where we were unavailable to each other. We were no longer able to be each other's support as we had thought we could. Although temporary, this was another loss.

The three things that give me a sense of stability and security (my home, job, and support network), were all significantly affected when we moved to Bangkok. The most damaging blow came when I discovered I was prohibited from working in the country because of my visa status. One of the things which makes me feel most secure, a job and a paycheck, was missing. I felt devastated, knocked off-balance, and angry.

I began to question whether I had made the right decision in agreeing to move overseas. I felt like the foundation under my feet had been pulled away from me instantaneously, and I was left to struggle to gain my equilibrium.

After an overseas move, your sense of stability and security often deserts you, either temporarily or permanently. In part, this depends on what represents or provides you with a sense of stability and security. The impact of the move on this sense may be minimal or significant, or it may lie somewhere in between. How the overseas move affects you depends on your attachment to those things that give you a sense of stability and security in your life.

For example, if being settled in your own home and community gives you security, what did the move do to you? If maintaining employment and having your own paycheck are important to your sense of stability and security, does your life still feel stable and secure when employment opportunities are taken away in the country you've moved to? If you felt a sense of stability and security when you lived near family or friends, how was this altered with your move? If you had to leave a support network or church that provided you with a sense of stability and security, how did this affect you when you moved?

In the following space, write about how the overseas move affected those things that you identified as representing your sense of stability and security before you moved.

_____
_____
_____
_____
_____
_____
_____
_____
_____
_____
_____
_____
_____
_____
_____

What We Mean by Re-establishing a Sense of Stability and Security

In the previous section, you identified the things that provide you with a sense of stability and security and we assume the move affected these things to some degree. When we talk about re-establishing your sense of stability and security as a tool, we are talking about consciously putting back into place the things you've identified as representing your internal foundation.

Re-establishing your sense of stability and security is about once again feeling safe and grounded within yourself. When you find ways to re-establish your sense of stability and security, you feel peaceful. Once again, you have some degree of control of your life. You can better cope with and complete the tasks of your daily life. By re-establishing your sense of stability and security, you're better equipped to meet the challenges in your life and take risks when you choose to.

Consciously putting back into place those things that bring you a sense of stability and security does not necessarily mean you have to return to where you previously lived, but rather that you gain a deeper understanding of what represents your sense of stability and security, the meaning of those things in your life, and how to make decisions based on this new knowledge.

Why Re-establishing a Sense of Stability and Security is an Important Tool for the Expatriate Woman

The primary reason Tool #1 is critically important for the expatriate woman is because having a sense of stability and security in your life is vital to your success overseas. From an internal need to survive, you'll spend most of your energy trying to re-establish your sense of stability and security, whether you consciously know you're doing it or not. Therefore, it's to your advantage to know what makes you feel safe and secure, and then proceed to put those things, in some form, back into place. Otherwise, you'll flounder. You'll operate from a disadvantaged or weakened position.

For example, if having a job and a regular paycheck provides you with a sense of stability and security, but you find yourself unable to work once you move overseas, your internal foundation will feel shaky and vulnerable. If you move to a country that allows you to work, your internal foundation will probably feel more stable and secure once you find meaningful employment.

However, what happens if you move to a country that prohibits spouses from working? Your need for a sense of stability and security still exists. Because having this security is critical to your success overseas, it will be essential that you explore the meaning of work in your life to determine whether or not you can achieve your sense of security in some other way.

You may, on the other hand, discover that you do need to work in order to achieve this sense. If you're prohibited from working in the country you've moved to, you'll need to make decisions based on this information. For example, you may decide to challenge yourself and explore other avenues that could help you achieve the same satisfaction. You might decide to challenge the system that prevents you from working. Or you may eventually decide that moving around the world doesn't work for you and your family because of the instability and insecurity you experience from not working.

Tool #1 is also an important tool for the expatriate woman because when you have a sense of stability and security in your life, it's easier for you to fulfill your other needs. For example, when your internal foundation is strong, you feel safe and secure, and you are better able to take risks. This is especially important in the overseas environment because the people, environment, language, and culture may be very different from your own. Having a sense of stability and security in your life gives you a feeling of confidence that a change will not collapse your entire foundation. You feel free to try new things or experiment with other ways of being.

⋖Exercise: Reflections ✧

The purpose of this exercise is for you to gain a better understanding of how the overseas move affected your sense of stability and security, so that you can begin to decide the value of Tool #1 to you as an expatriate woman.

To what degree was your sense of stability and security impacted when you moved overseas (i.e., minimally, significantly, or somewhere in between the two)?

_____

_____

_____

_____

_____

_____

_____

How would you describe the effect of this impact on your internal foundation (i.e., did you feel shaky, vulnerable, or strong internally)?

_____
_____
_____
_____
_____

Is your sense of stability and security affected by your overseas move to the point that the quality of your life has been interrupted, diminished, or interfered with?

_____
_____
_____
_____
_____

Is your move overseas at the root of what you're currently feeling, or are there other factors involved? For example, did you experience feelings similar to what you feel now even before moving overseas?

_____
_____
_____
_____
_____

Since moving overseas, what activity or pursuit have you spent the most time on _for yourself?_ Does this have anything to do with what you need for your sense of stability or security?

_____
_____
_____
_____
_____

After answering the above questions, do you have any ideas about what you want to do with this information? Please briefly explain your answer.

_____
_____
_____
_____
_____

Decision Point

Debra:

In the depths of my unhappiness and misery, I became aware that much of my internal state had to do with lacking a solid sense of stability and security, which was primarily linked to my lack of employment. Although Charise and I had not yet begun our work together, and I had no name for what I was doing, I made a conscious decision to try and change my situation for the better in an attempt to re-establish my sense of stability and security.

When I discovered I was prohibited from working in Thailand because I was on a diplomatic visa due to my husband's job with the U.S. government, I felt so many things. I was angry, confused, hurt, stunned, and bewildered. Most of all, I felt an incredible sense of loss. For a while, I was immobilized by my feelings and was unsure about which direction to go so I did nothing. I don't recall the exact moment that I made the decision to pursue employment, but I knew that to capture that sense of stability and security currently missing in my life, I needed to work.

Internally, I was miserable and at a personal low, but became reacquainted with a part of myself that, no matter what the odds, does not give up easily. Somewhere I found the energy and motivation to continue forward at two levels. I decided to explore other employment options while simultaneously I decided to try to obtain a legal Thai work permit from the Thai government.

In my exploration of other options, I contacted the U.S. Embassy for ideas. They told me I could apply for a job within the embassy. I didn't need a work permit for embassy positions because I'd be a temporary employee of the U.S. government. However, most of the jobs were secretarial or clerical support. I thought I'd be relieved, but I wasn't. I wasn't interested in these types of jobs. I still clung to the idea of working in my chosen profession in Bangkok.

In conversations with others I met through the embassy and in the expatriate community about other employment options, I continued to hear that I could volunteer in the community or work illegally and receive payment for services in cash or "under the table." However, I also discovered that I technically needed a work permit even to work in a volunteer capacity. All volunteer and work activities needed approval by the Thai government. Although the thought crossed my mind to work without a work permit and take my chances, I didn't feel comfortable. I couldn't do anything to jeopardize my husband's position or career.

I also contacted numerous organizations in the community that might be able to utilize my counseling and social work skills. However, my limited ability to speak Thai and my ineligibility for a work permit were constant barriers. Other people I contacted suggested joining organizations to "fill my time." I didn't want to just "fill my time." I wanted more. I wanted to work in my own profession, as a counselor, and I became increasingly frightened by the awareness that it might not happen. Every closed door I encountered increased my frustration, but, ironically, heightened my determination to succeed.

As I pursued employment options, I simultaneously set out to obtain a legal work permit from the Thai government. I wanted to do this so I could know that I tried everything in my power to be able to work. I also felt that if I tried everything I could think of, it would make it easier to "let go" of the idea of working in my profession if the effort proved unsuccessful. I knew I had a slim chance of succeeding. Others, many of whom were women, also frequently reminded me that I was taking on something that had low probability of success.

Out of respect for my own principles, I decided that if I could not obtain a legal work permit, I would not work as a volunteer in my profession. I found the assumption that expatriate spouses had to work for free ludicrous and insulting. I also felt that if I worked for nothing, I would be perpetuating a policy that ignored the needs of expatriate spouses. I came to a clear decision within myself that if my efforts to work were unsuccessful, I could close the door to that possibility with no regrets. I could look myself in the mirror and like who I saw. I felt free.

During the next few months, I focused my energy on trying to secure a legal work permit. I submitted an appeal to the Thai Department of Labor, basing my argument on the fact that my employment in the country was not taking a job away from a Thai national. Also, my employment in the country as a counselor would be beneficial to the expatriate community because I'd be helping foreigners living in Thailand resolve personal difficulties, and this, in turn, would be beneficial to the country. I made numerous trips to the Thai Department of Labor, CSB, and the U.S. Embassy for information.

At times, I felt like giving up. I spent an enormous amount of time talking to people, researching information, and collecting the necessary documentation for the Thai government. Often my efforts got me nowhere and resulted in closed doors. At other times I felt hopeful when I got a semi-positive response or someone said they were willing to help. Because I was trying to meet the requirements of two governments, I also relied heavily on the support of individuals within the two organizations.

My husband Brad became my greatest supporter. He helped me make contact with various individuals at the embassy, officials who could possibly help. He advocated on my behalf and also for our needs as a couple. Some individuals at the embassy resisted or ignored my requests, but, luckily, we found others who were incredibly helpful. We discovered that many other couples and families had experienced difficulties similar to ours and had undergone additional personal and family stress due to the spouse's inability to continue working professionally while abroad. What started out as my individual effort to attempt to secure a legal Thai work permit, evolved into an effort with potential benefit for other women in similar circumstances. This motivated me even more.

Because obtaining the work permit is not a major focus of this book, I won't go into further detail about the actual process. Instead, I'll summarize it by stating that several months later, the culmination of my efforts, and the efforts and support from individuals within the U.S. Embassy, the Thai government, the Thai Department of Labor, and CSB, were rewarded. The Thai Department of Labor granted me a work permit that would allow me to work legally in my profession as a counselor at CSB without jeopardizing my diplomatic passport, visa status, or my husband's position or career.

Initially, I was shocked, and it took some time for me to actually believe it was true. I felt tremendous relief that the struggle was over and that I could now work legally. I was also ecstatic because obtaining my work permit also served to help pave a path for other women like myself.

I found myself repeatedly looking at my permit, and reflecting on how much time and effort it took. I felt pride and contentment at my accomplishment. Most importantly, I began to feel a deeper sense of stability and security within myself as I began to work at CSB legally as a paid employee.

Do you *currently* feel a sense of stability and security in your life? In other words, do you feel safe and secure, content, and settled internally?

_____
_____
_____
_____
_____
_____

If you answered "no" to the previous question, what needs to occur for you to re-establish a sense of stability and security in your life?

_____
_____
_____
_____
_____
_____

What would the potential positive benefits be for you to re-establish your sense of stability and security?

_____
_____
_____
_____
_____

Would there be any potential negative consequences for you re-establishing your sense of stability and security?

_____
_____
_____
_____
_____

When you think about re-establishing your sense of stability and security, does this sound like a positive or negative experience for you? Please explain your answer.

_____

_____

_____

_____

_____

_____

After answering the above questions, do you want or need to pick up Tool #1 and use it? Please explain your answer.

_____

_____

_____

_____

_____

_____

If your answers to the preceding questions indicate that you have a sense of stability and security in your life, you may choose to skip the following section and go on to the next tool. However, if you discover that your answers reveal that your sense of stability and security has been affected by your overseas move to the point that the quality of your life has been interrupted or interfered with, you now face a decision. You need to decide whether you're happy or unhappy about your situation.

If you're unhappy with your current situation and your unhappiness is at least partly linked to a lack of a sense of stability and security in your life, you must consider your options. You can either choose to maintain the status quo or work toward making the changes that have the potential to bring more stability and security into your life.

The decision is yours. If you decide to pick up the tool, continue to the next section to discover how to use Tool #1.

How to Use Tool #1: Re-establishing a Sense of Stability and Security

What you identified as the foundation to your sense of stability and security is what you will need to re-establish, in some form, so you can once again experience it in your life. The guidelines on the next page will help with this process. We encourage you to modify this guideline to address your own unique circumstances and situation.

Guideline for Using Tool #1: Re-establishing a Sense of Stability and Security

Step 1: What represents or gives you a sense of stability and security?

_____

_____

_____

_____

_____

_____

Step 2: What is missing in your life that keeps you from feeling a sense of stability and security? What keeps you from this feeling?

_____

_____

_____

_____

_____

_____

Step 3: What needs to happen for you to be able to re-establish your sense of stability and security? Think about all the options that will help you reach this goal. You might want to brainstorm on your own or with someone you trust.

_____

_____

_____

_____

_____

_____

What *options* do you have to help you meet this goal? Make a numbered list.

_____

_____

_____

_____

_____

_____

Step 4: Consider the positives and negatives of each option you came up with.

Option 1: _____

Positives _____

_____

_____

_____

_____

Negatives _____

_____

_____

_____

_____

Option 2: _____

Positives _____

_____

_____

_____

_____

Negatives _____

_____

_____

_____

_____

Option 3: _____

Positives _____

_____

_____

_____

_____

Negatives _____

_____

_____

_____

_____

Option 4: _____

Positives _____

_____

_____

_____

_____

Negatives _____

_____

_____

_____

_____

If you have more than four options, continue on a separate piece of paper.

Step 5: Review your options and select the best one. My best option is:

_____

_____

_____

_____

_____

Step 6: Develop a plan.

Based on the option you selected, develop a plan that will help you re-establish your sense of stability and security. Consider steps you'll need to take, and in what order; think about people that can help you; and then estimate how long it will take you.

My Plan for Re-establishing My Sense of Stability and Security

Step 1:

_____

_____

_____

Who can help me with *Step 1?*

_____

_____

_____

How long will it take to complete *Step 1*?

_____

_____

_____

Step 2:

_____

_____

_____

Who can help me with *Step 2*?

_____

_____

_____

How long will it take to complete *Step 2*?

_____

_____

_____

Step 3:

_____

_____

_____

Who can help me with *Step 3*?

_____

_____

_____

How long will it take to complete *Step 3*?

_____

_____

_____

Step 4:

_____
_____
_____

Who can help me with *Step 4?*

_____
_____
_____

How long will it take to complete *Step 4?*

_____
_____
_____

If you have more than four steps, continue on a separate piece of paper.

Step 7: Evaluate your progress periodically.

Make sure you give yourself credit for all of the efforts you make, regardless of the outcome. Modify your plan as necessary. Ask yourself, from time to time, "How am I doing on completing the steps in my plan? Am I moving toward my goal of re-establishing my sense of stability and security?"

Date: _____

_____
_____
_____

Date: _____

_____
_____
_____

Date: _____

_____
_____
_____

Chapter 14

Tool #2: Communication with the Self

What We Mean by Communication with the Self

Communication with the self lets you connect with your soul, the real you, a very personal and introspective process where you get to know yourself better by exploring the depths of your soul. You take an inward journey that involves reflection about your life and who you are. When you communicate with the self, you take an honest look at yourself in the mirror of the soul. You ask yourself questions about what you want out of life, why you do the things you do, why you like or dislike certain things or people, or why you have certain values or morals. You take a personal inventory that includes your strengths and weaknesses.

Communication with the self involves thinking about your personal history and all that has influenced who and what you are today. This may include thinking about patterns in your family through the generations, important people or events that have helped shape your personality, where you've lived, or opportunities you've pursued or turned down. All that you do, all that you've done or have not done, has played a part in who you are today. You should note that when you communicate with the self, your self-knowledge increases, a personal resource that we discussed in Chapter 9 in Part Three.

While you're in the process of self-communication, you may experience a wide range of feelings. These feelings will vary depending on your situation, your personality, and your purpose for communicating with the self. You can use this tool to get to know your soul better, to resolve an issue you've been struggling with, or to ponder the meaning of your life. For example, if you communicate with yourself to get to know your soul better or to get in touch with the real you, you may feel anything from excitement to despair as you make discoveries about yourself.

If you communicate with yourself for the purpose of resolving an issue, you may experience feelings of sadness, hurt, anger, frustration, or abandonment. Once you've resolved the issue, you may experience hope, joy, a sense of loss, or relief. If you communicate with yourself to ponder the meaning of your life, you may feel anything from complete confusion to a strong sense of purpose about your life. If you think about your life as a quilt, the overall design makes your quilt unique and different from another person's. And, when you look closely, you can see more clearly all of the individual steps that have led to create the overall design of your quilt.

For example, some of the events that occur in your life are like the tiny stitches in the quilt. Each tiny stitch contributes in its own subtle way to make up the path creating and leading to the overall design. Some of the events in your life are similar to the pieces of fabric within the quilt. The size, color, and shape of each piece of fabric varies according to the importance and impact each event has had on your life.

To continue with this metaphor, communication with the self is the process of taking a closer look at the unique design of the quilt that is your life by examining the individual pieces of fabric, including the various shapes, sizes, and colors of fabric, and the stitches that connect the pieces of fabric.

Ways to Communicate with the Self

There are a variety of ways to communicate with your inner self. Activities such as journal writing, meditation, prayer, music, writing poetry, and self-expression through dance and art are all avenues that can help you communicate with yourself. These activities all help you access your soul.

In our opinion, journal writing provides one of the best ways to communicate with yourself and to connect with your soul. A private avenue for self-expression, you can do it anywhere. You can ask yourself very direct questions about topics or areas you want to understand better. In your journal you can reflect on some of the questions you have about yourself. It can help you both unleash and record your thoughts and feelings as well as provide a place for you to record your dreams and what they mean to you. Because we believe journals are one of the best ways to communicate with yourself, we'll discuss journal writing in more detail later in the last section, *How to Use Tool #2: Communication with the Self.*

Meditation, prayer, music, writing poetry, and self-expression through dance and art are other activities to help you communicate with yourself. We discuss these activities in more detail in *Tool #6: Seeking Out Internal Activities.* In Tool #6, we refer to these activities as "internal activities" because you pursue them by yourself for the primary benefit of your soul, and engaging in internal activities often leads to communication with the self. Therefore, communication with the self and internal activities are inextricably linked because they have a common connection: accessing your soul. We encourage you to refer to *Tool #6: Seeking Out Internal Activities,* for a more detailed discussion about these activities.

The way you choose to communicate with yourself, or connect with your soul, in large part, depends on your personality and your own personal preferences. All that is required of you, regardless of how you choose to communicate with yourself, is a genuine intention and willingness to be honest with yourself as you seek answers to questions you have about yourself. Communication with the self is simply a form of talking to your soul by asking yourself questions, and coming up with answers through one of the above-mentioned ways.

Debra:

In one form or another, communication with the self has always been a part of my life. From a very early age, the voice of my soul yearned to be heard and sought dialogue with me. But not until I was older did I understand that this voice was my soul. As far back as I can remember, I have always wondered about life, particularly my own. I guess you could say it comes naturally to me because it's difficult for me to imagine not thinking about those things. When I was in grade school, I often struggled to come up with answers to difficult questions. For example, I wondered what my life would have been like if I had grown up in another country.

I imagined all kinds of scenarios about my life in that country and played them out in my head. I wondered why my skin is white and what it would be like to be a different nationality or race. I questioned God and wondered why He would allow so many bad things to happen in the world. We moved twice while I was in grade school, and I often wondered about the direction of my life if we had stayed in Great Bend, Kansas, the small town where I was born. It seemed that I was constantly thinking about my life and my place within the world.

In junior high and high school, I continued to communicate with myself in various ways. One way was simply a form of self-talk. I would sit in a quiet place, often my bedroom, and ask myself questions like, "Why am I the way I am?"; "Why do I do things the way I do?"; "Why do I believe the things I do?"; and, "What is my purpose in life?" I'd ponder these questions and try to come up with definitive answers. In retrospect, I was doing a form of meditation, though at that time, I didn't really understand what that was. I also often prayed at these times, asking for guidance to my questions.

I also sporadically kept a journal. Most of my entries summarized the day's events, the latest love of my life, or a fight with a girlfriend. Since I grew up in a house with four brothers, and I was a teenager, I was guarded about what I wrote. So the benefits I obtained from journaling at that time were limited.

When I entered college, I naturally gravitated to classes in psychology, sociology, and social work. The reading for my classes always stimulated my thinking about myself. Even after I graduated from college, I read books related to psychology and self-improvement in my spare time. It seemed that I could always relate to something that I read. This would often spark further self-questioning, which led to personal growth. Somewhere during this time period I also realized that my self-questioning was a response to the voice of my soul seeking expression.

When I went to graduate school, I communicated with myself a great deal. My soul seemed to constantly tug at me. Even though I was studying to be a clinical social worker so I could counsel other people for a career, the intense program, internship, and course work seemed to expose my every vulnerability and unresolved issue.

After assurances by the head of the program that my experience was normal and common among students in the field, I decided to seek out counseling for myself to deal with some of the issues in my life that I had not fully resolved. I did this to benefit my soul and to be a better counselor. Entering into a therapeutic relationship (which is part of Tool #3: Communication with Others*) helped me open doors within myself that I was unable to reach on my own. Although at times I found it a painful process, therapy has enriched my life both personally and professionally.*

If you think about your life as a quilt, did you make a conscious effort to examine the stitches, fabric, and design of your quilt before moving overseas? Please explain your answer.

_____

_____

_____

_____

_____

In what ways did you communicate with yourself before moving overseas?

_____

_____

_____

_____

_____

How the Overseas Move Affects Your Communication with the Self

Debra:

After I moved to Bangkok, I communicated with myself frequently by keeping a journal. I initially planned on using a journal to record my thoughts, feelings, and impressions of Thailand and her people. Although I did this, I also came to rely heavily on my journal to help settle me internally after we first arrived in Bangkok.

As I have previously shared, I plummeted to a low within myself when I was initially unable to work in Thailand. I became angry and frustrated and my relationship with my husband suffered. I desperately needed to talk about my thoughts and feelings so I could better understand what was going on with me, but my friends and family were 14,000 miles away and I had yet to meet anyone that I trusted enough to share my true feelings with.

Gradually, and mostly out of desperation, I started using my journal almost daily in an attempt to understand what was going on with me, and achieve some sort of internal balance. I came to depend on my journal to help me reach my soul's inner voice when I was stuck on the surface somewhere, or engulfed by my feelings. By communicating with myself through journal writing, I unleashed my thoughts and feelings in a private, safe place. I was often disgusted by the words I wrote and I felt weak. I yearned for the strength I once had. And, at times I questioned whether I'd ever feel strong again. But communicating with myself through journal writing was the path that eventually helped me get back on track.

The only prerequisites for using Tool #2 are your willingness and presence, but your personality, situation, and history play a major role in how the overseas move affects your communication with the self. *Tool #2: Communication with the Self,* has the potential to arrive overseas with you in pretty good shape if you communicated with yourself before the move. For example, if you're an introspective person who reflects on things, you'll probably have this same tendency when you move overseas. You'll probably spend quite a bit of time thinking about yourself and your situation when you move. However, you may be the type of person who doesn't think about things much, and might not have communicated with yourself before you moved overseas. You may not know, or ignore, reject, or deny what you're thinking, feeling, and experiencing as a result of the move. This may cause you difficulty overseas because you may have trouble understanding your thoughts, feelings, and behavior.

Moving overseas is stressful and regardless of your personality and situation, it's probably unrealistic to assume that your communication with the self will not be affected. Because of the multitude of demands placed on you when you first arrive overseas, you may not have the time, or take the time, to focus on yourself. You may choose not to communicate with yourself in any depth initially while you arrange your external environment. Instead, you may choose to keep your communication with the self at a more functional and task-oriented level by asking yourself questions about where you want to live, where you want to shop, or where you'll enroll your children in school.

Because of all of the changes that have occurred in your life, the overseas move also has the potential to propel you into communicating with yourself more than you did in your home country. The change in culture alone can make you rethink your existence, and you may find yourself questioning your own culture, values, beliefs, and ways of doing things.

Whether you view the move as a positive or negative experience may affect your communication with the self. For example, if you view the move as a negative experience, your communication with the self may be more negative, take the form of self-criticism, doubt, anger, and/or it may be a way for you to vent your thoughts and feelings about the move. If you view the move as a positive experience, your communication with the self may take a more positive slant. For example, you may welcome the chance to learn more about yourself within the context of a different culture and your new surroundings.

How did the overseas move affect your communication with the self?

_____

_____

_____

_____

_____

Why Communication with the Self is an Important Tool for the Expatriate Woman

Debra:

Communication with the self was vital to my success and well-being overseas. Journal writing helped me figure out what I was thinking and feeling at times when I didn't have a clue about what was going on in my internal world. When faced with not being able to work when we

158

moved to Thailand, journal writing helped me process my thoughts and feelings about the situation. I think communicating with myself was perhaps even more important when we moved overseas, especially in the beginning, because I wasn't able to talk with my husband, friends, or family in the same way I had before the move. I had to rely on myself to figure things out.

After I began my work at CSB counseling clients, and once I felt my sense of safety and security returning, I continued to communicate with myself through journal writing to gain a deeper understanding of the meaning of work in my life. While in the middle of my struggle to work (that's what it felt like) my journal became my best friend, my most trusted confidante, as I attempted to figure out why I had felt so off-balance without work in my life.

Communication with myself through journal writing was vital to this process of self-reflection and looking inward. Some of the discoveries I made about myself were painful, but important. What I came to understand was that my sense of identity, or my sense of who I was, was defined primarily through my work role, and without it I felt lost.

Through journal writing, I discovered that I literally felt stripped of myself when my work was taken away from me. My life had always revolved around work. Without it, I felt naked. I was so uncomfortable not being in a familiar role that I actually "fought" to get my role back. Although I'm still grateful that I successfully obtained a work permit, I also had to face the realization that my life had become out of balance. I realized that it wasn't healthy for so much of "me" to be defined primarily through my work, and that I was so unhappy without this familiar role. Then I realized that I faced another decision. I needed to decide what to do about this discovery. In the next section, I'll talk more about that decision.

Communication with the self is an important tool for the expatriate woman because it can help you connect with your soul and help you gain a better understanding of yourself. It can help you process your thoughts and feelings when you're stuck. It can give you a more realistic view of yourself, such as your strengths, weaknesses, likes, dislikes, and limitations. This is important, because when you're more self-aware, you can trust that you're operating on behalf of your own best interests.

Communication with the self is also an important tool for the expatriate woman because it can help you make better decisions about your life. Communication with the self gives you a better understanding of who you are, and, in turn, helps you make more informed and suitable decisions about your life.

Communication with the self also fosters self-reliance. When you look inside yourself and find answers to questions you struggle with, you tap into your own personal strength. This, in turn, helps you to feel more in control of your thoughts, feelings, behavior, and the direction of your life. This is especially important for the expatriate woman. When you move around the world, others may not always be there for you to depend upon. Therefore, it's important for you to know you can rely on yourself.

Another exciting benefit of communication with the self for the expatriate woman is that it can provide you with an opportunity to deepen your awareness about who you are in the context of a foreign land. We've illustrated throughout this book that the process of moving overseas profoundly affects your identity. The effect of the overseas move on a woman's identity varies greatly and is unique to each woman going through the process. Therefore, the move itself can provide you with an opportunity to gain a better understanding about yourself in the context of a new country and culture.

✍Exercise: Reflections ✍

The purpose of this exercise is to help you gain a better understanding of your communication with the self before your overseas move, as well as how the overseas move affected this process. This will begin to help you decide whether Tool #2 may be of further value to you.

Did you communicate with yourself before moving overseas?

_____
_____
_____
_____
_____

Were you satisfied with your communication with the self before moving overseas, e.g., the way you communicated with yourself, the frequency and the benefits you experienced from the process?

_____
_____
_____
_____
_____

What was the most significant change in your communication with the self after you moved overseas? What was the effect on you?

_____
_____
_____
_____
_____

Do you currently communicate with yourself? If yes, are you satisfied with the way you communicate with yourself, the frequency and the benefits you experience from the process, etc.? If not, why do you think this is the case? Please explain your answer.

_____
_____
_____
_____
_____

After answering the above questions, do you have any ideas about what you want to do with this information? Please briefly explain your answer.

_____
_____
_____
_____
_____

As you completed the Reflections exercise, you discovered how your overseas move affected your communication with the self. Because communication with the self depends primarily on your presence and willingness to engage in the process, your communication with the self has the potential to arrive with you overseas fairly intact. What did you find for yourself? We'll highlight several possibilities below.

You may have found that you communicated with yourself before your overseas move, and that you continued to do so afterward. If so, give yourself a round of applause! You've established a continuing dialogue with your soul in the midst of a move.

You may have found that you were satisfied with your communication with the self before moving overseas, but that once you moved, your level of self-communication decreased or stopped altogether. Moving overseas is stressful, and getting settled in your new environment takes a lot of energy. During this time, it may have been difficult for you to take time for yourself or you may have been too tired or overwhelmed to do so.

You may have found that you communicated with yourself before moving overseas, but weren't satisfied with your methods, the amount of time you were able to spend, or the benefits you received. If this is what you found, be easy on yourself. Look at this as an opportunity to grow.

You may have discovered through the Reflections exercise that you didn't really communicate with the self before or after you moved. If this is what you found, this may also be an opportunity for you to grow in this area.

Decision Point

Debra:

After I discovered that my life was out of balance because of my over-identification with work, I made a decision to continue communicating with myself by spending time writing in my journal and reflecting on the discoveries I made about myself. Over the next several years, I began to work on this process of rediscovery and actively worked on achieving a better balance within myself. I realized that because of my over-identification with work and career, I had neglected my connection with myself and relationships with other people. So, I decided to spend time with myself to gain a better understanding of how this came to be.

I learned about other factors in my own history that contributed to where I was. For example, I grew up in a family that for generations has placed a high value on hard work. I also grew up in a large family where it was a lot of work just to complete the basics of daily existence. Working hard is an admirable trait that I have benefited from tremendously over the years. My work ethic has taught me to push myself to pursue goals and successfully achieve them. Yet, working hard also has a darker side for me.

I remember when I was growing up there seemed to be an endless amount of daily chores, and I became frustrated at times that the work needed to be done before I could enjoy myself. Often by the time the work was completed, I felt irritable and tired. I had strong feelings about wanting to have more fun and not wanting to work so much. But, as I grew into adulthood, I had already internalized the value of the work ethic and carried it into my adult life. It was very difficult for me to relax and enjoy myself unless my work was completed. My relationship with others and with myself suffered. I was not always available to fully experience the relationships I had.

Through my journal writing, I also reflected on my friendships and my ability to be a friend. I have always had friends and made friends easily, but I'm talking about the quality and closeness of those relationships. I had several long-time friends in the United States that I felt close to, but for several years (even before moving to Bangkok), I wasn't able to see or talk to them frequently because of geographic distance. They lived in the Midwest and I had moved to the East Coast after I got married. It was difficult to have a close relationship with them from that far away.

In relationships, I'm initially guarded with my feelings. I grew up in a home where I didn't always feel free to express my true feelings. In fact, feelings were rarely discussed in my family (although this has improved in recent years), and when I did express my feelings I often felt more vulnerable for that expression. As a result, it has been important to me to have friends and people in my life that I can share my thoughts and feelings with, and for them to accept them for what they are, and for me to be able to do the same for them. I have this type of relationship with my husband and with some of my family and friends I left in the U.S. By communicating with myself through journal writing, I became acutely aware that I missed having this type of relationship with other women in Bangkok. I felt lonely.

So, I made another decision. I decided to allow myself to be more vulnerable and to let my guard down. I decided to try and nurture some of the relationships I had with some of the women

I met in Bangkok. We spent time talking, going on day excursions to explore the city and traveling to other parts of Thailand to explore the country and her people. Some of these women didn't turn out to be friends, but, by allowing myself to be vulnerable, I also met two of my closest friends even to this day, Audrey and Tracy, while in Bangkok.

My new friendships led to new opportunities and personal growth. My friend Audrey and I volunteered to work on a play that was being performed by the expatriate Community Theater, and we were asked by the director to be co-producers. Although neither one of us had produced a play before, we took the challenge and had a lot of fun. We even ended up with a small part in it.

My friendship with Tracy evolved into a friendship that also included our husbands. Tracy and her husband Bill lived in our apartment building so we saw each other frequently. I also valued the frequent morning walks Tracy and I took. Some days our walks went on forever because we had so much to talk about. As we walked, we pushed each other to look deeper in ourselves to find answers to questions we each struggled with.

I also started exploring other parts of myself that had become stifled. I eventually reduced my hours at work, to work part-time. I learned to give way to a very playful part of myself and felt myself blossoming. I had always liked to stay in shape, and on the suggestion of a friend, I learned to play tennis. I also became more interested in the Eastern forms of preventive medicine, such as therapeutic massage and meditation. I also enjoyed entertaining friends, giving parties, and attending other social events.

As I became more self-aware, and as I began to make positive changes and feel better about myself, my relationship with Brad started to improve. We began to enjoy each other's company again and we spent a lot of time exploring the country and traveling to surrounding countries as well. We also got involved with an organization called WAR (Wild Animal Rescue Foundation) where we volunteered to care for gibbons and help reintroduce them to the wild.

When I look back at all of the personal and professional struggles I encountered after moving to Bangkok, I see that what started out as one of the most painful experiences of my life, evolved into one of the greatest experiences. Communicating with myself through journal writing and making decisions and changes based on some of the discoveries I made about myself was at the core of this. Bangkok came to symbolize an incredible odyssey of personal growth for me.

By the time my husband and I left Bangkok, I felt I had achieved a much better balance. Although work continued to be important to me, it was not all consuming and did not monopolize my time or energy. I also spent a lot of my time nurturing other interests and enjoying the time I spent with my husband and friends. I traveled frequently and took trips to spend time with my family. My relationship with Brad had improved and our marriage was stronger than ever. I felt more content and at peace with myself. I also enjoyed the time spent in quiet reflection, listening to the quiet voice of my soul. I felt at peace with myself and with my place in the world.

You too, have already used *Tool #2: Communication with the Self.* You used Tool #2 in Chapter 1 when you completed the "Who Was I?" exercise and in Chapter 5 when you completed the "Who Am I?" exercise. The "Who Was I?" exercise helped you gain a better understanding of how you defined yourself before you moved overseas. And, the "Who Am I?" exercise helped you gain more insight into how the overseas move and the cultural confrontation further impacted your identity. The purpose of reviewing these exercises now is to highlight your previous discoveries about yourself to help you determine whether Tool #2 may be of further use to you as an expatriate woman. After you review the exercises, answer the questions below.

After reviewing the *"Who Was I?"* exercise you previously completed, were you satisfied or dissatisfied with the person you saw on paper? For example, did you discover things about yourself that you were previously unaware of? Did you like or dislike certain aspects of yourself that you wrote down? Please explain your answer.

_____
_____
_____
_____
_____

After reviewing the "Who Was I?" and "Who Am I?" exercises you previously completed, do you have any ideas about what you want to do with this information? Please briefly explain your answer.

_____
_____
_____
_____
_____

Communication with the self can be an important tool for the expatriate woman because it can help you explore in more depth the discoveries you made about yourself in the "Who Was I?" and "Who Am I?" exercises. Communication with the self can also help you make choices about what you want to do with the discoveries you made about yourself in those exercises. (We'll discuss ways to do this in the following section on *How to Use Tool #2: Communication with the Self.*) But, only you can decide whether you want to pick up the tool and use it. To help you decide whether or not you want to use Tool #2, consider the following questions:

What would the potential positive benefits be for you if you communicate with yourself?

_____
_____
_____
_____
_____

What would the potential negative consequences be for you if you communicate with yourself?

_____

_____

_____

_____

_____

Would there be any potential positive benefits for you in *not* communicating with yourself?

_____

_____

_____

_____

_____

When you think about communicating with yourself, does this sound like an appealing process to you? Or does it sound like a process you fear or want to avoid? Please explain your answer.

_____

_____

_____

_____

_____

After answering the above questions, do you want or need to pick up Tool #2 and use it? Please explain your answer.

_____

_____

_____

_____

_____

If you decide to use *Tool #2: Communication with the Self*, continue to the next section. If not, you may skip the following section and go on to Tool #3.

How to Use Tool #2: Communication with the Self

Communication with the self is both easy and difficult. Tool #2 is easy to use because it is a form of talking to yourself. It requires only your presence, and you can use it anytime or anywhere. It's also difficult because it requires you to be vulnerable. It's often a very difficult decision to make, to sit and ask yourself questions about why you think, feel, behave, and/or do things a certain way.

There are three basic steps needed to communicate with the self. The first step is for you to make a decision to do so. The second step is a genuine intention and willingness on your part to be honest with yourself as you seek answers to questions you have about yourself. The third step is for you to select an avenue to help you communicate with yourself. As we said earlier, journal writing, meditation, prayer, music, writing poetry, and self-expression through dance and art are avenues that you can use to help you communicate with yourself.

Because we believe journal writing is one of the best ways to communicate with yourself, in the following section we will focus on how to communicate with the self through journal writing. We'll discuss how to get started with your own journaling process. We'll also show you how you, as an expatriate woman, can use journaling to help you further understand and make choices about the discoveries you made about yourself when you completed the "Who Was I?" and the "Who Am I?" exercises earlier in this book.

Communicating with the Self Through Journal Writing

1. Getting Started

First, purchase a blank journal to record your thoughts, feelings, and ideas in. Most bookstores and many drugstores or card shops carry blank journals in a variety of sizes, shapes, and colors. Choose one that reflects you and your personality. If you're in an area where such a book is unavailable, use a pad of paper or a notebook to record your thoughts. We do recommend that the paper you use be somehow bound together so you can keep all your entries together.

Since journal writing is a very personal process, it will be up to you to decide when and how often to write. Your journal can become a very special and treasured friend. Having your entries bound together in one journal makes it easier for you to put it away in a safe and protected place when you need to, and easier to pick it back up again when you're ready.

Another reason we like to have our journal entries in a bound book is because we've found it often helpful to go back and re-read previous journal entries. Often in retrospect, you can see more clearly what was going on in your life than you could during the actual time of your struggle. Looking back is also a good way for you to recognize ways in which you've grown and areas that you need to continue to work on.

Although we personally recommend writing in a journal the old-fashioned way, using pen and paper, you can also use a computer to record your thoughts. It's up to you to decide which method is best for you.

2. What to Write

Because journal writing is such a personal process, you need to decide what questions you need to ask yourself, and how you want to do it. That's the beauty of journal writing. There is no one right way to do it. Your journal is an expression of *your* unique creativity and personality. It's all really up to you. You can find several books at bookstores, the library, and on-line that illustrate various ways to journal. We highly recommend *The Complete Idiot's Guide to Journaling* by Joan R. Neubauer.[8] If you have difficulty getting started with journaling, you may want to review her very comprehensive and friendly book for ideas.

We, the authors, have each developed our own unique and different style of journaling, and we have each found answers to very difficult questions by trusting and using our own personal journaling methods. We trust that you'll be able to do the same for yourself.

Journal writing can also be used for very specific purposes. For example, as an expatriate woman, communicating with the self through journal writing can be an avenue to help you further explore the discoveries you made about yourself in the "Who Was I?" and "Who Am I?" exercises. In each of these exercises we outlined four facets which make up your identity; internal view, external factors, roles, and relationships. You can explore and re-evaluate your responses to any of these areas by communicating with the self through journal writing. (You may want to refer back to the Reflections exercise you previously completed earlier in this tool for ideas about areas you could explore further through journal writing.) Below, under each of the four facets of identity, we'll give you some examples of questions you could ask yourself to give you ideas about how you could communicate with the self through journal writing.

For example, under internal view, you may want to explore the answers to questions like those that follow. Is my self-perception accurate or is it distorted in some way? What are the origins of my strongest beliefs? How does my attitude influence how I see the world? Has my attitude changed since I moved? Which of my values defines me the most?

You can also use this time to reflect about these various aspects of your being within the context of a foreign culture. Under external factors, you may want to spend time re-evaluating external influences that have played a part in who you are. For example, in your journal, you may ask yourself questions such as those that follow. What people have influenced my life the most and why? Are my self-perceptions the same as others see me? If there is a difference, why do I think there is a difference? How have the communities I have lived in helped shape who I am? In what ways does living outside of my country and culture affect me?

Communication with the self through journal writing can also help you identify things that you no longer want in your life or that no longer "fit" you. For example, under roles, communication with the self through journal writing can help you explore your thoughts and feelings about various roles you occupy. One possibility is that you may discover through this process that you no longer enjoy a certain role, such as a volunteer in a certain capacity. Through journal writing, you can explore your thoughts and feelings about what you want to do with this information. Why do I continue to volunteer in a capacity I don't enjoy? What would it be like for me to refuse the next time I'm asked to volunteer when I don't want to? What would it be like for me to resign? What would it be like for me to "let go" of this role that no longer fits? What would I do with my time instead?

When you move, you often fall into new roles: expatriate woman, diplomat, "ma'am," etc. Communication with the self through journal writing may also provide an opportunity for you to process your thoughts and feelings about your new roles.

When you completed the "Who Was I?" and/or the "Who Am I?" exercises, you may have discovered that you're not satisfied with one or more of the facets that make up your identity. Communicating with yourself through journal writing can help you gain a better understanding of your dissatisfaction. For example, under relationships, you may have discovered the true significance of your relationships with family you left behind. In your journal, you may want to further explore the meaning of those relationships and their effect on your identity. Ask yourself some important questions such as: How important are the relationships I have with my family to my identity? How did the change and/or loss of the relationships with my family affect my identity when I moved overseas? Is this a temporary or permanent loss to my identity? Will new relationships with other people fill the void I currently feel in this area? When I think about living overseas without my family nearby, I feel_____.

Exploring such questions through journal writing may give you the insight you need to make decisions about what you want to do with the information you uncover. By continuing with our example, you may conclude that being close geographically to your family is central to your identity. If this is the case, then living overseas may not be for you. Coming to this understanding of yourself doesn't mean that you're wrong or that something is wrong with you. It simply means that living near your family is extremely important to you and you should carefully consider the impact of *not* living near them.

Or, you may decide that although your family is very important to you and central to your identity, you'd like to take a risk by moving away from them to experience living in a foreign country. So, instead of returning to your homeland to be near your family, you might decide to take the risk of developing other relationships, extending your support network beyond your family, and learning other ways to maintain close contact with your family even though you're continents apart.

We hope that by using this tool, you gain a deeper understanding of yourself; that you'll be more accepting of yourself and who you are, as well as accept the decisions you make, based on the information you learn about yourself through journal writing.

Communicating with the self through journal writing can also be a way for you to explore using other tools. For example, you may discover that participation in activities has been lacking in your life and you may want to try something new. By deciding to seek out an external activity, you use *Tool #7: Seeking Out External Activities*. Or, you may realize that your relationships with others have been lacking, and it may prompt you to seek out a new friendship (*Tool #3: Communication with Others* and *Tool #4:Re-establishing a Support Network)*. Communication with the self through journal writing can be a way for you to process the steps you need to take to use another tool, and the thoughts and feelings you have as you experiment with new ways of being.

In the space below, write some ideas about areas of your life or identity that you would like to explore further in a journal or perhaps some other format. Refer back to this exercise if and when you decide to begin this process.

Areas of my life or identity I'd like to explore further include the following:

_____
_____
_____
_____
_____
_____
_____
_____
_____
_____
_____
_____
_____
_____
_____

In summary, communication with the self is an important tool for the expatriate woman because when you're consciously aware of your life, that is, all the various pieces and shapes of fabric, and stitches that together make up the intricacies of your "quilt," you're better able to identify areas you need to work on, areas that can be left alone, and areas to let go of.

By using *Tool #2: Communication with the Self,* you also increase and strengthen your *self-knowledge,* a personal resource which you can draw upon when you need to. This enhanced self-awareness can prove very powerful because it enables you to meet your needs better and empowers you to make more informed and satisfying decisions about your life.

3. Begin Writing

After you decide what to write, the next step is to actually begin writing. You must decide when to do this. We suggest that when you begin journaling, you select a time in the day and a location free from distraction. This will help you be more in tune with yourself and your thoughts and feelings. At first, journal writing can feel a bit awkward. Don't worry, in time it will become second nature to you. As in any relationship, the beginning is always a bit awkward, and as time goes on it becomes more comfortable. The important thing is that you begin.

When you sit down to journal, write whatever comes to mind. Whether you're curled up in a chair with pen in hand or sitting at your computer, collect your thoughts, feelings, and ideas. Allow yourself to express your personal thoughts, feelings, and beliefs freely. Even if the words don't make sense, or seem ugly or distasteful to you, write them down. Don't censor your thoughts, ideas, or feelings. If you try to censor your thoughts, feelings, beliefs, or ideas, you'll inhibit your own self-understanding. Over time, what you write will make sense to you.

You don't have to write neatly or write in complete sentences. You don't even have to worry about correct grammar. Remember, the underlying purpose of journal writing is for you to ask yourself very direct and purposeful questions, and for you to give yourself permission to be vulnerable, and to allow yourself the freedom to respond to your questions as honestly as you can. The content of your journal writing is what matters, not the presentation of the material, not what it looks like on the page. We, the authors, both hope that journal writing will be as powerful and beneficial for you as it has been, and continues to be, for each of us.

Chapter 15

Tool #3: Communication with Others

What We Mean by Communication with Others

Communication with others involves people caring for people on a one-to-one basis, a reciprocal process whereby both parties mutually benefit from the relationship. It is about having someone to listen to you and try to understand you. It is also listening to someone else and trying to understand her/him. When you communicate with others, you learn about yourself. You allow yourself to be vulnerable in the presence of another person. By allowing yourself that vulnerability, you can share what's going on inside you. Part of communication with others involves taking the risk of sharing your most personal thoughts and feelings with another person. When you communicate with others, it can lead to greater emotional closeness or emotional intimacy.

Charise:

I tend to be cautious and selective in my communication with others. It can take a long time for me to develop a close relationship. I have to feel ready to jump in and reveal myself to someone new. Once I do jump in, I can grow tremendously in the course of communicating with this other person. Such a relationship becomes pivotal in my life, helping me to see things from a broader perspective than I could ever see by myself. But until I take the initiative to communicate with someone, I spend a lot of time alone or with limited contact with anyone outside of my family. I look inward and confer with myself, writing in a journal or thinking things through on my own. I have a good ability to communicate with myself, a skill I developed in high school when my parents were divorcing and no one talked about it.

It's easy for me to forget to communicate with others. I know I can get by on my own, if I have to. I can keep my feelings to myself; I can hide inside my own skin. Based on my experience, though, this is a very lonely condition. When I'm able to recognize how isolated I feel, and when I know that I want to feel more connected to other people, I begin looking for someone else to talk to.

171

Communication with others sounds very simple: just talk to another person. In fact, we do it most every day. During the course of a day most of us encounter other people. The people in our lives range from those we know at a surface level to those we feel very close to.

People we know at a surface level are acquaintances. We often encounter acquaintances during the course of our day, but these relationships are usually light and superficial. We say hello and make small talk with them as we complete the tasks of our lives. Our acquaintances include people we see at the grocery store, the doctor's office, in our neighborhood, at work, and at our children's school.

We feel closest to those people in our immediate emotional circle. We seek them out when we have important news to share, when something upsets us, or when we just want to enjoy their company. We don't have to see or talk to them every day to feel close to them. This inner circle may include our spouse, children, other family members, friends, a neighbor, or a colleague at work.

When life is going along fairly smoothly, we generally find it's quite easy to talk to both our acquaintances and the people we feel close to. We feel self-confident and good about ourselves. We easily engage in conversation with others. We openly talk about ourselves and the events in our lives. Our conversations are light and reflect what's going on around us. Relationships are easily maintained during this time.

Who were some of the acquaintances in your life that you communicated regularly with before you moved overseas?

_____
_____
_____
_____

Who were some of the people you felt close to in your life that you communicated regularly with before you moved overseas?

_____
_____
_____
_____

How the Overseas Move Affects Your Communication with Others

Charise:

When I left my home country, I was already feeling the loss of my peer support group. As a graduate student of social work, support and sharing was built into the structure of my program. Internships were done in pairs. Small supervision groups were held weekly. Informal discussions happened all the time; on the phone, in the car sharing a ride, outside the classrooms, or in the office at our placement site. Now I was a student overseas without any of these channels to communicate with my peers. I felt disadvantaged by the very fact that I was moving away from people who were integral to my learning process.

The dance and performing community I had belonged to was another niche which I doubted I could find overseas. It seemed that this move required me to make a sacrifice for my husband's sake, for his benefit, and to my loss. The experience of being a graduate student, or being a dancer, was not likely to be common overseas. If I was to be a counselor for fellow expatriates, then who would likely be my friend? With whom could I be vulnerable if the whole population was potentially my clientele?

If I wanted to succeed in my graduate program, I believed I needed to adjust well to life overseas. I needed to be available, as a counselor, to focus on other people's difficulties. I wondered how I could do this and also communicate with others about my personal feelings and concerns. This conflict was present in my mind when I embarked on my life overseas.

Moving overseas affects your communication with other people. When you move overseas, your relationships with others are in transition. You leave behind your acquaintances. You no longer see or make small talk with all those people you encountered as you went through your daily routine.

When you move overseas you also leave behind many of the people that you feel close to, for example, extended family, friends, neighbors, and work colleagues. You can no longer talk to them in the same way as before you moved. Although you want to maintain the closeness of these relationships with these people, the relationships often change significantly because of the geographic distance.

While you may feel close to your spouse and your children when you move overseas with them, your relationships with them are also in transition. They are experiencing the process of adjusting to new surroundings and the foreign culture just as you are. Each of you may feel differently about the move and you may have difficulty talking about the effect of the move with each other. As a result, you may feel detached from one another.

When you move, you're hit simultaneously with losses, changes, and additions to your life. Your losses may include friendships, roles, support systems, a house, a job, and living in a familiar culture and country. Changes in your life may include geographic location, relationships, job, and roles. Additions to your life may include a new job, residence, people, roles, relationships, and culture and country.

The combination of these factors can leave you feeling vulnerable and overwhelmed by your situation. This in turn affects your communication with others. Expatriate women in this overwhelmed and vulnerable state are actually in the most need of communicating with others, but are often hesitant to do so. Why?

Reasons Expatriate Women Hesitate to Communicate with Others after Moving Abroad

You don't want others' first impression of you to be negative.
You fear others won't understand you.
You don't want to reflect badly on your husband or his career.
You don't want to appear needy or unhappy.
You fear rejection.
You don't know whom you can trust with your thoughts and feelings.
Nobody likes a whiner.

The above reasons expatriate women hesitate to communicate with others are very real and valid concerns. However, we have found it vital to reach out to others even in a vulnerable and overwhelmed state.

Why Communication with Others is an Important Tool for the Expatriate Woman

Communication with others is an important tool for the expatriate woman because it can help reduce the stress associated with an overseas move. Moving is very stressful for the whole family, especially for women who primarily move in support of their husband's careers. When you move, once you reach your new destination, you're busy right away getting the boxes unpacked, perhaps enrolling the children in school and getting them adjusted to their new surroundings, and talking to your husband about his new job.

Your husband may not be available to support you emotionally when you first move. He's busy re-establishing himself in his job and may choose to spend more time at work to accomplish that goal, or he may be required to do so by his new boss. He may also feel guilty for moving you and the rest of the family abroad. He may respond defensively when you attempt to share with him your concerns, thoughts, and feelings about the move (ones he interprets as negative). He may cut you off when you attempt to tell him what you're feeling. He may not even ask how you're doing because he may not want to know the answer or fears your response. Unfortunately, this is when you probably need him the most.

It's important to give voice to your feelings, thoughts, and concerns, and for them to be validated by another person. If you find that your spouse is unable to hear you during this time or is unavailable, it's important to reach out to someone else who *can* listen to you. It's important for you to feel supported. During this time, talking with others can lessen the stress you feel as a result of the move. Talking about your feelings, problems, or situation can actually decrease the intensity of it.

Communication with others is also an important tool for the expatriate woman because it can help reduce the feelings of loneliness and isolation. When we talk about using communication with others as a tool, we are talking about taking a risk to talk to others about what you're going through, what you feel about the move, and what you expected vs. the reality. When you share with others how you feel about your situation or yourself, you'll feel less isolated and less lonely. The people you seek out can include your spouse or partner, friends, family, a minister, or counselor.

Communication with others is also an important tool because it can facilitate a support network. Women are experts at supporting others. Just look at the energy you spend (or have spent) getting yourself and your family settled into your new environment.

Communication with others provides the foundation to building a support network for *you.* Yes, a support network for you. It's important for you to have others you can talk to and provide you with support. By talking with others about what you're going through, you're increasing the number of people available to support you.

Communication with others can lead to additional friendships as well. Interacting with others, especially in a foreign land, presents you with a unique opportunity to get to know other women from all over the world. When you take the risk of sharing your true feelings, thoughts, and ideas with another person, you may develop a friendship that will last a long time. You may also gain a perspective on an issue that you may never have previously thought about or considered.

Communication with others is a vital tool for the expatriate woman because it can make the move overseas a more positive experience. When you think back to places that you've lived or jobs that you've had in the past, the people you knew there and were involved with probably determined whether it was a positive or negative experience for you.

The same holds true when you move overseas. People caring for people on a one-to-one basis makes the most difference. Having someone who listens and can understand is much more helpful than someone who just tells you what to do or offers advice.

❦Exercise: Reflections ❧

When you encounter new situations, or are in stressful situations, your ability to communicate is affected. Moving overseas is a stressful and new situation. In other words, when you moved overseas you were hit with several obstacles at once, all of which affect communication. The following questions will help you recognize how your communication with others was affected when you moved overseas. Answering them will help you decide whether you will find *Tool #3: Communication with Others* of value to you.

How did the overseas move affect your communication with the acquaintances you left behind?

_____

_____

_____

_____

How did the move affect your communication with those you identified as being close to you?

_____

_____

_____

_____

How did the overseas move affect your ability to communicate with your spouse and children?

_____

_____

_____

_____

Was there a difference in how you responded to your acquaintances, or the people you felt close to, or your spouse and children? Please explain your answer.

_____

_____

_____

_____

Think back to when you first arrived overseas. When others in your new environment asked, "How are you?" do you recall how you responded to them? Do you recall if you were honest with them? Did you share with others your feelings? Did you ever respond with "Fine" or "Okay," even when you weren't? Please explain your answer.

_____

_____

_____

_____

By completing the Reflections exercise, you discover how your move overseas has affected your communication with the people you left behind as well as those people you met after arriving overseas. Your contact and communication with acquaintances was probably immediately eliminated when you moved abroad. Although you felt close to certain people before moving overseas, they were no longer available to you in the same way because of distance. When they asked how you were doing, you may have also found yourself responding with "fine" or "okay" so you wouldn't worry or burden them.

You may have noticed that communication with your spouse or children was affected, and that an emotional distance developed between you because each of you was in the process of settling into the new country. You may have been reluctant to share with others how you really felt, especially if you initially wanted the move or change. You may have feared that if you did take the risk of sharing your negative feelings with others, they might have invalidated your feelings by telling you what a grand adventure you were on. Or, they might have reminded you that you wanted the very experience you were now struggling with.

When you moved overseas, most or all the people you met were new to you. As a result, you may have responded in a variety of ways when they asked, "How are you?" You may have responded to the question by claiming you were "fine" or "okay" when you weren't. You may have felt vulnerable or silly for feeling the way you did, so you may have avoided talking about your thoughts and feelings by diverting the conversation to another topic altogether. Or, you may have talked to anyone who would listen because you were overwhelmed by your move and needed to express your thoughts, feelings, or opinions about the situation.

Decision Point

Charise:

By the end of my first year overseas, I had made no effort to establish a meaningful relationship with open lines of communication. I had drifted far from the expatriate community, keeping my relationships with fellow expatriates on a superficial, acquaintance-only level. The less I communicated with others, the more I retreated into the active imaginings of my own mind, fantasizing about my tennis coach. I lived in a secret world, shared by no one else, where I believed I was in love with someone new.

I wasn't particularly interested in making my fantasy a reality. I just wanted to experience the feeling of love, connection, and passion that existed in the fantasy. Without this infusion of love and desire, I would have been forced to feel the lack of true intimacy in my life. I would have had to face my own needs. Perhaps I didn't want to know myself, or see myself, or acknowledge anything about myself that might not fit into my image of who I thought I should be. I had some superhuman idea of what a counselor was. I thought that a counselor should concern herself with other people's needs, not her own. I can attribute this belief partly to my own ignorance as a newly trained social worker.

Once I made the decision (as described in Chapter 7) to break my secrecy and communicate openly with my husband and counselor, I saw how empty my life was. My fantasy world was draining the vitality from my marriage. I had not developed any friendships. I had no female companionship. I hadn't experienced the kind of fun that comes from getting to know someone and doing things together. When I understood this lack in my life, I felt a great void. I longed for the type of connection with others that would allow me to be real, to let myself be seen and heard.

When you move overseas your communication with others is greatly affected. This is a normal process. Sometimes the change is temporary. However, if you currently feel a void in this area, or have discovered the lack of communication as a result of the overseas move, you may want to pick up and use *Tool #3: Communication with Others.*

To help you determine if you should pick up and use *Tool #3: Communication with Others,* answer the following questions.

Whom do you currently trust to talk to about personal issues and areas you're struggling with?

_____

_____

_____

_____

_____

Is that person or are those people emotionally available to you?

_____
_____
_____
_____
_____

Do you feel close to at least one person that you can talk to when you feel the need?

_____
_____
_____
_____
_____

After answering the above questions, do you want or need to pick up Tool #3 and use it? Please explain your answer.

_____
_____
_____
_____
_____

If you discovered, by answering these questions, that you do indeed have someone in your life who is available to talk to when you need to, you may skip the next section and go on to the next tool. However, if you think that your communication with others is lacking, continue with the next section to discover how you could use Tool #3 to enhance your communication.

How to Use Tool #3: Communication with Others

Charise:

On a whim, I took a four-day holiday with my daughter, Alexandra, to a beach resort while my husband traveled on business. Schools were closed, and I didn't want to stay in Bangkok for the duration of the holiday. The resort we went to offered activities for children, which would allow me some time to myself. Once Alexandra was set up for the morning, I went to the beach with a book in hand. Soon after, another woman whom I recognized from the international school community parked herself next to me. She also had a book with her.

Because we recognized each other, we began chatting. She was curious about the book I was reading, a philosophical work. She told me she was reading about myths and their symbolism. We became curious about each other through our choice of reading material for this retreat to the beach.

She was an American woman who had also come to the resort without her husband. She had brought her three children, one still in diapers, and her Thai nanny. Her eldest son was in the same kindergarten class as Alexandra, and she had volunteered at the same organization where I worked. Our curiosity about each other led to telling our stories to each other. As I shared with her how long I had known my husband, when we had met, and where we had lived, I felt a connection to my own past that I hadn't felt since I left the States. I described my history, my roots. I listened to her history, her roots. Over the four days, we met as much as possible, both with and without our children. We developed a kinship. We made plans to meet in Bangkok after the holiday. This was the beginning of a friendship that enriched my life in many ways.

We called ourselves "growing buddies." We spent hours talking together in her home or mine. We developed an interest in writing poems, primarily about being female. Unlike myself, she was outgoing and social and always had people stopping by her house. I met many others through her, and became more interested in including other people in my life.

On another whim, one day I went to a bookstore just to browse. I had an inexplicable hunch that there would be some purpose to this outing. While I was there, I saw a woman I had met once before. We recognized each other and noticed that we were both in the early months of pregnancy. She suggested we skip the browsing, and go have tea instead. As it turned out, she lived in my area, with a daughter slightly younger than my own. We were each expecting a second child within weeks of one another. Her husband was from Finland and she was from Malaysia. She had a circle of friends from all over the world, most of whom I came to meet through her. She introduced me to the amenities of the British women's circle, notably the mother's group of the British club. She excelled at finding fun things to do. We shared the experiences of pregnancy and birth of a second child together.

Clearly, these two key relationships with other women changed my life. By allowing myself to be spontaneous, to follow a whim or an intuition, I opened the door to opportunity. Once I became close to one person, I soon came in contact with a whole world of other people. To activate the tool of communicating with other people, I had to step out of my routine, do something different, go somewhere new or compelling.

I also had to trust the moment when another person entered the scene. When this happened on the two occasions I mentioned, there was an instantaneous mutual curiosity and a desire to know each other. Fueled by this desire we talked and listened. We shared ourselves and developed an emotional closeness. I now marvel at my ability, in the first year of living overseas, to live without this closeness to others. By not picking up the tool to communicate with others, I locked myself in emotionally and limited my own growth. But once I picked up the tool, I made friendships that continue to enrich my life.

Guideline for Using Tool #3: Communication with Others

Below are 4 steps to use as a guideline if you've identified that communication with others has been lacking in your life.

Step 1: Review the following list of traits. These attributes describe the ideal person for you to communicate with in an emotionally close relationship. The person should:
- be trustworthy;
- feel safe to be with, someone who will listen to you, give advice when you ask for it, and support you;
- respect your opinions, feelings, beliefs, and thoughts even if she/he disagrees with them;
- be likable;
- be a good listener;
- be emotionally available to you;
- care about you;
- keep your confidence.

Step 2: After reviewing the above list of traits, answer the questions below. These questions will help you evaluate your current communication with others and to identify people you may want to seek out to communicate with.

Who are the people in your life that you choose to communicate with?

_____
_____
_____
_____

Do these people have some of the traits listed in Step #1? If so, which traits?

_____
_____
_____
_____

Do you know of a person or persons who seem to possess some or most of the traits listed in Step #1 that you would consider getting to know better? If yes, who is this person or who are these people?

_____
_____
_____
_____

If you couldn't identify anyone you'd consider getting to know better, you may want to think about how you could increase your chances of meeting such a person. This could include places you could go or activities you could get involved with. Write your thoughts about this in the following space and then proceed to Step #3.

How can I increase my chances of meeting someone I'd consider getting to know better?

_____
_____
_____
_____
_____
_____
_____
_____
_____
_____
_____

Step 3: The third step in using Tool #3 is to either seek out the people you've identified in Step #2 to communicate with, or seek out the activities that will bring you in contact with people you can communicate with.

Step 4: The fourth step requires you to take a risk and allow yourself to be vulnerable so another person can get to know you. As the saying goes, "The only way to have friends is to be a friend yourself." You must risk sharing your thoughts, beliefs, ideas, opinions, and feelings with another. This is perhaps the most difficult step because you may already feel vulnerable due to all the changes you've weathered in your move. But, if you want to find these close relationships, a degree of risk is necessary.

We don't recommend that you tell someone your life story in your first encounter. Instead, be willing to let someone get to know you. Be willing to get to know them, slowly. Over time, you'll develop trust in each other and the relationship.

Chapter 16

Tool #4: Re-establishing a Support Network

What We Mean by a Support Network

In Chapter 11 we discussed *Resource #4: Your Ability to Access Support* and explained the two types of support: individual and group supports. Underlying both types of supports are people. In essence, a support is someone or something that helps you. Support can come to you through formal channels (parenting class through a local hospital) or an informal arrangement (friends or neighborhood playgroup). A support makes you feel good about yourself and your situation. A support can be something that you rely on frequently or something that you seek out when you can't handle things on your own. Some supports cost money, such as if you pay someone to clean your house so you have more time to spend with your children. Some supports are reciprocal or mutually supportive, such as a friendship. Generally, each person gives and receives support at various times in the relationship.

When we talk about a support network, we mean all the supports you've built into your life, the connected web of supports that allows you to live in a fuller, more satisfying way. With your support network in place, you can complete the tasks of daily life more easily.

The particular support network you build and connect to is composed of your relationships with individuals and/or groups in a variety of arenas. Together, they provide you with emotional and/or physical assistance, guidance, relief, and companionship when you need it. Your support network can include family members, friends, colleagues, organizations, an informal group of people with similar interests, a religious group, or counselor.

Having supports and establishing a support network is interwoven with another tool that we've already mentioned, *Tool #3: Communication with Others*. Communication with others leads to developing supports and a support network. Keep this in mind as you go through this section and refer back to Tool #3 as needed.

Charise:

When I think about my life before I moved overseas, I remember it in many different ways. I recall first and foremost my drive to succeed, to make it through graduate school, even with a two-year-old at home. I held a tenacious grip on my dance career at the same time, fitting in rehearsals and performances along with studies and parenting. Since my husband traveled a great deal for his work and I could never count on his availability to parent, my life became very complicated and challenging.

While it may seem that I was trying to attempt the impossible, other people participated in holding together the structure of my life. Without them, this structure would have collapsed. When you have a toddler, you need more than one other person to fill in when you can't be there. For example, my child developed chicken pox and wasn't allowed to return to day care for two weeks, which happened to coincide with my mid-terms. My husband began searching for an interim child-care solution and recruited a babysitter from the local college.

Whenever my husband was out of town, and I couldn't find a sitter for rehearsal nights, either my sister or my neighbor came to my aid. Of course, I had to ask for their help. All of these people, my sister, my neighbors, my husband, my day care provider, my sitters, provided a safety net to ensure care for my daughter while I fulfilled other obligations.

At that time in my life, I was 31, and had started redefining my career path. I wasn't interested in having any more children, and I was not confident about my marriage. Something was starting to bubble up inside me, some sort of need to follow my own inner voice. I wanted to make things happen, even though I knew that our stay in Atlanta was most likely temporary. I needed to stake out my own life. I wanted to put down roots. I had an unrealistic thought that I might not join my husband for his next move. Maybe I could stop him. Maybe he'd do what I wanted instead. Maybe I could walk away.

Unfortunately, I didn't discuss these thoughts and feelings with anyone. I didn't divulge them to my counselor, who was there to support me emotionally. As I proceeded with my day-to-day life, this emotional component went underground, for the time being. The friendships I developed with other students and dancers were "buddy" type of relationships. We didn't reveal too much about ourselves. We just enjoyed the experience of being together, hanging out, getting silly, or chatting. These relationships provided me with a feeling of belonging and being liked. Together, they were like a circle of warmth around me, a comfort zone.

Take a few moments and think back to your life before moving overseas. What individuals, groups, and/or organizations together made up your support network?

_____

_____

_____

_____

_____

How the Overseas Move Affects Your Support Network

Charise:

In Atlanta, I had several key people involved in the care of my daughter. They enriched her life and mine, and it was a sad day when we had to leave them. I had no idea who would help care for Alexandra in a foreign country, but I knew it would be an altogether different experience. Once I arrived in Bangkok, I had two weeks to figure out a plan before starting my social work internship. The pressure was on and I didn't even know anyone. I couldn't enroll Alexandra in a preschool until I knew where we were going to live. I had been told that it could take up to six weeks to find housing. I'd need to locate a Thai maid whom I could trust with my child, and quickly. All I could do was be optimistic and be on the lookout. My survival skills were put to the test immediately.

As a graduate student in Bangkok, I was an anomaly in the expatriate community. In the States, after initial introductions, the next question is usually, "So what do you do?" In this community, no one asked what an expatriate wife "did." It seemed to be a given that these women were simply living, doing nothing of any importance. I remember that one woman remarked on how I looked cheerful, and that this was a characteristic of being new to Bangkok. She assured me that after a while, this cheerfulness would wear off.

Wow! I thought. Something to look forward to!

Where was my comfort zone? Did I want to hang out with these people? My initial impression of expatriate wives was not favorable. In fact, I started to view them as a group of losers. They seemed, for the most part, to be bitter. They were excluded from the world of adventure that belonged to men. Many of them had chosen this time in their lives, while they had domestic help, to have children. Their pregnancies and postpartums separated them even more from the man's world. I decided this was not going to be me. I was not going to recede into the background. I was going to push myself to the frontlines, as an independent woman with a professional job. No second-class status for me. In my effort to escape the negativity of the expatriate wife experience, I nurtured my more masculine side. I focused on my need to feel successful through achievement. I neglected to scout out emotional supports. I began to deny my emotional needs. I became a loner.

Generally, when you move overseas, your support network *as you knew it,* no longer exists and you notice the loss almost immediately. The people, groups, and/or organizations that supported you are no longer available to you in the same way they were before you left. For example, you may have had a neighbor and best friend who was a vital component of your support network. Now you can no longer go next door to borrow a cup of sugar when you need it, share a laugh, or talk things out when you feel overwhelmed. This has an affect on you. Leaving a place involves a sense of loss, both emotional and physical.

When you leave, you can no longer participate in relationships, groups, or organizations in the same manner in which you did when you were physically present. You experience a sense of loss due to the changes in your relationships and the loss of your support network as you knew it. (There is also an emotional effect on others when you leave, but since we are focusing on how the overseas move affects you, we won't discuss that in this section.) To begin to get an idea about how the overseas move has affected your support network, answer the question on the next page.

How did your move overseas affect the support network you had before moving overseas?

_____

_____

_____

_____

_____

What We Mean by Re-establishing a Support Network

When you leave your homeland to live overseas, you leave important relationships behind as well as the roles that helped define you, and your culture which provided you with a context and structure to your life. In addition to these losses, you also leave the support network that you had in place for yourself. Once you arrive overseas, however, your need for support still exists. In fact, at least initially, you're probably even in more need of support because of the sudden changes in your life that have occurred as a result of the move.

When we talk about re-establishing your support network, we are talking about putting back into place supports for yourself that will allow you to complete the tasks of your daily life more easily while living overseas. And, when you connect the various supports into a network, you'll be able to live your life in a fuller and more satisfying way. By re-establishing your support network, in essence, you're re-establishing where you belong within the overseas environment.

Why Re-establishing a Support Network is an Important Tool for the Expatriate Woman

Charise:

When I cut off my association with other expatriate wives, I believed I was steering clear of the negative part of the expatriate wife experience. I pictured myself as different from these other women, less susceptible to a negative experience. This is a little bit like imagining you're not a woman when you are. No matter what I did to cast myself in a different light, I was still an expatriate wife, and I had not come to terms with my own feelings about it. Because I had disassociated myself from the community of expatriate wives, I was floundering. I didn't know where I belonged. My life felt confining. I became aware that I wanted something, something that seemed out of reach. I wanted to feel good about myself, yet couldn't seem to accomplish this on my own.

My ability to sustain my own happiness was limited. Then I asked myself why was I trying to sustain my own happiness by myself, anyway? Where were the other players in my life? Hadn't I felt better about myself when I had the camaraderie of fellow students in Atlanta? Had I forgotten about the importance of camaraderie altogether? Had I forgotten the importance of sharing my mothering experience with other mothers? Could I deny my need for connection with other people, the type of connection that allows me to see who I am inside whatever my role is? In fact, I couldn't deny my need for connection. I channeled that need into a romantic fantasy

185

that would never materialize. At least that was a start. There was a part of me that couldn't let me stay so isolated. This part of me was hunting for a way to connect in a roundabout, backwards way.

Re-establishing a support network is an important tool for the expatriate woman because when you arrive overseas you arrive virtually alone. Although your husband or partner is with you, he may not be available to support you emotionally, at least initially, because he finds himself in a similar situation. In addition, if you have children, it's crucial that you do not view them as a primary support. If this has occurred or occurs in your family, we encourage you to address the situation immediately and to seek professional help if necessary. Although children can be a support to parents, you must allow your children to be children. You need to find supports independent of your husband or partner or children.

Re-establishing a support network enables you to better complete the tasks of your daily life. In addition, this network helps to feed you emotionally. With your own physical and emotional needs met and supported, you can provide better support for your husband or partner, children, and others.

Re-establishing a support network is an important tool for the expatriate woman because once you build this new network into your life, your experience overseas will be more satisfying. You'll feel better about yourself and the situation. You may even find that you like living overseas or you may actually surprise yourself and like it much more than you thought you would.

Re-establishing a support network is an important tool for the expatriate woman because it helps reduce stress and feelings of isolation and loneliness as well as leads to additional friendships, and makes the move overseas more positive. We talked about these same factors in *Tool #3: Communication with Others*. Since these same benefits also apply to re-establishing a support network, refer back to the section in Tool #3 if needed.

✥Exercise: Reflections ✥

The purpose of this exercise is to help you gain a better understanding about how the overseas move affected your support network. Your answers will help you decide if you might find Tool #4 useful to you as an expatriate woman.

Did you have supports or a support network in place for yourself before moving overseas?

_____

_____

_____

_____

_____

Were you satisfied with the supports or support network that you had in place for yourself before moving overseas? Please explain your answer.

_____
_____
_____
_____
_____

Previously in this section on Tool #4 you answered a question about how the overseas move affected your support network. How did you feel as you responded to the question? (For example, did you feel or experience a sense of loss as you identified those things that had made up your support network? Were you surprised at how much your support network was affected?) Please explain your answer.

_____
_____
_____
_____
_____

What was the most significant change in your support network after you moved overseas and what was the effect on you?

_____
_____
_____
_____
_____

Which individuals support you now?

_____
_____
_____
_____
_____

Are these individuals available to you to offer you support when you need it?

_____
_____
_____
_____

What groups or organizations support you now?

_____

_____

_____

_____

_____

Are these groups or organizations available to you to offer support when you have a need?

_____

_____

_____

_____

_____

After answering the above questions, do you have any ideas about what you want to do with this information? Please briefly explain your answer.

_____

_____

_____

_____

_____

As you completed the Reflections exercise, you discovered what supports you had, how satisfied you were with the supports you had in place before the overseas move, how your supports were affected when you moved overseas, and what supports you currently have in place for yourself.

Most likely you discovered that the supports you had in place for yourself before you moved overseas are now no longer available to you in the same way. Although the relationships you had and the organizations to which you belonged can continue their support when you move abroad, the degree in which they can help changes because of distance. For example, if you and your best friend used to get together for hours and talk over coffee or tea, this support is no longer available in the same way. Your girlfriend can continue to be supportive after your move, but on a less frequent basis. The support you can give to each other is limited to your letters, phone conversations, e-mails, and perhaps infrequent visits.

You may have discovered through this exercise, or in Chapter 11 on *Resource #4: Ability to Access Support*, that your support system was lacking even before your overseas move. If so, you might have been unaware of this when you moved. You may have just blamed the move itself for your unhappiness. And, when you moved overseas, the lack of support you had in your life intensified.

What you may discover now, is that the root cause of your unhappiness may be a combination of the move and the lack of support you feel in your life. If so, this may indicate your need to spend some additional time thinking about what you need in the way of a support network.

Regardless of your responses, you probably discovered a significant change in your support network after the move. Your next step is to make a decision about where you go from here.

Decision Point

Charise:

My crisis point occurred when my romantic fantasy could no longer sustain me emotionally. I wanted real contact. To achieve that, I thought I needed to pursue my fantasy. I was afraid I'd have to end my marriage. I saw myself separating from my husband, completely altering my life, and staying in Thailand indefinitely. After all, I had a job and my own independent visa. When I discussed these thoughts with my husband, I found that my emotions had not caught up with the imaginings of my mind. I became physically sick in my effort to pull away emotionally from my husband. I felt an ache in the pit of my stomach and I vomited. I cried that all I really wanted was to "go home," but didn't know where home was anymore.

My husband offered himself as a comfort and a refuge but I didn't like how much I needed him. I hated feeling so vulnerable, but didn't have the strength to fight this feeling. I was deep into my own crisis. This degree of vulnerability finally brought me to a decision. I decided to go to a counselor. I felt overwhelmed and needed perspective.

When my counselor told me I didn't have to make a choice between one man and another, I felt enormous relief. I had another option. We could look at my emotional needs, the very thing I had come to deny! We discovered that I tended to deny myself nurturing in the form of relationships. It was as if I put myself in a barren landscape, a desert, with just enough to survive. Somehow, that had become my safe place. Where I really wanted to be was in a lush garden, with bountiful life all around me. To shift landscapes required me to reassess myself in my world. I was pretty starved in the area of supportive relationships. I was beginning to get on track, however, through my own crisis. I had a supportive counseling relationship. My husband and I had become emotionally close, which reawakened our love for each other. I could see that I was missing out on friendship and companionship, and I could open myself to the possibility of putting these back into my life. I was finding opportunity within my dilemma.

Like Charise, you, too, will need to make a decision about which direction you want to go. By completing the Reflections exercise, more than likely you've discovered that your support network was greatly affected when you moved overseas. This was not done purposefully or maliciously, this is just a reality of most overseas moves. However, it's up to you to decide whether or not you want to pick up and use *Tool #4: Re-establishing a Support Network*. To help you, consider the questions on the next page.

What would the potential positive benefits be for you to re-establish a support network?

_____

_____

_____

_____

_____

Would there be any potential negative consequences for you by re-establishing a support network?

_____

_____

_____

_____

_____

When you think about re-establishing a support network, does this feel like a positive or negative experience for you? Please explain your answer.

_____

_____

_____

_____

_____

After answering the above questions, do the potential benefits of re-establishing a support network outweigh the potential negative consequences? Please explain your answer.

_____

_____

_____

_____

_____

What would need to happen for you to think about re-establishing a support network?

_____

_____

_____

_____

_____

After answering the above questions, do you want or need to use Tool #4? Please explain your answer.

_____
_____
_____
_____
_____

If you decide to use *Tool #4: Re-establishing a Support Network*, continue to the following section. If you decide not to use Tool #4, you may skip this section and go on to *Tool #5: Acceptance.*

How to Use Tool #4: Re-establishing a Support Network

Developing Supports

Although re-establishing your support network may seem daunting, we see it as a vital ingredient to your success overseas. In order to re-establish a support network you must develop supports. Since there is a relationship involved, the nature of the support depends on you just as much as it does on the other person, group, or organization. Your part in developing supports is threefold: first, recognize your own need for support; second, recognize where support can come from; and third, allow yourself to accept support.

Recognizing Your Need for Support

In our opinion, we believe that no matter who you are, no matter your strengths or previous experiences, you need support when you face the challenge of an overseas move, and it is a very real challenge. At the deepest level of your self, you know this already. Remember that no one else is doing a better or worse job at meeting this challenge than you. Everyone is equally challenged and in need of support.

Without supports and taking steps to fill that need, your stint overseas will be much lonelier than necessary. In addition, ignoring this need can lead to more serious difficulties, such as problems in your marriage or with your children.

How do you know when you need support?

_____
_____
_____
_____
_____

Recognizing Sources of Support

Where do you turn for support? Since moving overseas, you're probably meeting a lot of people. In fact, you've probably met an entire community or set of communities at once. Inevitably, you'll develop relationships for purposes other than support for yourself. For example, you may develop relationships with people associated with your husband's job, or the parents of your children's playmates and schoolmates. But the supportive relationship, whether an individual or group support, is in a category by itself. As we mentioned earlier, there are individual and group supports.

For interaction with another person to become an individual support, someone needs to take a risk. The risk involves saying something more personal, something that goes beyond the pleasantries of conversation. With practice you'll develop the ability to screen people, to choose someone based on their self-awareness, a fact you can determine in the course of conversation. Pay attention to how you feel in their presence. Consider whether she shows a willingness to look within herself. The extent to which a person demonstrates such self-awareness, can give you some idea of her awareness of you.

A group support consists of people who share similar interests or goals with you. For example, group supports can be found through your affiliations with a church, temple, or place of worship, organizations you belong to, play groups, sports, or hobbies. There are also expatriate websites and chat groups that can serve as a source of support for you while you live overseas. For example, our site, *www.aportableidentity.com*, is designed specifically for expatriate women who are the trailing or accompanying spouse during an international relocation. In addition to providing information about our book and us, the site has other valuable resources and links, news articles, and a chat group. Our chat group provides a place where you can participate in a community of support with other women to discuss how to take charge of the changes in identity that occur at each stage of the move overseas.

Above all, when you're in the process of developing individual and group supports, it requires you to reach out. More than likely, this means you're reaching out to other people by communicating with them. As you recall, *Communication with Others* is *Tool #3* and is interwoven with *Tool #4: Re-establishing a Support Network*, because communication with others is the foundation to building your support network. When you reach out to others, you're using Tool #3 which leads to Tool #4.

Is it easy or difficult for you to seek out support?

_____
_____
_____
_____
_____

Re-establishing your support network also draws heavily from *Personal Resource #4: Ability to Access Support* in Chapter 11. Knowing your ability to access support will be very helpful to you in using *Tool #4: Re-establishing a Support Network*. For example, if you know that it's difficult for you to ask for or seek out support when you need it, you may want to establish some type of safety net, something within your network that reaches out to you if you're not in contact with the group. For example, in advance, you could ask several members of your support network to call you if they don't see or hear from you in a while. Or, if you know that it's difficult for you to ask for or seek out support when you need it, then you know that you'll need to really push yourself to get the help or support you need.

Accepting Support

Accepting support is the grand finale in developing supports! All of your effort in identifying potential supports and taking risks pays off when you need help. Some women have difficulty allowing others to help them. We hope that you'll find ways to allow others to support you. If you find this difficult, then look at this as an opportunity for you to grow in your ability to accept the help and support of others.

Often when you accept support, you'll find yourself returning support as well. A supportive relationship tends to be mutually beneficial for the people or group involved. You could call it a "growing" relationship, one in which each person supports the other's growth. Obviously the people involved need to be willing to grow in order to experience this type of relationship, but it can be very rewarding for all parties involved.

Is it easy or difficult for you to receive support?

_____

_____

_____

_____

_____

Guide to Developing Supports and a Support Network

We have designed the following eight-step exercise to help you identify the various supports that you'll link together to make up your support network.

Step 1: Brainstorm

Write down anything and everything that comes to mind about what you need to feel supported. Be as specific as possible.

_____

_____

_____

_____

_____

_____

Step 2: Prioritize

Prioritize the supports that you've identified in Step 1 that you need in your life from most to least important.

Most Important: _____
_____
_____
_____
_____

Least Important: _____
_____
_____
_____
_____

Step 3: Supports Currently in Place

List the supports you currently have in place.

_____
_____
_____
_____
_____

Are these supports actually supportive to you, i.e., are you satisfied with the supports you have in place?

_____
_____
_____
_____
_____

If not, what can you do to increase your satisfaction?

_____
_____
_____
_____
_____

Do you need to modify any of these supports in any way? If yes, which ones and how can you do this?

_____
_____
_____
_____
_____
_____

Step 4: Supports Currently Missing

List the supports currently missing from your life.

_____
_____
_____
_____
_____
_____
_____

What are your options to put these supports back into place for yourself?

_____
_____
_____
_____
_____
_____
_____

Step 5: Steps to Take to Re-establish Supports

List at least two steps you can take to re-establish each support that you've identified as missing in your support network.

Support Missing:_____
*Step 1)*_____
*Step 2)*_____

Support Missing:_____
*Step 1)*_____
*Step 2)*_____

Support Missing:_____

*Step 1)*_____

*Step 2)*_____

Support Missing:_____

*Step 1)*_____

*Step 2)*_____

Support Missing:_____

*Step 1)*_____

*Step 2)*_____

Step 6: Risk-Taking

Write down what risks you'll need to take to re-establish supports.

_____
_____
_____
_____
_____
_____

If you find it difficult to take risks, how can you help yourself be able to do this?

_____
_____
_____
_____
_____
_____

Step 7: Draw a Picture of Yourself

Draw a picture of yourself surrounded by the supports you'll re-establish for yourself. This picture will reflect you surrounded by all your newly created elements of your new support network.

My Picture

Step 8: Surrounded by Supports

After drawing your picture, write a few words about what this will be like for you once you have re-established your support network.

_____
_____
_____
_____
_____
_____

Chapter 17

Tool #5: Acceptance

Acceptance is a difficult word to define, and each of us probably has a slightly different interpretation of the word. Think back over your life and try to recall a time when you either told yourself or someone else told you that you needed to accept some situation, person, condition, or event. What did such acceptance mean to you? Was it an easy process, or was it painful? Did it happen quickly, or did it take a period of time? Was the process a graceful one, or was it bumpy? Does acceptance mean that you have to agree to something that deep down you really want to resist? Does it mean that you have to like what is happening? Does it mean that you have to approve of something you don't want to? Does it mean that once you accept something, that it becomes your fate? Is it positive, or negative, or somewhere in between?

It's important for you to understand how you view acceptance. Some people associate acceptance with giving in or weakness. Others equate it with peace of mind and tranquility. And for others, it can vary, depending on the situation.

Debra:

Acceptance has meant different things to me at various stages in my life. When I was younger, acceptance had a negative connotation to me. I thought that if I accepted something that I didn't want or like, it meant I was giving in and was weak. Somewhere along the line, I learned that my lack of acceptance of a person, event, or situation only hurt me. I was the one who was stuck. More recently, I've come to understand that acceptance actually helps me. Once I accept what I initially find unacceptable, I can then more easily deal with whatever situation I've been struggling with.

What does acceptance mean to you?

_____

_____

_____

_____

_____

What We Mean by Acceptance

Because we view acceptance as a tool for the expatriate woman, we think it's important for us as the authors to give you our definition and perception of acceptance in relation to the overseas move. We define acceptance *in relation to the overseas move* as an internal state of being that allows you to come to terms with what your life was like before the move while also acknowledging the reality of your present situation. Acceptance includes the ability to acknowledge and accept your thoughts and feelings associated with your life before the move, after the move, as well as the life you now have as a result of the move.

Acceptance includes allowing yourself to feel and experience a range of feelings such as frustration, sadness, anger, and loneliness about what you left behind and what you're struggling to let go of. It also includes feelings such as uncertainty, anticipation, excitement, joy, and hope for the future. Within this state of acceptance you're also able to acknowledge that your present cannot be the past. When you achieve this state of acceptance, you're able to focus on your present and your future.

We also believe that letting go is intertwined with acceptance. The *Ability to Let Go (Personal Resource #1)* leads to acceptance. In Chapter 8 we talked about your ability to let go and how letting go is a process that occurs over time. In the same way, acceptance is also a process that occurs gradually over time. Acceptance does not happen overnight, nor does it happen smoothly. Inevitably, you'll have gains and setbacks.

How the Overseas Move Affects Your Acceptance

Debra:

After we moved overseas, I initially refused to accept many things, ranging from trivial details that seem silly now, to more significant information that could have had a profound effect on my life. For example, when Brad told me I couldn't get my own mail at the embassy because I wasn't the employee, I argued with him about it several times. When I initially learned I couldn't work in Thailand because of my visa status, I refused to believe it. I cited numerous examples of information I had been given before the move that turned out to be incorrect when I arrived in Thailand, as if this would matter and provide the justification to allow me to work. Although part of me knew that I was not being very rational, I couldn't stop myself. In hindsight, I can say that I felt that my life seemed to have changed overnight, leaving me with little sense of control. Instead of accepting the changes, I initially resisted them with all my might.

Moving overseas will probably highlight for you how you've accepted other situations and changes in the past. For example, if you easily accepted change in the past, you may easily accept the changes that are occurring to you now. If change has been difficult for you throughout your life, it's probable that the changes occurring to you now as a result of your move will be difficult for you to accept.

Acceptance also closely links to your ability to let go. You may want to refer back to the personal resource section to review your answers. For example, if you discovered that you tend to remain attached and that you have difficulty letting go, then this probably intensified when you moved overseas. In this case, acceptance may be more difficult for you.

As we have said throughout this book, when you move overseas you encounter a barrage of changes to your life simultaneously. Moving overseas affects and changes how you view yourself, how others view you, your roles, and your relationships. During this process, you may feel that you've lost control of your life. As a result, you may try to reassert control. This need to regain control can make it difficult for you to accept your situation, because acceptance requires you to relinquish control.

The change in culture is an added component unique to the experience of moving overseas. In fact, many of the things you may be struggling to accept may have to do with dramatic differences in culture. For example, you may be having difficulty accepting that because you're a woman, people treat you like a second-class citizen in your new country. Consider the role the new culture plays in this. Does the difference in the way you're being treated have more to do with the change in culture than it has to do with you? Knowing this may not make things any easier to accept, but it may give you added insight into your situation.

How has your move overseas affected your acceptance?

_____
_____
_____
_____
_____

Why Acceptance is an Important Tool for the Expatriate Woman

Debra:

When I think back over events in my life that I have resisted, painfully, I must admit, I see that I often initially made the situation worse because I refused to accept the situation, person, or event as it was. I found myself bargaining with myself, my spouse, another, or God that I could accept the situation, but only if certain conditions were met. This left me feeling like a bucking bronco trying to get the rider and saddle off my back. No matter how hard I tried, they remained and I felt more weighed down than ever. But, once I accepted the saddle and the rider, and the weight of the situation, I found myself more easily able to maneuver gracefully within my boundaries. I also felt at peace and at ease within myself. Time and time again, I found that the harder I resisted, the more difficult my situation became.

The same held true when I moved to Thailand. I initially found my situation turning out very differently than I had anticipated. In my mind and in my actions, I refused to accept things the way they were, and as time went on, I became more and more miserable. However, once I learned to accept things the way they were presented to me, life became easier and more manageable. I felt freer and rediscovered peace within myself.

Acceptance is an important tool for an expatriate woman because ultimately, it allows you to gain a sense of power and control over your new situation. Ironically, acceptance frees you from the very situation you're struggling with. Once you accept the situation as it is, you'll be free to make choices about what you want to do. This makes you powerful.

Acceptance allows you to move on. This gives you the freedom to enjoy today. Acceptance gives you inner peace, thus freeing you to focus your energy in a more positive way. This lowers your stress level and allows you to experience the joy of living. Acceptance in general, as well as accepting situations like your overseas move, takes courage, but in exchange you'll find the strength to better deal with your situation.

◄Exercise: Reflections ◄

To help you determine whether *Tool #5: Acceptance* might be of further use to you as an expatriate woman, answer the questions below.

What people, situations, things, or events do you currently resist accepting?

_____
_____
_____
_____
_____

Do any of the above have to do with your overseas move? If so, which ones?

_____
_____
_____
_____
_____

How has your lack of acceptance affected you?

_____
_____
_____
_____
_____

How has your lack of acceptance prevented you from enjoying life in the present?

_____
_____
_____
_____
_____

Do you feel that the more you resist, the greater your chances are to change your situation?

_____
_____
_____
_____
_____

Do you feel stuck between the past and the present? If yes, how so?

_____
_____
_____
_____
_____

After answering the above questions, what do you want to do with this information? Please briefly explain your answer.

_____
_____
_____
_____
_____

Decision Point:

Debra:

When we moved overseas, the most difficult thing I had to accept was the possibility that I might not be able to work while in Thailand. As I said in Tool #1, working had been the foundation of my sense of stability and security. However, the feelings I had and the emotions I expressed after finding out that I might not be able to work were linked to my lack of acceptance of what I had been told. For several months I resisted with all my might and I was miserable. I ranted and raved and had a scowl on my face (at least in private) most of the time. My heart felt heavy and I felt weighed down. I had difficulty experiencing pleasure in things that I had been looking forward to, like living in and experiencing a foreign culture. My relationship with my husband became strained. Nothing seemed to be going right. My emotions felt toxic and I felt out of control. I didn't like the way my life was going. I got to the point where I was sick of feeling angry and not having any fun. I realized I was stuck between the life I had left behind and the current reality of my situation in Thailand. I needed to decide whether I was going to stay stuck between the past and the present and continue in my misery, or do something different.

I decided to do something different.

This was the beginning of acceptance for me. After I realized that the amount of my resistance would not change the fact that I might not be able to work in Thailand, I stopped resisting. I was amazed at how much more energy I had from this alone. My resistance had only been hurting me. Although I felt out of control, I also realized I was trying desperately to control things that were beyond my control. When I relinquished control, I actually felt more in control of myself because I felt free to make choices. This felt liberating. When I stopped blaming myself, my husband, others, and life itself for the things that were different from what I had been told before the move, things improved, but only because I decided to accept the situation just as it was.

Acceptance can be an important tool for the expatriate woman to use because it can free you from being stuck between the past and the present. However, it's up to you to decide whether you want to pick up the tool and use it. To help you decide whether or not you want to use Tool #5, consider the following questions:

What do you think will happen if you accept what you don't want to accept?

_____

_____

_____

_____

_____

How would it benefit you to accept what you don't want to accept?

_____

_____

_____

_____

_____

Do you see any negative consequences in accepting what you don't want to accept?

_____

_____

_____

_____

_____

When you think about acceptance, does this sound like a positive or negative experience? Please explain your answer.

_____

_____

_____

_____

_____

After answering the above questions, do the potential benefits of acceptance outweigh the potential negative consequences? Please explain your answer.

_____

_____

_____

_____

_____

What would need to happen for you to think about accepting those thing(s) you don't want to accept?

_____

_____

_____

_____

_____

Do you want to pick up *Tool #5: Acceptance*, and use it? Please explain your answer.

_____

_____

_____

_____

_____

If you decide to use *Tool #5: Acceptance*, continue to the following section. If you decide not to use Tool #5, skip this section and go on to Tool #6.

How to Use Tool #5: Acceptance

Using Acceptance as a tool is first about deciding to unconditionally accept your situation as it is. You don't have to like it. If you attempt to put conditions on it, for example, telling yourself or others you could accept the situation only if…(you fill in the blank), you'll only remain stuck.

As you read this, you may be wondering how you can accept the very situation, person, or thing that causes you so much grief. In fact, you might think we're crazy for even suggesting such a thing, or that we're just adding to your problem. That's not our intent at all. In fact, our intention is to help free you from your problem.

For example, in many situations you actually make your situation worse or more complicated when you refuse to accept it as it is. Take a minute to think back on a situation that you didn't initially want to accept. Did your resistance to the situation actually change anything? Probably not. In fact, your reluctance to accept the situation at that moment probably only increased your frustration and made matters worse.

Until you accept the very situation causing you grief and frustration, your life will feel out of control. The more you resist, the greater your grief. Once you accept the situation, you'll immediately gain power and control over the situation. When you refuse to accept a situation, your energy focuses on resistance, not resolution. However, when you finally come to acceptance, you free your energy to channel it in more positive and productive ways.

Exercise: Acceptance

Below is a five-step exercise, an example of how you may use *Tool #5: Acceptance*. The exercise outlines how you can begin to free yourself from your problem, help you channel your time and energy more productively, and refocus your thoughts more positively as you begin your journey down the path of acceptance.

Step 1: Make a Decision

I'll accept the following unconditionally regarding the overseas move:

_____

_____

_____

_____

_____

Step 2: Benefits of Acceptance

What benefits will I receive for accepting those things which I have stated in Step 1?

_____
_____
_____
_____
_____

Step 3: Practice Moving On

By accepting those things which I have stated in Step 1, I can refocus my time and energy on:

_____
_____
_____
_____
_____

My thoughts will focus on:

_____
_____
_____
_____
_____

Step 4: Observe Myself

I understand that acceptance is a process that occurs over time. As I go through the process of acceptance, I'll observe myself and periodically record my gains and setbacks.

My gains:

_____
_____
_____
_____
_____

My setbacks:

_____

_____

_____

_____

_____

Step 5: Allow Myself Time

Acceptance takes time, and I must be patient with myself and with my situation. In the process of acceptance, I'll recite the following when I feel I need a gentle reminder:

Acceptance is a process that occurs over time. No matter how much I may want to "rush" the process, it's not possible. I need to be gentle with myself and give myself permission to have setbacks and gains. I may experience a wide range of feelings. All of my feelings are important and valid. Acknowledging and honoring all of my feelings will give me a greater understanding of the depth to which I have been struggling with acceptance. Acceptance is a messy process, with good days, bad days, and in-between days. All of this is necessary and normal in the process of acceptance.

Chapter 18

Tool #6: Seeking Out Internal Activities

What We Mean by Internal Activities

Internal activities are specific types of activities that you engage in by yourself for the primary benefit of your soul. Generally, internal activities make you feel good inside. When you engage in an internal activity, you'll experience an internal response. For example, you may feel happy, peaceful, powerful, relieved, content, relaxed, or energized in the process of participating in an internal activity for your soul's benefit. Sometimes internal activities can be utilized to facilitate your personal growth, which can be a painful process. During these times, you may experience feelings such as hopelessness, sadness, despair, frustration, or depression when you are working through a difficult issue.

Internal activities are activities that you pursue on your own. For the most part, your participation does not depend on others or the outside world. Internal activities are separate from other people, although you may participate with others such as in a yoga class. While internal activities often also have a recreational component to them, their primary purpose is to help you reconnect to or stay connected to yourself.

Types of Internal Activities

In this section we'll provide a brief overview of some activities that we consider internal activities. One popular internal activity is journal writing, a private avenue of self-expression. It can be done anywhere at anytime. It only requires paper and a pen or pencil, and you don't have to follow any rules. You can use it to record everything from the funny things that happen in your life to extremely painful events. In your journal, you can freely record your thoughts and feelings about anything on your mind. Journal writing is an excellent internal activity because you can explore the depths of your soul. It provides a place where you can ask yourself questions then record and explore the answers in a written format to better understand yourself. Over time, your journal will serve as a record of your soul's journey.

We discuss journal writing in more detail in *Tool #2: Communication with the Self*. In our opinion, journal writing is one of the best ways to communicate with yourself. If you're interested in learning how to use journaling in your own life, we encourage you to refer to Chapter 14, Tool #2 for a more detailed discussion.

Listening to music is another example of an internal activity. Although some form of pre-recorded music and a listening device is required, the actual process of listening to the music can provide a very private avenue for you to discover how the music affects you and explore the meaning it has in your life.

Another enjoyable internal activity is reading. You must have heard the expression, "You are what you read." Many believe the type of books you read are a window into your soul because they reflect your personality, interests, and hobbies. For example, if you read books about safaris in Africa, perhaps you long for adventure, or have a love of animals, or are fascinated with that continent. If you read romance novels, perhaps you seek more romance in your life, or because you're a romantic yourself.

Meditation and yoga are other examples of internal activities which you can practice individually as well as with others. One of the main purposes of practicing meditation is learning to center yourself. It teaches you how to gain peace and calm even when you may be feeling uptight and stressed out. Meditation helps teach you how to separate yourself from the outside world while still remaining aware of it, thus allowing you to get in better touch with yourself. Meditation helps those who practice it, better listen to the voice of their soul, free from distraction.

There are various forms of yoga, but the underlying thread in most forms is the connection of the body, mind, and spirit. Yoga helps your physical body become healthier by stretching and strengthening muscles and increasing flexibility. These same benefits also apply to your mind and the way you think about life. As your body gains strength, so does your mind. The spiritual element of yoga, establishing a connection between the body, mind, and spirit comes into play by using the postures and breathing as vehicles to link all three together.

Prayer is also an internal activity. You can pray anywhere, at anytime, to the deity who corresponds to your belief system: God, Buddha, Allah, or a Higher Power. Your religious orientation will influence how you pray. People pray for many reasons in many ways. They pray for some type of peace for themselves, others, or for the world. They often pray for answers to questions, to help others, or for forgiveness.

Self-expression is another type of internal activity that you can accomplish in a variety of ways. You can express yourself through dance, drawing, painting, writing poetry or music, playing an instrument, or singing. For example, when you dance, you express your thoughts and feelings through your body and the way you move. When you draw or paint, you express yourself through the images or pictures you create. When you write poetry or music, you express your inner feelings through your words or lyrics. When you play an instrument, you use the instrument as the medium. And when you sing, the words you choose, your vocal range and tone of your voice convey your thoughts and emotions.

By seeking out an internal activity, you're also using *Tool #2: Communication with the Self.* Internal activities are vehicles which you can use to help you communicate with yourself by exploring the depths of your soul. Tool #6 and Tool #2 are inextricably linked. In most cases, when you use one of the tools, you use the other as well.

Charise:

I think of internal activities as a means to look inward, into my psyche. My psyche, the place where I truly exist, lies beneath several layers of social conditioning, personality traits, and coping mechanisms. It's the raw me. I want to know and see the raw me, but it's invisible. I have to call upon some vehicle to access it, to make it more visible to me. I have to seek out an internal activity so I make a deliberate choice to access my psyche. The alternative is to turn a blind eye to my inner world, and forge ahead with my life.

Before I moved overseas, I made the alternate choice. I can't think of a single internal activity that I consciously participated in, other than the occasional writing of a poem. My involvement in dance was not for the purpose of accessing my psyche, though at times it happened. Putting dance on the stage made it a show, something I acted out rather than something I experienced for its own sake.

I could argue that I was too busy to seek out an internal activity: my schedule was crowded with classes, homework, rehearsals, home, and family duties. But the primary ingredient in picking up a tool is choice. Before I moved overseas, I chose not to pick up the tool. At that time in my life, I was simply in survival mode. I had recently uprooted from my home in Baltimore. I was concerned with my survival in the job market, as well as my ability to cope with being a parent and a wife in my new situation. I had no sense of stability or security in my life. Perhaps I needed to establish that sense of stability and security first. Seeking out an internal activity might have helped me experience some stability, but I didn't take that route. Looking back, I regret the neglect to my psyche. That neglect caught up with me later, as I'll describe in the next section.

What forms of internal activities did you participate in before moving overseas?

_____
_____
_____
_____
_____

How the Overseas Move Affects Your Internal Activities

Charise:

When we knew for certain that we were bound for Thailand, one of my social work supervisors suggested I purchase a journal to take along. She had lived briefly overseas herself, and found that keeping a journal was a good way to record her experiences. I pictured her at that time, sitting in a window, looking out over the bustle of people, with her journal in hand. I imagined her recording what she observed, her impressions. I developed a similar picture of myself, as the observer.

The journal I selected for my trip was pretty but tiny. Each page could only hold a few lines. Once I arrived in Thailand, I began to jot down my thoughts. I found it easy to fill a page and be done with it. It was as if I were completing a homework assignment. I was doing it because someone said it was a good idea. I hadn't developed the ability to talk with myself through journaling. I still maintained some distance from the voice of my psyche. I felt safer with this distance, and I needed the safety of distance, especially in the course of moving overseas. Therefore, my early attempts at journaling were superficial. I had the means to access my psyche, but lacked the intention. I had not yet made the commitment to track my internal process in relation to the move. Without that commitment, I had no way to get closer to my psyche.

If you pursued internal activities before you moved, out of all of the tools, this tool probably has the potential to arrive with you at your overseas destination in the best shape, because for the most part, it has no dependence on the outside world. However, this doesn't mean that it will come with you unaffected.

Because the overseas move throws you off balance, at least temporarily, you may find yourself not seeking out the internal activities you engaged in before the move. You have so many other things to deal with, including getting you and your family settled in. As a result, you may totally ignore your need to seek solitude or solitary activities. You may think you don't have enough time or can't take the time for yourself. Or your musical instrument may still be in transit, or your dance studio may be oceans away, or your yoga mat may still be packed in a box somewhere.

If you prayed, meditated, or practiced dance, or yoga in a particular place, you might assume after the move that because this physical place is no longer available to you, you may no longer engage in that activity. Or you may not even feel like practicing because that would mean finding another place. You may not be ready to start again because you may still feel the loss of leaving the original place. If you prayed before the move, you may not even want to now out of fear of what you might say in your prayers. You may even be angry at the Higher Power you believe in. Similarly, if you wrote in a journal or wrote poetry, you may hesitate to write about your thoughts and feelings because you're not sure what would come out once you started, or whether what you're thinking or feeling is valid.

If you danced before, the type of dance you did may not be available in your new country or you may not have access to a dance studio. Initially, you may not have the energy to dance. Or you may be too tired to even think about it.

Internal activities, for the most part, are affected to the degree you allow them to be when you move overseas. When you move you probably have more control over this tool, than any other. Most internal activities such as prayer, meditation, yoga, dance, or singing only require *you* to do them. Some internal activities may require props, such as drawing paper and art supplies, a journal, books, dancing shoes, musical instruments, sheets of music, or pre-recorded music and some form of listening device. But, it's up to you to make the time to do them.

How were the internal activities you participated in before moving overseas affected by the move?

_____

_____

_____

_____

_____

Why Seeking Out Internal Activities is an Important Tool for the Expatriate Woman

Charise:

I learned from my own experience, and from counseling others, that you can only ignore your psyche for so long. It calls your attention in various ways, as a need or a longing or a symptom or a disease. For me, my distancing from my own psyche left me feeling lonely. The overseas move served to magnify my feelings of loneliness. Cut off from the buffering of my culture, my neighborhood and my school pals, I grew acutely aware of a void in my life, though I didn't know what it was. I felt a longing to fill that void, and so focused my attention in that direction.

I focused on how to fill up my loneliness, rather than attending to my loneliness itself. I developed a fantasy world, with a Thai man at the center. My longing to fill the void of my loneliness developed into a longing to be with him, either in person or in my mind. While part of me became enchanted with him, another part of me was terrified at the power of my attraction to him. I practically quivered under my skin in his presence, as I stayed just on the edge of pouncing on him.

With great restraint, I began to watch myself. A part of me would not allow me to touch him, would never allow me to touch him. I imagined how I could get lost in my own passion, that it would consume me, that I would never stop wanting him. He would be like a drug. Even now, as I write this, I can feel myself slipping away toward his memory, like falling into a spell. I become dispossessed. If I fail to embrace my own psyche, this is what happens to me. I begin looking for my own soul in someone else's body.

I find it easy to explain this phenomenon in retrospect, but at the time I had no idea what I was doing. I felt such a combination of powerlessness, longing, fear, need, and desire. I also felt responsible to account for these feelings to my husband and, through him, to myself. My inner world, rather quiet and hidden before the move overseas, was now on display. It was as if someone had just turned up the volume of the sounds that had always been there, but had not previously been heard.

I recognized a new intensity in my life, an intensity that wanted expression, and my romantic fantasy grew into a frustrating and unfulfilling obsession. A voice from inside me kept calling me. "Hello, is anyone home?" I didn't know how to answer the call. I was too steeped in my own quagmire of emotions and disillusion about relationships. That's when I decided to seek counseling. I needed to take this step first, to pick up the tool of communication with others, in order to find my way back to myself.

My counselor acted like a mirror for me, showing me who I was. I began to find other ways to look inward, as well. I began journaling, documenting what I learned in counseling. My journaling expanded to include my dreams, and other thoughts and feelings about my life. I also began what I called a talking journal, where I spoke spontaneously into a tape recorder. I found speaking out loud a very different experience from writing. It was like unraveling bits of a story, and then listening to it play back in my own voice. These were ways I developed to communicate with myself, the next tool I needed to pick up. I sought out internal activities specifically to help me engage this other tool. Communicating with myself and sorting through the process of understanding myself better was a lot of work. I was making up for past neglect. With the guidance of my counselor, and the love and support of my husband, it became less frightening to see my true self.

One of the main reasons *Tool #6: Seeking Out Internal Activities* is an important tool for the expatriate woman is that it's highly accessible and depends only on you (with the exception of minimal props required for some of the activities). This is especially important to the woman who moves around the world frequently. When everything is changing or being left behind, this is one tool that you may not have to re-create everywhere you go. You can take it with you when you move and wherever you go.

You also need some activity just for you, something that doesn't depend on or involve anyone else. View your internal activities as a gift to yourself, or a celebration of yourself, your thoughts, feelings, and talents. They enrich and replenish your soul or your psyche. The particular activity you choose reflects that part of your soul that needs attention, expression, and release.

Internal activities also help to keep you grounded or connected to yourself. Moving overseas takes you out of your familiar environment and catapults you into a whole new culture. As you see the differences around you, new sights, sounds, smells and behavior, you may find these differences very unsettling. You may begin to question why and how you do things, or why you behave or think the way you do.

Questioning yourself isn't a bad thing. In fact, you can learn much about yourself by asking such questions. But it's also important for you to have an activity that keeps you grounded as you question yourself or change the way you think or behave. And, seeking out internal activities is an excellent way to stay grounded and connected to yourself during this time of change and reflection.

Another advantage of pursuing internal activities is that you can spend as much or as little time as you have available. For example, when you first move overseas, you may find yourself overloaded with the demands of getting you and your family settled. During this time, you may only be able to spend a few minutes each day or each week making time for yourself. Later on, when the dust has settled somewhat and you have more time, you may be able to devote more time each day or each week on an internal activity.

Internal activities can also reduce the stress associated with moving overseas, be a refreshing break from the external chaos, and they help you by allowing you to seek solitude when you need it.

❧Exercise: Reflections❧

The purpose of this exercise is to help you gain a better understanding of how the overseas move affected your internal activities. Your responses will help you decide whether Tool #6 may be valuable to you as an expatriate woman.

Did you seek out internal activities for yourself before moving overseas?

_____
_____
_____
_____
_____

Were you satisfied with the internal activities you had in place for yourself before moving overseas, i.e., the types of activities, the frequency in which you were able to participate in them, and the benefit you experienced from them, etc.?

_____
_____
_____
_____
_____

What was the most significant change in your internal activities after you moved overseas and what was the effect on you?

_____
_____
_____
_____
_____

After answering the above questions, do you have any ideas about what you want to do with this information? Please briefly explain your answer.

_____
_____
_____
_____
_____

As you completed the Reflections exercise, you discovered how the overseas move affected your internal activities. As we said earlier, the internal activities you had in place for yourself before the move have the potential to arrive with you overseas the least affected, the least disturbed and in the best shape, compared to the other tools, because they depend primarily on you. Is this what you found for yourself? If so, congratulations for taking the time to replenish yourself and your soul in the midst of moving!

If not, be gentle with yourself. What you may have found instead is that you didn't pursue the internal activities you normally would have because of all of the other demands on you and your time. Sometimes when in the midst of trying to satisfy multiple demands, wants, and needs associated with such a move, we sideline our own wants and needs. Perhaps you're just too tired to take the time for yourself. Or perhaps through completing the Reflections exercise, you may have discovered that you did seek out internal activities for yourself after moving, but found that you're not satisfied with the frequency or amount of time you've been able to take for yourself.

Or, you may have discovered through the Reflections exercise that before you moved overseas you didn't really seek out any form of internal activity, or that the one(s) you did pursue weren't that satisfying. In any case, view this as an opportunity to grow in this area.

Decision Point

Charise:

Eventually, the relationship I developed with myself became more central to my life. After awhile, the journaling I did for the sake of my counseling process came to serve a different purpose. My journal became a conversational tool, a place to write my story as I lived it. To this day, I still write that story, in bits and pieces, filling up numerous blank journal books. It is an internal activity for its own sake, for the benefit of my soul.

In Thailand, I experienced a shift in focus. After my marital crisis, after the struggle to understand what was happening to me, I became aware of my soul. I can only say that it was like remembering an internal flame that somehow stayed lit, flickering in the cold numbness I had surrounded it with. I made a decision to honor that flame, to feed it, to let it blaze into a torch. To do this, I had to consciously let my fantasy go.

On my knees, in front of the Buddha altar in our Thai home, I released my attachment to the man I had wanted so strongly, and visualized my inner flame growing. I was certainly empowering myself. The decision to honor my soul led to a great need to seek out internal activities. In addition to journaling, I began writing poetry effortlessly. I also discovered Motherpeace tarot cards,[9] and began to play with these, relating the images on the cards to the different facets of my psyche. I reexamined my religious and spiritual inclinations, and started going to church again.

I chose to read books that were handbooks for the soul: Care of the Soul: A Guide for Cultivating Depth and Sacredness in Everyday Life, *by Thomas Moore and* Women Who Run with the Wolves: Myths and Stories of the Wild Woman Archetype, *by Clarissa Pinkola Estés, Ph.D. I also joined a meditation group. The church, meditation group, the books, and tarot cards all came my way only when I was looking for them. It was clearly my desire and my effort to look for ways to feed my soul that allowed me to find these things. I would like to emphasize that it was the action of seeking out internal activities that made them manifest in my life.*

Most likely, any internal activities you participated in before moving overseas were affected in some way when you moved overseas, and in large part depended on your personality and situation. It's now up to you to decide whether you want to pick up the tool and use it. To help you decide whether or not you want to use *Tool #6: Seeking Out Internal Activities*, consider the following questions.

Does your soul have or need an avenue for self-expression?

_____
_____
_____
_____
_____

Do you have something that you do for yourself that makes you feel good on the inside, is independent from other people and the environment, and helps you to connect with yourself or stay connected to yourself?

_____
_____
_____
_____
_____

What would the potential positive benefits be for you to seek out internal activities?

_____
_____
_____
_____
_____

Would there be any potential negative consequences for you seeking out internal activities?

_____
_____
_____
_____
_____

When you think about seeking out internal activities, does this sound like a positive or negative experience for you? Please explain your answer.

_____

_____

_____

_____

_____

After answering the above questions, do you want or need to pick up Tool #6 and use it? Please explain your answer.

_____

_____

_____

_____

_____

If you discovered that by answering the previous questions, your responses indicate that you already seek out internal activities for yourself and that you're satisfied with what you do, you may choose to skip the following section and go on to the next tool. However, if you think that you need to seek out internal activities, continue to the next section to learn how you can start using Tool #6.

How to Use Tool #6: Seeking Out Internal Activities

If you haven't been satisfied with your previous level or quality of internal activities, the amount of time you've been able to devote to them, or if you don't know what type of internal activity would reach your soul, view this as an opportunity for you to grow in this area. The following activity will help you identify internal activities that could benefit you.

Step 1: Take an Inventory

The first step in pursuing internal activities is to reflect on your life and identify activities you engaged in by yourself that primarily benefited your soul. For example, when you were a young girl, did you write in a diary or spend hours in your room reading or listening to music? Did you enjoy dancing in your room or writing poetry to express yourself? In the following space, take an inventory of those internal activities that you engaged in over the years that have made you feel good on the inside and benefited your soul.

_____

_____

_____

_____

_____

Write whatever else comes to your mind about those internal activities you listed in the previous question.

_____

_____

_____

_____

_____

Of those activities you identified, which ones were the most satisfying to you and why?

_____

_____

_____

_____

_____

Step 2: Identify Current Internal Activities

What internal activities do you currently seek out for yourself?

_____

_____

_____

_____

_____

Are you satisfied with the current internal activities you seek out, i.e., the type of activities, the frequency in which you're able to participate in them, or the benefit you experience from them, etc.?

_____

_____

_____

_____

_____

Is there any overlap between the internal activities you've done throughout the course of your life and the ones you currently engage in?

_____
_____
_____
_____
_____

Step 3: Identify Internal Activities You've Thought About Trying

In the following space, write down internal activities that you've thought about trying or would like to try for yourself. You may want to review the section on "Types of Internal Activities" found near the beginning of the text on Tool #6.

_____
_____
_____
_____
_____

Step 4: Develop a Plan

Review what you've written about internal activities from your past and present, and those that you have thought about trying. From these internal activities, make a decision about which one(s) you would like to seek out now based on your current situation and write them in the following space.

_____
_____
_____
_____
_____

Begin to develop a plan about how you'll go about seeking out the internal activity(ies) you listed above by answering the following questions.

Do you feel comfortable by yourself or engaging in activities on your own?

_____
_____
_____
_____
_____

If doing activities on your own is not something that comes easily to you, this is an opportunity for you to grow. Think of some ways to reward yourself for taking the risk to grow in this area and write them in the following space.

_____

_____

_____

_____

_____

How will you go about seeking out the internal activity(ies) you've chosen to pursue?

_____

_____

_____

_____

_____

How will you make time for solitude to spend on your internal activity(ies), i.e., how will you carve out the time for yourself with your existing commitments?

_____

_____

_____

_____

_____

Is there anything you can change, rearrange, or eliminate from your schedule that will give you the time and space you need to spend on your internal activity(ies)?

_____

_____

_____

_____

_____

Can you activate any of your supports to help give you the time and space you need to seek out internal activities?

_____

_____

_____

_____

_____

How many days per week will you seek out the internal activity(ies) you've identified? Which days?

_____

_____

_____

_____

_____

Approximately how long will you spend each time on the internal activity(ies) you've identified?

_____

_____

_____

_____

_____

Step 5: Benefits to Myself

Write a statement about the benefits you believe you'll experience as a result of giving yourself the time and space needed to use *Tool #6: Seeking Out Internal Activities.*

_____

_____

_____

_____

_____

Chapter 19

Tool #7: Seeking Out External Activities

What We Mean by External Activities

External activities are activities that are directed outside yourself. They provide avenues for you to actively seek out fun and enjoyment in your life. For the most part, you enjoy external activities with others, although you can engage in some individually. External activities often depend on other people and your environment and they often include a recreational component.

Internal activities and external activities have similarities. Like internal activities, external activities make you feel good on the inside and benefit your soul. You also experience an internal response. For example, participating in an external activity may make you feel excited, energized, challenged, relaxed, happy, or competent. Or, you may gain a sense of connection with others as a result.

You may also use external activities to facilitate personal growth. For example, you may need to seek out another person or a group of people to participate in some external activities. If this doesn't come naturally to you, then you must take a personal risk in seeking them out. Although this may make you nervous or a bit anxious, you grow when you do so. The key difference between external and internal activities is this: the primary purpose of internal activities is to benefit you and your soul, while the primary purpose of external activities is for you to have fun while you interact and connect with others. In essence, external activities do more than benefit you, they also benefit those you interact with.

Types of External Activities

You have many types of external activities available to you, and they vary according to the country or region you live in. In this section, we'll provide a brief overview of some activities that we would include as examples of external activities.

Team sports provide a popular form of external activity. Softball, baseball, football, soccer, cricket, ice hockey, volleyball, basketball, rugby, fencing, rowing, and polo are good examples. Team sports bring people together in a competitive atmosphere of play. They foster teamwork and focus toward a common goal. Although individual skill and effort have importance, collaboration and cooperation between team members are equally important.

Aside from the fun of friendly competition, team sports offer the opportunity to meet and socialize with others while getting physical exercise. People seek out team sports for various reasons. Some people play team sports for fun, companionship, and exercise. Others love the opportunity to compete, improve an existing skill, or to learn a new one.

Recreational activities such as: golf, swimming, bowling, dancing, hiking, walking, running, aerobics, working out at a gym, playing pool, and playing games or cards are also examples of external activities. Although you can participate in these activities individually, we have included them in this section because people often enjoy them with or around other people. For example, people often join a gym so they can interact with others while they work out. It also makes working out more fun. People often look for recreational activities to interact with others and have fun at the same time. Friends getting together to play games or cards, take a hike or dance are good examples.

Socializing is another type of external activity. People are social creatures who love getting together to talk and enjoy each other's company. An informal or impromptu example of socializing is when a friend telephones to ask you to come over for a cup of coffee or tea and a chat. On a formal level, you socialize when you receive an invitation to a dinner party and your host asks you to respond by a certain date. Whether formal or informal, socializing provides people with a way to get together with people they care about, to meet others they might like to get to know better, or to just interact with others.

Traveling is another external activity. Most people travel in the company of others. Even if you travel alone, it's almost impossible to avoid interacting with people along the way. Traveling gives you the opportunity to get away from your regular routine while visiting and exploring new and different places. Traveling can relax, refresh, educate, and excite. However, it can also be frustrating: lost luggage and/or cultural barriers. Traveling is a good external activity because when you leave the structure of your daily life, like work, you can connect better with those traveling with you. You can spend more time with someone away from the distractions and stresses of your daily life, while enjoying the destination you've traveled to together.

Community clubs and organizations such as groups affiliated with your church or temple, your profession, your children's school, or an interest you may have, are other forms of external activities. Participating in such groups allows you to interact with others while working toward a common goal. Members of these groups often share a sense of camaraderie and have fun together. They also offer leadership opportunities, a sense of accomplishment when goals of the group are met, and, the chance for new friendships.

Charise:

Before moving overseas, I had enjoyed two activities that encouraged frequent contact with other people: dance and socializing. Socializing with other students eased the pressure of graduate school. With my peers, I could talk freely about my fears, as well as my hopes about entering the field of social work. I felt that we were going through the experience together. We were a team trying to score a goal and cheering each other on. I looked forward to spending time with my classmates, and this alone often motivated me to go to class. Beyond my intention to finish the program, and keep up my grades, I wanted the company of my peers.

What I enjoyed most about dance was rehearsing as a group. During rehearsals, we could make mistakes and laugh, or chat while someone else was doing their part. It was fun to work out the movements as a group, and try them out with music. Moving in synchrony feels wonderful to me. Joined to others in rhythm, I transcend my body as a single unit. I become part of the hum of the universe. It can be ecstatic; it can be spiritual; it can be sensual. It is energizing. Since age three, when I began dance classes, I have found no other endeavor that compares.

What forms of external activities did you participate in before moving overseas?

_____
_____
_____
_____
_____

How the Overseas Move Affects Your External Activities

Charise:

The activities I participated in before I moved overseas were closely linked to the people who were involved and to the places where they happened. When I left those people and those places, I lost the activities as well. Being a graduate student overseas was no longer a social experience. I had no peers to chat with. I no longer went to the places where we met to study, to eat, or to talk, and the places we frequented were gone as well. The built-in socialization network no longer existed.

As for dance, I felt that I was leaving the art for good. I didn't know how long we'd be living overseas (three years minimum), and did not expect to find anything in Bangkok comparable to what I had done in the U.S. I knew that my dance skills would suffer from lack of practice and I'd probably lose my competence as a modern dancer. I felt that I had no choice but to resign from the world of dance and give up. I felt that my link to dance and my social life came through the people and places that supported these activities while I lived in the U.S. When I moved overseas, this link was broken.

Since external activities are usually dependent on others and/or the environment, they will be affected in some way when you move overseas. Leaving behind the people you interacted with, your peers, your team, your groups, is often difficult. You may feel sad and experience a sense of loss when you do so. You may feel like the fun in your life is gone, that you're leaving part of yourself behind.

Then, once you arrive overseas, you undertake the enormous task of getting yourself and your family settled. You may need to locate housing, schools for your children, markets and stores, doctors, and/or a church or temple. Completing these tasks takes a lot of time, especially in a foreign culture. With so many things to do, you may feel guilty for taking time out for fun.

Some external activities may not be available in the country you move to. However, some countries may provide more opportunities to participate in such activities. It's more likely that you'll find similar external activities available to you in countries that have a culture similar to your own or where you find a large expatriate community from your country.

For example, if you played a team sport such as softball before you moved, and the country you move to has a large expatriate community, chances are good that the community will already have an organized league. If, on the other hand, you enjoyed bowling and you move to a remote Third World country, don't count on getting your bowling ball out of the bag too soon.

If you enjoyed socializing, you'll most likely find this available to you overseas. In fact, in some communities, people actually have more opportunities to socialize or are required to do so with their job. On the downside, since the people you socialized with before the move will no longer be available to you, you may experience this as a sense of loss. However, you can view this as an opportunity to meet new people and develop new friendships. While this requires you to take a risk in reaching out to these new people, this is another opportunity to grow.

If you enjoyed traveling before moving overseas, your new situation may actually increase your opportunity for travel. Many people find that when they move overseas they not only have a new country to explore, but they can also explore surrounding countries more easily and affordably than if they were still living in their homeland. In addition, a common benefit for people who move overseas is increased time off, and, therefore, you may have more time available for travel.

If you participated in community clubs and organizations before moving, you'll necessarily leave behind the other members of the group(s). This loss may make you feel sad, especially if the country you move to doesn't offer a similar group. However, some organizations may have international chapters and you may be able to transfer your membership to the chapter in your new country, or even start a new chapter.

How were the external activities you participated in before moving overseas affected when you moved?

_____

_____

_____

_____

_____

Why Seeking Out External Activities is an Important Tool for the Expatriate Woman

Charise:

After living overseas for several months, I began to feel the lack of physical exercise. Other than occasional outings to the pool, I sat around a lot. During the week, I devoted most of my time to sitting and talking with clients. When I wasn't with a client, I sat at my desk or in meetings. I sat in the car wading through traffic. I was also more sedentary at home since I didn't need to sweep, or mop, or carry hampers of laundry up and down the stairs. Someone else handled all the physical tasks of maintaining a home and family. I became desperate for some fun activity to get me moving again. I also hoped to find something that my husband and I could do together.

Within walking distance of my house sat an elementary school with a tennis court. I noticed that adults used this court after school hours. I had played tennis during high school. My best friend and I would opt out of whatever team sport was going on in the gym, and request to use the tennis courts instead. She and I enjoyed equal levels of skill, or lack of, and we felt no pressure to compete. We happily shunned the competition going on in the gym and often fell into stitches of laughter over our mistakes. That was my memory of tennis. Here was my chance to pick it up again. I had the time and the need for activity.

My husband and I made a plan to begin lessons together, but no sooner had we made the plan than my husband got called away to Nepal. Regretting his absence, I started lessons on my own. Twice a week, I drove home from work, changed into shorts, a T-shirt, and sneakers, then walked or biked to the tennis court.

Although my lesson began at 5 p.m., it was still hot. I felt like jumping or sprinting my way through the lesson, no matter how sweaty I got, because here I had the space to move! My coach laughed at my antics, as I sought to satisfy my need to dance through tennis. Gradually I learned to position myself for proper tennis form. After each lesson, I returned home to shower, still flushed from the heat. It took a long time to cool down. Once I did, I felt tired yet energized. With tennis I gained a sense of strength and power that I had not previously found through dance. I felt capable, strong and fast, attributes that I had not identified with before.

One of the main reasons why *Tool #7: Seeking Out External Activities* is an important tool for the expatriate woman is because it lets you have fun in your life. When you first arrive overseas, and you're surrounded by packing paper and boxes, and the contents of your life are scattered across the floor, it's hard to imagine taking time for fun. But, it's for this very reason that you need to do so. Moving overseas is hard work and very stressful. Often it takes months to prepare for such a move, and once you arrive, you're faced with a great number of tasks to get yourself and your family settled into your new environment. The whole process can drain you, but by building in breaks for yourself with external activities and having fun, you'll feel more refreshed and better able to deal with whatever comes your way.

Tool #7: Seeking Out External Activities also provides an ideal way for you to meet other people. You leave your friends behind when you move, creating a void in your life and you arrive overseas with this void. When you participate in external activities, you often meet others with similar interests. External activities can be the connecting link between you and meeting new people.

External activities are an important tool for the expatriate woman because like internal activities, external activities are good for the soul. Not only do external activities allow you to connect with other people, they also help you connect or stay connected to yourself. External activities provide you with an avenue to help express parts of yourself through activity. For example, external activities can help you express your playful side, your athletic ability, your need to be challenged, your desire for adventure, or your need for companionship.

External activities are also good for your mental health. Having fun and being with others can give you a sense of well-being and have a positive effect on your attitude. This, in turn, can make you feel better about yourself and your situation. By participating in external activities, you may also experience a sense of pride or accomplishment for completing personal goals you've set for yourself. And this, in turn, can increase your self-esteem.

External activities also help reduce stress. As we have said throughout this book, moving overseas is stressful. External activities provide you with a diversion from your daily routine. Having something else to think about and focus on can reduce your stress level. Many external activities also have a physical component to them, which provides for a physical release of tension and stress. When you participate in external activities, you often have the opportunity to get to know others and friendships can blossom.

◦ჹExercise: Reflections ჹ◦

This exercise will help you gain a better understanding of how the external activities you participated in before moving overseas were affected by your move. Your responses will help you begin to decide whether Tool #7 may be valuable to you as an expatriate woman.

What type of external activities did you seek out for yourself before you moved overseas?

_____
_____
_____
_____
_____

Were you satisfied with the external activities you had in place for yourself before moving overseas, i.e., the types of activities, the frequency in which you were able to participate in them, and the benefit you experienced from them, etc.?

_____
_____
_____
_____
_____

What was the most significant change in your external activities after you moved overseas, and what was the effect on you?

_____
_____
_____
_____
_____

After answering the above questions, do you have any ideas about what you want to do with this information? Please briefly explain your answer.

_____
_____
_____
_____
_____

You made discoveries about yourself as you completed the Reflections exercise. You discovered what types of external activities you participated in before moving overseas and how satisfying you found them. You also discovered how the external activities you participated in were affected when you moved and those possibilities are many. The degree to which your participation in external activities was affected when you moved has to do with the following factors: the type(s) of external activities you participated in; your satisfaction with them; where you moved to; and, your priorities and personality.

For example, you may have found that the overseas move did not affect your external activities because the same activities you enjoyed at home are also available in the country you've moved to. Or, you may have discovered that the country you've moved to offers the same activities as the country you left, but that you're not satisfied with the frequency or amount of time you can spend participating in these activities. You may have discovered that, because of your priorities and personality, you're spending time completing tasks, settling in, and meeting other demands that have been placed on you, and not taking time for yourself.

Another possibility is that your external activities may have been negatively affected when you moved overseas because the activities you participated in at home are not available in the country you've moved to. Or, on the other hand, you may have discovered that the overseas move has had a positive effect on your external activities because it has provided you with more opportunities than ever before.

Decision Point

Charise:

One day, in the course of conversation with one of my good friends, I came to a sudden realization. I said to her, "I look for meaning in everything!"

We laughed. We were talking about playing tennis, and how I analyzed my game. My coach frequently told me that I needed to watch the ball. Whenever I messed up, he said, "You're not looking at the ball!" Then my mind would spin off of his comment.

I wondered why I wasn't looking at the ball. I would begin thinking about my distractibility and lack of focus, and judge my actions. While thinking about all those other things, I messed up the very next stroke. This made me feel even worse about myself. I forgot to have fun, to let go, and relax into the game.

Somehow, I had turned tennis into something other than an external activity. It had become part of my inner life, how I thought and felt, how I saw myself. My attraction to my coach complicated things further. As I talked about this with my friend, I saw the situation through her eyes, that I was making myself miserable when I could be having fun. I wondered if I could rescue the simple pleasure of tennis from all the stuff that I had layered on top of it. I wanted to enjoy tennis for its own sake.

I also wanted to find other avenues for fun. My personality and the type of work I chose to do tended toward the serious. I was counseling people who had complicated issues, including the process of grieving. Some people were grieving the loss of a relationship, or were coming to terms with other losses (loss of independence or loss of supports, for example). At times I took on their pain. I had to learn to clear myself so that I didn't carry their burdens for them.

I began to crave relationships with people who did not demand my mind to follow a therapeutic track and I needed to balance my caretaker role (as a counselor, a mother, and a wife). I found myself gravitating toward my peer group, other expatriate women. Gradually I learned to drop my counselor role outside the office, and enter the expatriate community with my own need to belong. I found expatriate women incredibly interesting, with all kinds of talents and life histories of how they had arrived at this point in their lives. The people I met through my first, and closest overseas friend I made, were fun to be with. They had a familiarity with each other which I had missed out on by keeping myself so aloof. They also liked activity, to do things and create situations. When with them, I felt a connection to my more playful side. I realized that play had been a very small area of my life, barely tapped into since I had moved overseas. I was also beginning to tire of the commute to work, which took more time as traffic continued to increase.

My work schedule deprived me of opportunities to meet with other women who were not working. I wanted the freedom to join them more often for socializing, traveling, exploring, and organizing projects. After a year-and-a-half in Bangkok, I decided to cut back on my work schedule to three days a week. This allowed me to continue my work while expanding my social life. I found that both of these areas of my life benefited as a result.

External activities are an important tool for the expatriate woman because they help connect you with other people as well as incorporate fun into your life. After completing the Reflections exercise you may have a better idea about whether you want or need to pick up the tool and use it. To help you decide whether or not you want to use Tool #7, consider the following questions.

Would you like to have more interaction with other people?

_____

_____

_____

_____

Would you like to have more fun in your life?

_____

_____

_____

_____

_____

What would the potential positive benefits be for you to seek out external activities?

_____

_____

_____

_____

_____

Would there be any potential negative consequences for you to seek out external activities?

_____

_____

_____

_____

_____

When you think about seeking out external activities, does this sound like a positive or negative experience for you? Please explain your answer.

_____

_____

_____

_____

_____

After answering the above questions, do you want or need to pick up Tool #7 and use it? Please explain your answer.

_____

_____

_____

_____

_____

After answering the above questions, you may have discovered that you already seek out external activities for yourself, and are satisfied with them, the people you include, and the amount of fun in your life. If so, you may choose to skip the next section. However, if you've decided that you need to seek out external activities, continue to the following section to see how you may use Tool #7.

How to Use Tool #7: Seeking Out External Activities

Tool #7 may provide an opportunity for you to grow in this area if: you haven't been satisfied with your current set of external activities; you haven't been satisfied with the amount of time you've been able to spend on external activities; or if you don't know what type of external activity would help you connect with other people and have fun. This may give you an opportunity to grow.

Life is often about allocating and balancing our time, including the time we spend alone and with other people. The time we spend with others allows and nurtures our connections to them, and they often bring fun and enjoyment into our lives as well.

The following four-step exercise will help you learn to use Tool #7.

Step 1: Take an Inventory

The first step in seeking out external activities for yourself is to identify external activities you've engaged in throughout your life that you've enjoyed. List them in the following space.

_____
_____
_____
_____
_____

Of the activities you listed above, which ones were the most satisfying to you and why?

_____
_____
_____
_____
_____

Step 2: Identify External Activities Available Where You Currently Live

What external activities are available in the city or country you now live in? You may want to review the section on "Types of External Activities" found near the beginning of the text on Tool #7 for ideas.

_____

_____

_____

_____

_____

Is there any overlap between the external activities that you've enjoyed throughout your life and the external activities available in the city or country you now live in? If so, which ones?

_____

_____

_____

_____

_____

Are there any activities available in the country you now live in that you would like to try? If so, which ones?

_____

_____

_____

_____

_____

Step 3: Develop a Plan

Review what you've written about external activities you enjoyed in the past, and the activities now available to you. From these external activities, make a decision about which one(s) you'd like to seek out based on your situation and write them in the following space.

_____

_____

_____

_____

_____

Answer the following questions to help develop your plan about how you'll go about finding the external activities you listed above.

Are you comfortable participating in activities with other people?

_____
_____
_____
_____
_____

If participating in activities with other people doesn't come easily to you, embrace this as an opportunity to grow. Think of some ways to reward yourself for taking the risk to grow and write them in the following space.

_____
_____
_____
_____
_____

How will you go about finding the external activities you've chosen to pursue?

_____
_____
_____
_____
_____

How will you make yourself available (with your existing commitments), to spend time engaging in external activities with others?

_____
_____
_____
_____
_____

Is there anything you can change, rearrange, or eliminate from your schedule that will give you the time and energy you need to spend on your external activities?

_____

_____

_____

_____

_____

Can you activate any of your supports to help give you the time you need to seek out external activities?

_____

_____

_____

_____

_____

How many days per week will you seek out the external activities you've identified? Which days?

_____

_____

_____

_____

_____

Step 4: Benefits to Myself

Write a statement about the benefits you believe you'll experience as a result of taking time to participate in activities with other people and having fun by using *Tool #7: Seeking Out External Activities.*

_____

_____

_____

_____

_____

CB   CB   CB

By completing Part Four, picking up and using Tools for Change, you have completed Step 3 in reconstructing your identity. Your identity is taking shape according to the choices you have made at this final step of The Wheel. In Part Five, we will look at the positive outcome of setting The Wheel in motion as it relates to your current overseas experience, as well as to future moves and repatriation.

Part Five

The Wheel in Motion

Chapter 20

Your Portable Identity:
Using The Wheel Wherever You Go, Including Repatriation

In Part One of this book you gained an understanding about the loss of identity associated with an overseas move, including the effect of living in a foreign culture. We tracked, step-by step, the entire process of identity loss over time, beginning with how you defined yourself before the decision to move overseas. We illustrated how your original identity picture goes through several alterations: first from the decision to move; then by the actual departure; third, by the entry into the foreign country; and, finally, by the addition of new roles and new relationships in your life overseas.

By illustrating these changes and phases, you were able to understand the effect of the move on your identity. You learned that after an overseas move, your identity is in transition and that experiencing a wide range of feelings is normal within the context of so much change.

In Parts Two, Three, and Four, we showed you how having an identity in transition puts you on the threshold of personal growth and change. We introduced The Wheel, a model we developed to help you take charge of reconstructing your identity based on choice, rather than circumstance. We discussed the process of reconstructing identity as a series of three steps and illustrated how, as you proceed through these steps (making a commitment, accessing your personal resources, and picking up tools) you set The Wheel in motion and move toward a positive outcome in your identity's transition. By setting The Wheel in motion, your identity becomes what you envision and what you reconstruct based on what is important to *you.*

The Positive Outcome

To refer to an earlier metaphor, when you set The Wheel in motion, your identity begins to take shape again, like the crab that gradually grows a new shell. In essence, by creating a shell that "fits," you bring resolution to the state of transition your identity has been in. The results of your efforts are twofold. First, you put back into place the four facets of your identity (internal view, external factors, roles, and relationships) altered by the move. This will support the success of your current overseas experience. Second, your identity becomes portable. You'll have an identity rooted to your sense of self which can thrive outside of your home country and culture. This will serve you well when you face the next move, either to another country or when you return to your home country.

In the next section we'll look at the positive outcome of setting The Wheel in motion as it relates to your current overseas experience. We'll look at how the benefits of setting The Wheel in motion during future moves, including repatriation, can result in a positive outcome as well.

A Successful Overseas Experience

When you first move overseas, the four facets of your identity are in flux. Internal view, external factors, roles, and relationships are altered by the event of the move. The three steps of The Wheel, commitment, personal resources, and tools, provide the means to re-establish these four facets of identity in the context of your life overseas.

You have many ways to move within the steps of The Wheel. Remember that these three steps exist inside The Wheel, which is not a linear form. Therefore, it offers plenty of interaction between the steps. Ultimately, The Wheel adapts to your use, based on your individual needs and choices.

For example, your commitment may lead you straight to a tool, bypassing the resources altogether. It's perfectly okay to go to a tool first; it will probably link you back to your resources anyway. You could, for instance, discover that the most challenging aspect of the move is accepting it. *Acceptance* (Chapter 17) is a tool. When you pick up that tool, you'll likely engage your *Ability to Let Go*, a resource (Chapter 8).

Using one tool may also lead you to another companion tool. For instance, when you want to *Re-establish a Support Network* (Chapter 16), you'll need to *Communicate with Others* (Chapter 15). You'll use these two tools together. You might engage a resource and two of the tools simultaneously. If you want to improve your *Ability to Manage Stress* (Chapter 10), for example, you might *Seek Out Internal Activities* (Chapter 18) as well as *Seek Out External Activities* (Chapter 19). The successful use of a tool may lead you back to your commitment, where you find the motivation to address another area in the process of reconstructing identity. These are examples of movement within The Wheel.

The positive outcome of The Wheel in motion is a stable identity in which you redefine your internal view, external factors, roles, and relationships. These four facets of identity will fall into place according to the choices you make. For example, your internal view may shift in such a way that you become more open and tolerant of beliefs and values other than your own (such as a different religion in the country you've moved to). You may find that external factors (such as the new community and culture you've moved to) have helped you grow as an individual by exposing you to another way of life.

You might carve out a new role (such as Debra's work role) or gain a new relationship (such as Charise's two key friendships). Just as the crab's new shell gradually hardens, your identity eventually takes on a solid form. Where the four facets of your identity were previously in limbo, you can now see them gaining clarity and definition. You can now see the results of reconstructing your identity. You no longer struggle as you did when you were in the transitional state. You've regained your inner equilibrium for a successful overseas experience.

Successful Future Moves and Repatriation

As an expatriate woman, you move between cultures. You have the opportunity to become an expert at managing change. The Wheel gives you the means to navigate the changes. Wherever you go, The Wheel applies. A key aspect of The Wheel is that it has no outer, enclosing boundary. Not anchored to any particular place, it is moveable. The Wheel can carry you from one country to another, since it exists outside of the mandates of culture. It has the capacity for openness, flexibility, and adaptation to a new environment. It represents an identity more aware of internal processes, and less dependent on external elements such as culture and environment.

Once you work with The Wheel, it becomes yours, integrated into your experience. You'll view any future move in light of what you discovered via The Wheel the first time. When you move to another overseas posting or repatriate to your home country, your identity will be, once again, in transition. Because of your prior experience with The Wheel, you can set it in motion any time you choose. You have the advantage of knowing how to move through this transitional state while you're in it. Because you're already familiar with how it works, you can refer to The Wheel in a more shorthand approach. Use the diagram of The Wheel as a visual tool to help you identify where you are in the process of reconstructing identity.

How to Use the Diagram of The Wheel as a Visual Tool

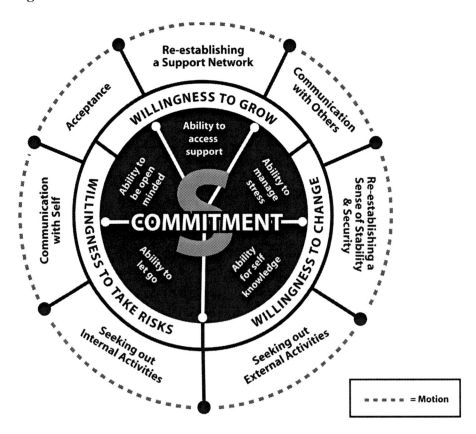

240

During your current overseas experience, a future move, or repatriation, you can scan the diagram of The Wheel illustrated on the previous page to see how well you're working with it. Always enter The Wheel from the center each time you begin the process of reconstructing identity. That's where you check in with your commitment. Ask yourself, "How am I doing with my commitment to take charge of what's happening to my identity?" If you determine that your commitment is lacking, then this is where you need to focus your attention. Remember, your commitment is your foundation and it is essential for it to be strong in order to make the changes you seek. If you feel your commitment is strong, then continue around The Wheel, pausing at each personal resource and each tool to ask yourself, "How am I doing in this area?" Using The Wheel like a checklist, you'll determine which areas need your immediate attention and which are working well for you. Using The Wheel in this way puts you fully in charge of your process.

In the course of using The Wheel as a visual tool to assess how you're doing in reconstructing your identity, you may discover that you are using the various components of The Wheel to your satisfaction. Or you may discover that one or both of the following scenarios is happening to you. You may find that you're not accessing your personal resources. Or, as you continue to work your way around, you may discover that you're stuck because you're not picking up tools and using them in the way you identified as most beneficial to you. If you find that either one of these two scenarios is true for you, the following exercise can help you identify what is happening and help you find a starting place to put The Wheel back in motion.

Centering Exercise

This exercise can be especially beneficial in the early stages of a move, when your sense of self is less secure. It's also a means to check in with yourself anytime when: you need to gain clarity or perspective on a particular situation; when your life is not going in the intended direction; when your life seems out of balance; or when you'd like to make a change, but aren't sure where to begin.

In this exercise you'll put your full and undivided attention on yourself. To gain a sense of how you're doing on a deeper level, you'll separate yourself from the daily routine. You'll be tuning in on a physical and energetic level to your sensations which will provide clues to your feelings and what you're experiencing on a deeper level than you may be aware of.

We have purposefully made the directions simple, so that you won't have to rely on thinking. However, you should read through the directions first, and then practice the exercise. If you find you don't remember what to do, you can either pause to look at the directions again, or you can simply do what feels most natural and genuine. You may end up developing your own way to tune in. The most important thing is to come back to your breathing anytime your attention drifts, breathing consciously, in and out.

Tuning In

Find some quiet time for yourself, at least twenty minutes. Pick a place where you can have privacy and where you feel comfortable. Purposefully shut the door on any possible distractions. When alone, lie on your back on a rug, or a mat, or a bed. Make yourself comfortable. If you need a pillow under your head or under your knees, use one. Settle against the surface and notice where you feel uncomfortable in your body.

Check your shoulders and your neck for tightness. Move these areas slightly, to allow the muscles to loosen. Relax your jaw by allowing it to drop slightly. Check other areas where you might be tight, such as your back, belly, thighs, your hands, and feet. Allow yourself to sink further into the surface underneath you, feeling the heaviness of your body. Breathe into your chest and allow it to soften when you exhale. Do this a few times. Then breathe into your belly, allowing it to expand as you inhale. Do this a few times. Then gently slide your feet toward you, bending your knees so that the soles of your feet rest on the surface you're lying on.

Lift your arms to the ceiling and just let them float, keeping elbows and wrists slightly bent to avoid tensing in your arms. Explore the space above you with your arms as you float them in an arc above you. You don't need to direct this movement. See where they want to go. Then gently lift your feet off the floor and float your legs toward the ceiling, keeping the knees slightly bent. Move your legs freely in your hip sockets, allowing them to float along with your arms while you're still lying on your back. When you're ready, bring arms and legs down closer to you and let yourself roll over to your side.

Bring your knees in close and curl into a fetal position. Feel as though you're safely tucked away from the outside world. Breathe slowly in and out. With each breath, imagine you're letting go more and more of anything you're holding that you don't need. Let your self soften and melt. Stay there quietly breathing and softening. You deserve this rest. Notice any sensations. Notice how the mat or the bed feels under you. Notice how the air around you feels against your skin. Notice if you feel like falling asleep or if you feel like jumping up and doing something. Let yourself stay present, without falling asleep and without getting up.

At some point, roll over to your other side and continue quietly breathing and softening. When you're done, take your time to sit up and notice how you feel. What are you most aware of? Are you tired? Are you jumpy? Are you numb? Do you feel heavy or light? Do you feel warmth or coolness inside you? Is there an emotional component to what you're experiencing on a physical level? If so, what is it? Is what you're experiencing on a physical and/or emotional level related to your move? Do any thoughts come to mind about what you're going through and how being in a new environment affects your identity? Recognize anything that calls your attention, even if you don't have a name for it. Stay tuned in to your process as long as you can. You can come back here anytime, and repeat the exercise.

Like meditation, this exercise establishes a "ground" in your being where you can locate your experience. While you're literally shifting ground by moving from one country to another, or repatriating to your home country, you can cultivate the ground within your self, your center. In the course of doing this exercise, you choose to *risk* opening yourself to discover what is occurring within you at a deeper level. You demonstrate a *willingness to grow* by allowing yourself to learn more about your experience on an emotional and physical level.

To continue with the spirit of this exercise, would mean demonstrating a *willingness to change* by following through on the discoveries you made about yourself. By doing so, you once again re-engage The Wheel by *making a commitment* to take charge of the outcome of your identity. To fully set The Wheel in motion, you would use the other two steps of The Wheel, *personal resources and tools*, to continue the journey of rediscovering who you are in the context of another move.

ೞ   ೞ   ೞ

From first hand experience we know that any move is stressful and can affect your identity in a number of ways. We also know that an overseas move carries with it a whole unique set of circumstances. We hope this book with its insights and exercises will give you a way to cope, grow, and handle the move with grace and joy.

Notes

1. Nancy J. Adler is an expert in the field of international human resource management. Her book, *International Dimensions of Organizational Behavior*, serves as a reference and guide for business executives, managers, educators, and students who seek an understanding of cross-cultural aspects of global business. Her research shows that an international move is particularly difficult for the expatriate wife. Nancy J. Adler, *International Dimensions of Organizational Behavior* (Cincinnati: South-Western College Publishing, 1997), p. 263.

2. Cross-cultural awareness, communication, and adaptation are essential ingredients for a successful overseas experience. These topics are explored in *Survival Kit for Overseas Living,* a practical guide written for Americans planning to move overseas. L. Robert Kohls, *Survival Kit for Overseas Living: For Americans Planning to Live and Work Abroad, 3rd edition* (Yarmouth: Intercultural Press, 1996), p. 23.

3. The application of developmental theory (historically which has been based on observations of men's lives) to the lives of women is challenged by Gilligan in *In A Different Voice.* Through her research, she differentiates women's moral and psychological development from that of men's. Carol Gilligan, *In A Different Voice: Psychological Theory and Women's Development* (Cambridge: Harvard University Press, 1993), pp. 5-23.

A pivotal work based on interviews with 100 girls which explores the significance of relationships in the psychological development of girls' identity in adolescence. The authors illustrate how girls give up their voice and disconnection occurs. Ideas are offered on how to help adolescent girls during this critical time. Lyn Mikel Brown and Carol Gilligan, *Meeting at the Crossroads: Women's Psychology and Girls' Development* (Cambridge: Harvard University Press, 1992), p. 3.

This book focuses on the origins of depression in women and provides valuable insight into how relationships play a significant role in depression in women. Dana Crowley Jack, *Silencing the Self: Women and Depression* (Cambridge: Harvard University Press, 1991), pp. 3-16.

245

4. Focusing is a method to heighten awareness of the physical aspect of a problem or situation, as a felt sense in the body. This method is simple to apply, does not require an expert to assist you, and has proven effective in bringing about a process of change. Eugene T. Gendlin, *Focusing* (New York: Bantam Books, 1981).

5. Prostitution is an entrenched tradition in Thai society, a fact which Victoria Combe develops in "A Few Home Truths," *The Bangkok Nation*, October 22, 1991. pp. C1, C8-9.

6. The crab metaphor was taken from Gretchen Janssen's book which is now out of print. According to Ms. Janssen, she paraphrased the metaphor from the Robert Raines book, *To Kiss the Joy.* Word Books, Waco, Texas, 1973, on pp. 9-10. Gretchen Janssen, *Women on the Move: A Christian Perspective on Cross-Cultural Adaptation* (Yarmouth: Intercultural Press, 1992), p. 18.

7. Robin Pascoe is the author of four best-selling books on expatriate life and she is best known as the Expat Expert. She is an inspirational speaker and advocate for the needs of expatriate families, especially women. In *A Moveable Marriage,* Robin discusses the unique challenges and stresses international relocation places on a marriage, including the following topics: the role of the company; dual career issues; isolation and dependence; money, sex, and intimacy; parenting; restoring balance in the marriage; and, what to do if the marriage goes wrong. Robin Pascoe, *A Moveable Marriage: Relocate Your Relationship without Breaking It* (Vancouver: Expatriate Press, 2003).

8. Journaling has been with us since the ancients. Over time, diarists have discovered the many benefits of keeping a journal. For a fresh guide to journaling, its uses and benefits, *The Complete Idiot's Guide to Journaling* is an excellent guide for the beginner or the veteran. Joan R. Neubauer, *The Complete Idiot's Guide to Journaling* (Indianapolis: Macmillan, 2001).

9. Tarot cards have existed since the Renaissance, and have been used for many purposes. The *Motherpeace Round Tarot* was created to assist self-understanding through visual, dream-like images. This particular deck challenges the traditional look of Tarot by incorporating more female and racially diverse images on round, or circular, cards. Karen Vogel and Vicki Noble, *Motherpeace Round Tarot* (Stanford: US Games Systems, Inc., 1983).

Bibliography

Adler, Nancy J. *International Dimensions of Organizational Behavior, 3rd edition.* South-Western College Publishing: Cincinnati, Ohio, 1997.

Anderson, Joseph. *Social Work Methods and Processes.* Wadsworth Inc.: Belmont, California, p. 112, 1981.

Aptheker, Bettina. *Tapestries of Life: Women's Work, Women's Consciousness, and the Meaning of Daily Experience.* The University of Massachusetts Press: Amherst, Massachusetts, 1989.

Bateson, Mary Catherine. *Composing A Life.* Plume: New York, New York, 1990.

Black, J. Stewart, and Hal B. Gregerson. *So You're Going Overseas: Spouse Workbook.* Global Business Publishers: San Diego, California, 1998.

Brown, Lyn Mikel, and Carol Gilligan. *Meeting at the Crossroads: Women's Psychology and Girls' Development.* Harvard University Press: Cambridge, Massachusetts, 1992.

Combe, Victoria. "A Few Home Truths." *The Bangkok Nation*: October 22, 1991. pp. C1, C8-9.

Estés, Clarissa Pinkola. *Women Who Run with the Wolves: Myths and Stories of the Wild Woman Archetype.* Ballantine Books: New York, New York, 1992.

Gendlin, Eugene T. *Focusing.* Bantam Books. New York, New York, 1981.

Gilligan, Carol. *In A Different Voice: Psychological Theory and Women's Development.* Harvard University Press: Cambridge, Massachusetts, 1993.

Hall, Edward T. *Beyond Culture.* Anchor Books: Garden City, New York, 1977.

Hantrakul, Sukanya. "Feudalism and the Politics of Sex in Thailand." *The Bangkok Nation*: August 1, 1993. p. A10.

Hantrakul, Sukanya. "Of Liberty, Equality and Prostitution." *The Bangkok Nation:* August 4, 1993.

Hartman, Ann, and Joan Laird. *Family-Centered Social Work Practice*. The Free Press: New York, New York, pp. 288-294, 1983.

Hess, Melissa Brayer, and Patricia Linderman. *The Expert Expatriate: Your Guide to Successful Relocation Abroad: Moving, Living, Thriving*. Intercultural Press: Yarmouth, Maine, 2002.

Hughes, Katherine L. *The Accidental Diplomat: Dilemmas of the Trailing Spouse*. Aletheia Publications: Putnam Valley, New York, 1999.

Jack, Dana Crowley. *Silencing the Self: Women and Depression*. Harvard University Press: Cambridge, Massachusetts, 1991.

Janssen, Gretchen. *Women on the Move: A Christian Perspective on Cross-Cultural Adaptation*. Intercultural Press: Yarmouth, Maine, 1992.

Kalb, Rosalind, and Penelope Welch. *Moving Your Family Overseas*. Intercultural Press: Yarmouth, Maine, 1992.

Kaplan, Paul S. *The Human Odyssey*. West Publishing Company: St. Paul, Minnesota, 1988.

Khantipalo, Phra. *Buddhism Explained*. Mahamkut Rajavidyalaya Press: Bangkok, Thailand, 1973.

Kohls, L. Robert. *Survival Kit for Overseas Living: For Americans Planning to Live and Work Abroad, 3rd edition*. Intercultural Press: Yarmouth, Maine, 1996.

Lester, Robert C. *Theravada Buddhism in Southeast Asia*. The University of Michigan Press: Ann Arbor, Michigan, 1992.

McCollum, Audrey T. *The Trauma of Moving: Psychological Issues for Women*. Sage Publications: Library of Social Research, 1990.

McCoy, Mildred M. "Focus on the Expatriate Woman," in Proceedings of The Expatriate Experience: A Symposium, In Touch Foundation, Inc.: Philippines, 1986.

Meltzer, Gail, and Elaine Grandjean. *The Moving Experience: A Practical Guide to Psychological Survival.* Multilingual Matters: Clevedon, England, 1989.

Moore, Thomas. *Care of the Soul: A Guide for Cultivating Depth and Sacredness in Everyday Life.* HarperCollins: New York, New York, 1992.

Mulder, Niels. *Inside Thai Society: An Interpretation of Everyday Life.* Editions Duang Kamol: Bangkok, Thailand, 1992.

Neubauer, Joan R. *The Complete Idiot's Guide to Journaling.* Macmillan: Indianapolis, Indiana, 2001.

Northern, Helen. *Clinical Social Work.* Columbia University Press: New York, New York, pp. 45-46, 1982.

Orbach, Susie. *Hunger Strike: The Anorectic's Struggle as a Metaphor for Our Age.* W. W. Norton & Company, Inc.: New York, New York, 1986.

Otaganonta, Wipawee, and Chanyapron Chanjaraen. "Looking at Love and Non-Marriage." *Bangkok Post*: March 28, 1994.

Pascoe, Robin. *Culture Shock! Successful Living Abroad: A Wife's Guide.* Graphic Arts Center Publishing Company: Portland, Oregon, 1998.

Pascoe, Robin. *A Moveable Marriage: Relocate Your Relationship without Breaking It.* Expatriate Press: North Vancouver, BC, Canada, 2003.

Piet-Pelon, Nancy J., and Barbara Hornby. *Women's Guide to Overseas Living, 2nd edition.* Intercultural Press: Yarmouth, Maine, 1992.

Raines, Robert. *To Kiss the Joy.* Word Books: Waco, Texas, 1973.

Raymond, Ronald J., and Stephen V. Eliot with Marilyn Mercer. *Grow Your Roots Anywhere, Anytime.* Peter H. Wyden: Ridgefield, Connecticut, 1980.

Redmond, Mont. "Sadness: The Smile of Secrecy and Denial." *The Bangkok Nation*: January 30, 1994. p. B2.

Roman, Beverly D. *Home Away From Home: Turning Your International Relocation Into a Lifetime Enhancement.* BR Anchor Publishing: Wilmington, North Carolina, 1999.

Roman, Beverly D. *The Insider's Guide to Relocation: Expert Advice to Move Across the State, the Country or the World, 1ˢᵗ edition.* The Insider's Guides, Inc.: Manteo, North Carolina, 1996.

Schlossberg, Nancy K. "Taking the Mystery Out of Change." *Psychology Today*: May 1987. pp. 74-75.

Seidenberg, Robert. *Corporate Wives-Corporate Casualties?* Anchor Books: Garden City, New York, 1975.

Specht, Riva, and Grace J. Craig. *Human Development: A Social Work Perspective.* Prentice-Hall, Inc.: Englewood Cliffs, New Jersey. pp. 200-201, 1982.

Storti, Craig. *The Art of Crossing Cultures.* Intercultural Press: Yarmouth, Maine, 1990.

Vogel, Karen, and Vicki Noble. *Motherpeace Round Tarot.* U.S. Games Systems, Inc.: Stanford, Connecticut, 1983.

Winfield, Louise. *Living Overseas.* Public Affairs Press: Washington, D.C., 1962.

About the Authors

Debra R. Bryson

Debra Bryson's career has been dedicated to helping others maximize their full potential for over twenty years. She is a licensed clinical social worker and her experience includes providing mental health, educational, and vocational counseling services to clients from diverse backgrounds, nationalities, and age groups in a variety of multicultural settings.

Debra graduated Summa Cum Laude from Missouri State University in 1985 with a Bachelor of Science Degree and a major in Social Work. In 1991, she earned her Master's Degree in Social Work with a specialization in mental health counseling from Virginia Commonwealth University. She is a member of the National Association of Social Workers and is an honored member of Empire Who's Who Among Social Workers and Executives and Professionals in Mental Health.

Debra has moved over fifteen times, including twice while writing *A Portable Identity*. She currently resides in Austin, Texas with her husband and two daughters. She enjoys outdoor activities, weightlifting, biking, journaling, and spending time with her family and friends.

Charise M. Hoge

Charise Hoge has worked in the field of health and healing for over twenty years in the disciplines of social work, dance therapy, polarity therapy, and yoga. Her experience includes four years counseling expatriates in Thailand, where she developed an expertise in cross-cultural issues. She received her Bachelor of Arts Degree from Sarah Lawrence College in 1980, followed by a Master of Arts Degree in Dance/Movement Therapy from New York University in 1984. She earned a second Master's Degree in Social Work from the University of Georgia in 1992.

Charise lived overseas as a child in Panama City, Panama, as a college student in Paris, France, and as a military spouse in Bangkok, Thailand. Overall she has relocated more than ten times, including once while writing *A Portable Identity*.

Charise currently lives in the Washington, D.C. area with her husband and two daughters. She teaches SynergyYoga and performs with the Ancient Rhythms Dance Troupe. She also enjoys writing, getting together with friends, and going with her family to the wilds of West Virginia for the occasional weekend getaway.

Our Vision

Our vision is to reach expatriate spouses worldwide with the message that changes in identity are normal for the accompanying spouse during an international relocation. Our goal is to empower women who move overseas in support of their husbands' or partners' careers to take charge of the changes in identity that occur, for a more successful transition to life overseas.

We are also dedicated to advocating for the needs of the accompanying spouse by educating employers, sending organizations, human resource managers, and relocation specialists about the effect of an overseas move on the accompanying spouse's identity so that they can offer support from an organizational level to ensure success during an international relocation.

www.aportableidentity.com

Our website, *www.aportableidentity.com*, is a companion to this book and is another source of support for women who are the accompanying spouse during an international relocation. The site provides information about our book, news articles, contact and order information, links to other resources, and a chat group.

The chat group is a special feature of *www.aportableidentity.com* because it provides a place where a woman can focus on the effect of the overseas move on her identity, where her thoughts and feelings about the move can be voiced and validated, and where she can ponder questions such as "who am I in this move?" By participating in this community of support, a woman has the opportunity to share ideas about how to take charge of the changes in identity she is experiencing, so that women around the globe who are going through a similar process, or who have gone through the process already, can benefit from her experience, and she can benefit from theirs.

CPSIA information can be obtained at www.ICGtesting.com
Printed in the USA
LVOW121141161111

255233LV00001B/15/A